The Narrative Study of Lives

Volume 3

The Narrative Study of Lives

The purpose of this Series is to publish studies of actual lives in progress, studies that use qualitative methods of investigation within a theoretical context drawn from psychology or other disciplines. The aim is to promote the study of lives and life history as a means of examining, illuminating, and spurring theoretical understanding. *The Narrative Study of Lives* will encourage longitudinal and retrospective in-depth studies of individual life narratives as well as theoretical consideration of innovative methodological approaches to this work.

Guidelines for authors:

The editors invite submissions of original manuscripts of up to 35 typed pages in the areas described above. As a publication of an interdisciplinary nature, we welcome authors from all disciplines concerned with narratives, psychobiography, and life-history. In matters of style, we encourage any creative format that best presents the work. Long quotations in the protagonists' voices are desirable as well as discussion of the author's place in the study.

References and footnotes should follow the guidelines of the *Publication Manual of the American Psychological Association* (4th ed.). A separate title page should include the chapter title and the author's name, affiliation, and address. Please type the entire manuscript, including footnotes and references, double-spaced, and submit three copies to:

Ruthellen Josselson, Ph.D., Co-Editor
The Narrative Study of Lives
Department of Psychology
Towson State University
Towson, MD 21204

Interpreting Experience
Volume 3
of
THE NARRATIVE STUDY OF LIVES

Interpreting Experience

■ ■ ■

The Narrative
Study of Lives

Ruthellen Josselson
Amia Lieblich
editors

The Narrative Study of Lives ■ Volume 3

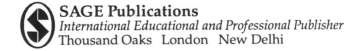

SAGE Publications
International Educational and Professional Publisher
Thousand Oaks   London   New Delhi

For information address:

SAGE Publications, Inc.
2455 Teller Road
Thousand Oaks, California 91320

SAGE Publications Ltd.
6 Bonhill Street
London EC2A 4PU
United Kingdom

SAGE Publications India Pvt. Ltd.
M-32 Market
Greater Kailash I
New Delhi 110 048 India

Printed in the United States of America

Library of Congress Cataloging-in-Publication Data

ISBN 0-8039—7106-0 (cloth); ISBN 0-8039-7107-9 (paper)

ISSN 1072-2777

This book is printed on acid-free paper.

95 96 97 98 99 10 9 8 7 6 5 4 3 2 1

Sage Production Editor: Yvonne Könneker
Copy Editor: Gillian Dickens

Contents

Introduction

$\mathcal{T}$he ultimate aim of the narrative investigation of human life is the interpretation of experience. But in this postmodern age, what it means to interpret and what it means to experience become highly relative, contextual concepts. Recognizing the futility of ever describing a universalized orderly human social world, Clifford Geertz recommended that we orient ourselves instead to "local knowledges," aspects of human experience that are individualized and contextualized. But Geertz wryly observes, "To turn from trying to explain social phenomena by weaving them into grand textures of cause and effect to trying to explain them by placing them in local frames of awareness is to exchanged a set of well-charted difficulties for a set of largely uncharted ones" (1983, p. 6).

Narrative approaches to understanding bring the researcher more closely into the investigative process than do quantitative and statistical methods. Through narrative, we come in contact with our participants as people engaged in the process of interpreting themselves. We work then with what is said and what is not said, within the context in which life is lived and the context of the interview in which words are spoken to represent that life. We then must decode, recognize, recontextualize, or abstract that life in the interest of reaching a new interpretation of the raw data of experience before us.

"What is utterly strange to us at the moment—because, whenever we attempt to engage in rational discussion of its nature, we mystify ourselves by routinely adopting a decontextualized, theoretical stance— is our ordinary world of everyday social life," says John Shotter (1992, p. 69). In this volume of *The Narrative Study of Lives,* we present work of investigators who are not simply theorizing the process, but are actively engaged in studying some aspect of "everyday social life" by using narrative as a tool of inquiry. Inevitably, such effort brings these researchers into close contact with questions of methodology, epistemology, and ontology, and these they explore in the context of their work. They undertake their shared aim, to interpret experience, from different standpoints, viewing diverse others through varying lenses.

In our continuing effort to carry forward our task of being an international and interdisciplinary forum, in this third volume of *The Narrative Study of Lives,* we present work from four countries (Canada, Israel, Swaziland, and the United States) and three disciplines (psychology, sociology, and education). We recognize that increasingly our colleagues who use narrative methodology cross disciplinary lines and integrate multiple perspectives; thus our writers also bring grounding in anthropology and literature to bear on their work.

This volume brings together the work of people who are interested in interpreting experience and who are concerned with both the method and practice of working toward this holistic—but often ephemeral—goal. They regard the analysis of human action, in Geertz's words, as an "interpretive science in search of meaning, not an experimental science in search of laws" (1973, p. 5).

The first two chapters focus on methodological issues. Thinking about what it means to "take narrative seriously," Susan Chase critiques standard modes of sociological interviewing styles and advocates the importance of making space for interviewees to frame their experience in their own terms. Using examples from others' work, her own work, and her own experience as an interview participant, Chase reflects on what it means to invite the "story" of another.

Ruthellen Josselson is similarly concerned with how we approach narrative understanding as she asks about how we enter the experience of another and how we decide what to highlight for investigation. She believes that the architectonics of the self are uniquely accessible through narrative in which the diaglogic aspects of the self are given voice. Applying some of Mikhail Bakhtin's work to narrative investigation, she stresses the importance of attending to the polyphony of interview texts.

Jaber Gubrium and James Holstein, writing from the standpoint of what they term "the new ethnography," discuss the ways in which accounts constitute rather than just reflect the realities of the social world. Using material drawn from nursing homes, family therapy, and community mental health centers, these authors explore the ways in which participants interpret their experience in the context of available interpretive horizons, which, despite common concrete realities of setting, can be highly individual and diverse. They build on Susan Chase's argument for taking narrative seriously.

The next chapters take a biographical approach to explore some questions that might not be accessible in any other way. Steve Weiland asks about how an individual professor's career trajectory can offer fresh perspective on the development of faculty lives within academic cultures. His effort to understand the experience of a colleague leads him to consider issues of doing biography, of the relativity of contextual influence, and of the relation of this perspective to conventional understanding of academic life.

Also in the realm of academic biography, but from a quite different perspective, Ada Zohar's chapter reflects on her interviews with most of the women mathematicians in Israel as well as two male mathematicians. Adding biographical exploration to her previous work on genetic transmission of outstanding mathematical ability, Zohar uncovers some developmental commonalities in these people's histories.

In the following chapters, two psychologists make use of narratives to enlarge and deepen their understanding of current topics of psychological interest. Adital Ben-Ari looks at the process by which people restructure their worldviews as a result of disclosing a previously hidden "secret." Tracing the process of a gay man "coming out" to his family, she explores the reverberations of "telling."

Using interviews and narrative analysis to look behind a quantitative measure, Hadas Wiseman tries to capture some of the subtle differences in the experiences of young people who all score high on the UCLA Loneliness Scale. In a longitudinal investigation, she also explores how the loneliness of four young people changes over their college years and identifies the complex dimensions of experience that underlie feeling (and not feeling) lonely.

The final two chapters present narratives from groups little represented in social science literature. Sarah Mkhonza takes a sociolinguistic approach to the experience of domestic workers in Swaziland during the colonial period. Vividly portraying the experiences of five women, she demonstrates the role of language in shaping and maintaining social and power relations.

Ardra Cole and Gary Knowles explore the use of narrative to document and understand the experience of two teachers who exchange positions for a year. Tracking the common patterns and divergence in their journals, the authors elucidate the process in which these teachers used the change in context to construct new meanings.

We are often asked how each volume of *The Narrative Study of Lives* represents an advance over previous ones. Are we documenting and tracking "progress" in this field? We think that this is a burgeoning area of scholarship, the development of which is nonlinear. Each successive issue of our Annual, then, does not build on the previous one so much as it continues to encourage and present the creative and reflective use of narrative in the search for understanding of experience. We applaud authors struggling with and for the form in which to tell what they have learned (and how they have learned it) and leave it to our readers to consider their own responses to the varying approaches we present and to judge which formats shall become models for work that they themselves might like to undertake. Our aim in this Annual is to continue to try to navigate the challenges of this relatively uncharted terrain.

RUTHELLEN JOSSELSON
AMIA LIEBLICH

References

Geertz, C. (1973). *The interpretation of cultures*. New York: Basic Books.

Geertz, C. (1983). *Local knowledge: Further essays in interpretive anthropology.* New York: Basic Books.

Shotter, J. (1992). "Getting in touch": The meta-methodology of a postmodern science of mental life. In S. Kvale (Ed.), *Psychology and postmodernism.* London: Sage.

❦ 1 ❦

Taking Narrative Seriously

Consequences for Method and Theory in Interview Studies

Susan E. Chase

*F*or years, humanities and social science scholars have debated the nature and significance of narrative in literature, historical writings, the popular media, personal documents such as diaries and letters, oral stories of various kinds, as well as in the academic disciplines themselves.[1] Although they disagree about what constitutes narrative and develop divergent approaches to the relation between narrative and life, narrative and subjectivity, narrative and culture, and narrative and fiction or truth, most scholars point to the ubiquity of narrative in Western societies and concur that all forms of narrative share the fundamental interest in making sense of experience, the interest in constructing and communicating meaning.

Despite the significance of narrative, qualitative researchers rarely focus specifically on eliciting narratives in the interview context and pay little attention to the narrative character of talk produced during interviews. Among others, Elliot Mishler (1986) argues that conventional methods of sociological interviewing tend to suppress respondents' stories, and that conventional methods of interpretation ignore the import of stories that they manage to tell despite our attempts to

1

stifle them.[2] Mishler suggests that the impulse to narrate is such an integral part of human experience that interviewees will tell stories even if we don't encourage them to do so.

I have found, however, that asking for and attending to another's story in the interview context is not a simple matter and that it requires an altered conception of what interviews are and how we should conduct them. If we take seriously the idea that people make sense of experience and communicate meaning through narration, *then in-depth interviews should become occasions in which we ask for life stories.* By life stories, I mean narratives about some life experience that is of deep and abiding interest to the interviewee. Furthermore, taking narrative seriously has consequences for how we use those life stories to pursue our sociological interests. As many have argued, narration is a complex social process, a form of social action that embodies the relation between narrator and culture. Taking narrative seriously means directing our attention to that process of embodiment, to what narrators accomplish as they tell their stories, and how that accomplishment is culturally shaped. A major contribution of narrative analysis is the study of general social phenomena through a focus on their embodiment in specific life stories.[3]

Inviting Stories Rather Than Reports During Interviews

Livia Polanyi's (1985) distinction between stories and reports provides a good starting point for articulating how and why interviews should become occasions to ask for life stories. She writes that *"stories are told to make a point, to transmit a message . . . about the world the teller shares with other people"* (p. 12). In telling a story, the narrator takes responsibility for "making the relevance of the telling clear" (p. 13). By contrast, a report is "typically elicited by the recipient," and "the burden of assigning differential weighting to the various narrated propositions thus falls to the receiver of the report" (p. 13). To illustrate this distinction, Polanyi offers the familiar example of a parent asking her child what happened at school today. We all recognize the difference between an obligatory chronicle and an animated story of the day's events.

In the interview context, whether we hear stories or reports has to do with who takes responsibility for the import of the talk. If we want to hear stories rather than reports then our task as interviewers is to *invite* others to tell their stories, to encourage them to take responsibility for the meaning of their talk. A successful interviewer manages to shift the weight of responsibility to the other in such a way that he or she willingly embraces it.

But how does this shifting of responsibility happen (or fail to happen) in the course of actual interviews? How do we go about inviting others to tell their stories? The answer lies in the questions we ask, and more deeply, in the orientation to others embedded in our questions. Qualitative researchers certainly agree that the questions we ask make a difference to the quality of the information we collect; that our questions should be phrased in everyday rather than sociological language; that we need to ask about participants' experiences, thoughts, and feelings to gather data thick enough to shed light on our sociological problems; and that the relationships we construct with interviewees affect the quality of their responses to our questions. Nevertheless, even when interviewers put these widely accepted ideas into practice, they may end up inviting reports rather than stories. Shifting responsibility to the participant requires something more. By way of illustration, I present examples from three different interview studies.

Karen Sacks's Study of Working-Class
Women's Workplace Militancy

In her research on the union drives by service and clerical workers at Duke Medical Center, Karen Sacks (1988, 1989) sought to understand, among other things, working-class women's militancy and leadership in the workplace. She suspected that there was a strong connection between what women learned from their families and their resistance to oppression at work. When her participant observation produced no evidence of this link, she began to interview women about their families.

> In the spirit of feminist collectivity, though naively, I put my problem to as many of the women as I knew who were willing to discuss it: I had a strong hunch that women learned the values and skills to resist oppression at work from their families. Did they share that feeling? If so, could they figure out what they learned and how they learned it?

> The questions I posed to the women were sociological, and women responded in that mode, giving me answers that linked sociological variables to personal militance. At first there was no definitive pattern: maybe birth order was important, maybe race, or working mothers, marital status, and so on. Their answers were as abstract and uninformative as my own thinking. (1989, p. 88)

By sharing her thoughts and interests—her sociological questions—Sacks treated research participants as equals, as persons as capable as she was of analyzing the social factors that have shaped their lives.[4] Indeed, Sacks got what she asked for, but not what she was looking for. Because her questions were sociological, the women offered sociological responses. Together, they speculated on significant factors that might have shaped their family lives and thus their actions at work. But the abstraction of such talk—its disconnectedness from their actual lives—made it hollow. Sacks concluded that the idea of putting sociological questions on the table is naive—even when done in a collective, feminist spirit—because such questions produce answers that have little to do with how people live their lives. The problem lay not in the wording of her questions but in their orientation; they directed others to her research interest rather than to their own life experiences.

Sacks dropped her sociological questions and began to ask for life stories—something she had no intention of doing when she started the study—when she realized that the general processes she sought to understand are embedded in women's lives.

> There were a few women whose constructions of their life narratives and analyses became exemplars of how family learning empowered women to rebel, and whose experiences

became central for developing that model. *This happened when I finally asked them how they learned about work and what it meant to them.* That question generated narratives about work—childhood chores, and a progress report about the kinds of tasks and responsibilities each woman had at different ages. (1989, p. 88, emphasis added)

Sacks finally stumbled on the specific questions that *invited* women to tell stories about growing up, taking on increasing responsibilities at home, developing self-respect as a result of the work done at home, and recognizing the importance of demanding respect from others. She learned from these stories that the sense of responsibility and self-respect developed at home conflicted with the poor treatment working-class women encountered at work; as she listened to these stories, she realized that conflict was at least one important source of working-class women's workplace militancy.

My Study of Women's Experiences in the White- and Male-Dominated Profession of the Public School Superintendency

In our interviews with women of various racial and ethnic backgrounds who are public school superintendents in rural, small town, and urban districts across the Unites States, my coresearcher, Colleen Bell, and I asked about the work they do, the professional and interpersonal contexts in which they work, their work histories, and the relationship between their personal and professional lives. At certain points in the interviews, we also asked about the inequalities these educational leaders have faced in their profession, which is 95% white and 96% male (Bell & Chase, 1993). Generally speaking, our interest lay in hearing about their work experiences in this white- and male-dominated leadership occupation. Nonetheless, in the course of our early interviews, we learned about the difference between questions that invite stories and those that invite reports.

In our earliest interviews, which were with white women in rural and small-town districts, we included a set of questions about what it is like to be one of a few women in a male-dominated context: Are you treated as a representative of women in general? As an exception? Do other women look to you as a role model? What are the effects of your visibility? Do you experience social awkwardness with male colleagues? Was there any particular point in your career when you began to think that being a woman might make some kind of a difference? We presented these questions much like Sacks presented hers, in the spirit of asking women to help us check out sociological understandings through the reality of their own experiences. We introduced these questions by giving a brief overview of what sociologists say about the experiences of women in male-dominated professions. This introduction was important, or so we thought, because it allowed the women to hear where the questions came from. By offering this background, we attempted to make the questions less abstract and to make the research relationship collaborative. Like Sacks, we thought we were inviting others to speak "in the spirit of feminist collectivity." Listen, for example, to the following exchange between me and Laura Stuart, a white superintendent from a working-class background.[5] This exchange came near the end of a 3-hour interview. Notice that I state in five different ways that I'm interested in hearing "your experience."[6]

SC: OK now *this* is a set of questions about um [p]
experiences that women have who work in male-dominated
   professions
so what I—what we've done is read the sociolog
what the sociologists *say* about these things
and what *I'd* like to do is ask for *your experience* of them
like *you're* the informant
you know the sociologists have theories and they say these
   things and
I'd like to ask you *whether* you have experienced them
whether you think they are true or not
so I really want your opinions about them
um one thing they say happens is that a woman who's in a male-
   dominated profession gets treated as a representative of women in
   general
because she's the only *woman* up there as the leader

that other people don't really know what to do with her
and and they might do things like
if she does the job poorly then they'll say
"oh women can't do that job"
if she does the job well then they'll say
"oh yeah I guess women can do that job."
Have you experienced anything like that?

I'm clearly doing my best to invite Laura Stuart to share with us whatever she has to say about these sociological formulations of women's experiences. Here is her response:

LS: No I really haven't.

I have every reason to believe that Laura Stuart answered my question honestly and in the collaborative spirit in which I asked it. In effect, she communicated something like this: "If you want to know whether my experiences fit with sociologists' ideas about women's experiences in male-dominated professions, I'm happy to help you out." In other words, she heard my question as requesting a report, which meant that the burden of interpreting the significance of her response rested with me, the one who asked for it in the first place. Despite my repeated statements of interest in her experience, she heard that my primary interest lay in the connection between her experience and sociological ideas. In the case of this question she felt no such connection, and so she had nothing to say but "No I really haven't." Our exchange continued:

SC: What about other women treating you as a role model
looking up to you
you've talked a bit about that
LS: Well [sigh] um I hope that I have been
and I've I've had two people call me since I've been here
to ask uh *my* advice *my* help with them applying for
   a superintendency
I've given them a copy of my resume
things I have prepared
shared with them the black book I I prepared for my interview

and this sort of thing.
So I always hope to be a *helping* for someone and not ever
  a hindrance you know.
I don't have any [p]
I've read articles you know
in some journals on women on how hard when a
  woman is the boss
but I haven't experienced that
SC: you mean when they say it's harder to work ||for a woman||
LS: ||uh huh yes||
SC: you haven't had that problem with men or women?
LS: no

After reporting on my question about others treating her as a role model, Laura Stuart anticipates and answers a third sociological question. Interestingly, I articulated that question—"you mean when they say it's harder to work for a woman . . . you haven't had that problem with men or women?"—only after she answered it.

Not every woman had so little to say in response to these sociological questions. And even Laura Stuart had more to say as we went along; she began to supplement her reports with stories about her workplace relationships. But the excerpts offered here capture the problematic character of these questions in any case: They *invite* reports. They do not invite the other to take responsibility for the import of her response because the weight of the question lies in the sociological ideas. Although some women did tell stories in response to these questions, they did so in spite of rather than because of the questions. In fact, when Stuart added stories to her answers, she apologized for doing so, stating, "Go on with your question. I got way off base." And later, "I get off on the wrong stories."

The exchange surrounding my sociological questions stands in sharp contrast to the lively, lengthy, and engrossing story Laura Stuart told earlier in the interview about her upward mobility from secretary to superintendent. Indeed, my brief request for her work history allowed her to launch into a story that continued with little interruption from us for more than an hour.

SC: So [p] the story of your work life [small laugh]

LS: OK I started [p] some 15-16 years ago as secretary to to
the superintendent.

I was a *nurse* at the time.

CB: ||Oooh||

LS: ||I was|| working for a doctor and the superintendent of
schools called me at Libertyville and said "would you be
interested in going to work for *me*?"

And I had had a little secretarial training course that was
manpower

they don't even have that I think they call it something else
now (CB: hm hmm)

but back at that time it was a manpower program

and so I went to that for 6 months and and got *re* [p]

oh uh *trained* myself.

But I didn't use the secretarial training at that time.

The hospital called and said "would you be interested in coming
back to work?"

I had worked there previously till the kids were born

as a nurse and then went back and did private duty

and I said "well I just finished school

I'm really interested in getting into another line of work"

and I said you know "besides you don't pay enough."

"Well we will pay you."

So they *upped* the salary to what I I felt like I could get as
a secretary.

So I I really *liked* nursing and uh so I went back to work at
the hospital.

I didn't have my license but I had had RN training.

I I just quit did not finish uh and in a little small rural town
like that well that you know if you have any training at all that
was a plus.

My request for Laura Stuart's work history was brief and required
no explanation in part because we had begun the interview by telling
her about the kinds of questions we would ask, including this one. More
importantly, my request required no explanation because *this was the
story she most wanted to tell during the interview.* In this excerpt, her
story tumbles out, with different events toppling over each other as

if each event is so tied to all the others that she can't talk about one without immediately bringing up the rest.

Like Karen Sacks, my coresearcher and I eventually dropped our sociological questions because they were too external to women's experiences; they encouraged reports rather than stories.[7] The problem with those questions did not lie in their wording—the excerpts show that I used everyday language—but in the way they pulled women away from their experiences. When we asked the sociological questions, we got what we asked for, but not what we were most interested in hearing. Those questions distracted us from the deeper and broader life story the interviewee had to tell.

My Own Experience as a
Subject in a Study of Academic Women

Rose Jones, a student in another social science department at my university, asked whether she could interview me as part of her study of women in academe. I agreed, thinking it would be fun to be the interviewee for a change. During the interview, I noticed that some of her questions invited me or at the very least allowed me to tell the story of my own experiences. For example, her first question was "What were the motivating factors that got you into the academic profession?" Rather than listing motivating factors, I chose to talk about how I ended up in graduate school, what graduate school was like for me, and how I made the transition from graduate school to an academic job. Interestingly, my answer suggests that I was not actually motivated to get into the profession because I did not orient to the profession even as I worked my way toward it. I began graduate school with an interest in getting a better education, never imagining that I would come out of it with a Ph.D. and that I would end up as a full-fledged academic with a real job in the profession.[8] Although Rose asked for motivating factors, I answered a broader life story question: "How did you end up in academe?" Nonetheless, her question was close enough to the one I wanted to answer that it did not inhibit my story. She asked a number of other questions that permitted me to tell my own stories, such as: How do you manage teaching versus research? What is keeping you in the profession?

By contrast, some of the questions she asked were not about my experiences at all, but about my opinion concerning the difference gender makes in the profession. For example, What do you think about the issue of tenure for women in academe? How do you think women are represented in institutions of higher education? How do you think your male colleagues manage teaching versus research? I felt impatient with these questions but not because I had nothing to say about them. Indeed, I have plenty to say about the differences gender makes in this and other occupations, differences that I talk about in my courses as well as during everyday conversations with friends, colleagues, and students. I was impatient because this was neither a classroom interaction nor a casual conversational context; this was supposed to be an interview about *my* experiences. I did not want the focus to shift away from me and my stories. These questions asked me to speak as a sociologist, something I am perfectly capable of doing but which I didn't want to do here. In short, these questions felt like work. Not surprisingly, I offered sociological responses to her socio-logical questions. Listen, for example, to part of my answer to her question about women and tenure:[9]

SC: Women tend to do more service activities because of the low representation of women on campuses, but when it comes to ten-ure that doesn't count. It's not intentional discrimination, it's insti-tutional discrimination.

This is not a description of my own experience but a summary of what I assume to be many women's experiences. Rose Jones's socio-logical questions invited me to report my observations of what women in general do rather than to recount what I in particular have done.

In sum, all three examples suggest that sociological questions fail to invite the other's story because they orient the interviewee to the researcher's interests. Even when the researcher phrases such ques-tions in everyday speech and intends to produce a collaborative research relationship, sociological questions direct the other to the researcher's concerns and away from her own life experiences. In some cases, of course, participants willingly enter such a conversation to help the researcher with his or her questions. But even in those cases, the researcher invites a report rather than a story because the weight or import of the question remains on the researcher's side, with the interviewee acting at best as a willing reporter or informant.

What, then, does it mean to invite the other's story and how do we articulate a good life story question? Unlike sociological questions, questions that invite the other's story encourage a shift of responsibility for the import of the talk. Our task as interviewers is to provide the interactional and discursive conditions that will arouse her desire to embrace that responsibility. We are most likely to succeed when we orient our questions directly and simply to life experiences that the other seeks to make sense of and to communicate.

But even if we aim to invite the other to tell her story, it's not always clear in advance which question will serve as an invitation. Sacks did not know she had asked a good question until she started to hear stories about how childhood chores produced a sense of responsibility and self-respect. In her case, the good questions were: How did you learn about work? And what did work mean to you? In my study of women educational leaders, the request for work histories invited them to take responsibility for determining the direction and significance of their talk. But even though my coresearcher and I asked that question from the beginning of the project, I did not recognize it as the pivotal question until later.

Our work as interviewers, then, includes careful formulation of questions that will invite the other's story. Before we start interviewing, we need to begin with, or at least work our way toward, some sense of the broad parameters of the other's story, the life experience he or she seeks to make sense of and to communicate. And we do this by articulating what makes this group of people's life experiences interesting in the first place.

In the case of my study, the anomaly of women holding positions of power makes their experiences interesting, not only to themselves, but also to researchers, journalists, and the public at large. As public school superintendents, these educators occupy influential positions in their communities. As white women and women of color, they are continuously subject to gender and racial inequalities in a male- and white-dominated profession. It is the coexistence of power and subjection in their work lives that makes their experiences interesting within the context of contemporary American society. Although we did not articulate it at the time, my coresearcher and I, as well as the women we interviewed, *assumed* that as highly successful professional women, they would have stories to tell that others want and need to hear, stories about how they rose to such influential leadership positions despite the anomaly of their gender or race, stories about what it is like to work in such positions, stories about the inequalities they face and how they handle them. These assumptions reveal the broad parameters of the life stories women educational leaders have to tell. Hence the appropriateness of the request for their work histories.

Encountering Narrative
Difficulties and Reiterating the Invitation

Knowing the broad parameters of the other's story prepares us to ask a good question. However, the very thing that makes any group of people's life experiences interesting may also produce narrative difficulties. For example, as women educational leaders recounted their work histories, they told stories about themselves *both* as highly accomplished, successful professionals *and* as women who are subject to sexism and racism in the profession. As I analyzed their narratives, I discovered that women often have difficulty bringing together these two distinct experiences of self. That difficulty is not psychological or personal (although it might have psychological or personal consequences). Rather it is cultural and discursive. In narrating their work experiences, successful professional women work at integrating two kinds of talk—two discursive realms—that do not usually belong together in American culture: talk about individual achievement and success, and talk about gender and racial inequality.[10]

In articulating the general parameters of the other's story, then, we need to attend to what may be culturally problematic about that story and what may produce narrative difficulties or complexities. In listening to the other tell her story, we need to remain attentive to the ways in which its culturally problematic character may produce silences, gaps, disruptions, or contradictions. Thus, inviting the other's story requires more than a good life story question, it also requires reiterating the invitation throughout the interview. This means that we may need to ask questions that will encourage her to fill in what she has left out or to articulate more fully her contradictory feelings.

I return to Laura Stuart's work history to illustrate how a narrative difficulty arose that my coresearcher and I should have explored in more depth. In recounting her career story, Stuart emphasized her hard work and determination in her upward mobility from the humble position of secretary to the powerful position of superintendent of schools. Throughout that story she wove the theme of her growing self-confidence through mastery of new responsibilities and recognition of how much she had accomplished with so few resources. Yet a less obvious theme bubbled to the surface at certain points: her nagging feeling of inadequacy. The gap or contradiction between her growing self-confidence and her persistent lack of self-confidence indicates a narrative difficulty.

In the following excerpt, Laura Stuart concludes her discussion of how she managed to finish her bachelor's, master's, specialist's, and administrative degrees while working full-time in jobs with increasing responsibility: secretary, secretary-teacher, business manager, and administrative assistant to the superintendent.

LS: And I graduated from [university] [p]
same weekend I became a grandmother.
It was a *very* exciting weekend.
CB and SC: [laugh] yeah
LS: But anyway it's been a very uh [p] uh *exciting* period. (CB: hm hmm)
People *anyone* could have what I have attained
if they had the determination and willing to make the sacrifices that I had to do
because I haven't been blessed with
I mean I'm not *super* intelligent like I think Ruth Porter is

like Adrienne like Mary [other women superintendents]
I feel like they're just head and shoulders above me
you know I feel so in*adequate* sometimes when I'm in their
   presence because I think they have so much.
I guess because I've come up that way that my you know a lot
   of mine has been *practical* experience. (**CB:** hm hmm)
But I *honestly* do not feel like I could have handled this job here
   had I not had the background of that secretarial you know
   training and coming up . . .
it has been a *great* benefit to me
I think if you interviewed any one of my employees here from
   the cooks to the custodians
they will tell you you know that uh I've made them feel
   important . . .
this belongs to them too
and I think that comes from my background.

In terms of narrative process, Laura Stuart sandwiches her statements about her inadequacy between more convincing and fully developed descriptions of her strengths. At the beginning of this excerpt, as she summarizes a busy, exciting period in her life—one filled with many accomplishments—Stuart points to her own determination and willingness to make sacrifices as the source of her success. And at the end of the excerpt, she articulates the strengths she has gained from her practical experience. Virtually all superintendents enter the educational system as teachers (a professional occupation); Stuart's beginning as a secretary (a working-class job) is unusual. She claims that her unique background has provided her with the insight and skills to make all school employees feel part of the educational community.

It is unclear from this passage why Laura Stuart thinks she is not as intelligent as the women superintendents she names; indeed, she provides no evidence of that claim. The disjunction between her feelings of inadequacy and her descriptions of her strengths points to a narrative difficulty.[11] How can a professional woman who occupies one of the most influential positions in her community make sense of her recurrent lack of self-confidence? Cultural discourse about professional work makes it easy for Laura Stuart to tell a story about increasing responsibilities and thus increasing self-confidence. In other words, that is an intelligible, recognizable story in our society. In contrast, it is difficult to narrate her feelings of inadequacy because they do not make sense within conventional discourse about professional work. Thus her lack of self-confidence surfaces in her narrative without becoming integrated into it. My point is not that it is impossible to imagine her feelings of inadequacy—what professional has not felt inadequate at times in comparison to peers?—but that the undeveloped description of those feelings indicates the limited character of professional discourse within which she has been telling her story.

Interestingly, neither my coresearcher nor I pick up on Laura Stuart's feelings of inadequacy at this point. Here is how we continue:

SC: I'm I'm missing a little piece of the story.
How did you decide when you were administrative assistant
    to the superintendent
how did you decide that *you* would start applying for superintendencies yourself?
LS: OK the superintendent was going to retire
and uh I felt like I was next in line for the job there. . . .
BUT guess who he recommended
CB: the high school principal
LS: and I said "I'm not going to train another high school
    principal.
This is it.
I have carried the ball for you." . . .
That last superintendent had [emphatically] the *best* job of any
    of my superintendents
because I had *grown* and matured *professionally*
had assumed more responsibility you know as time went on. . . .
[emphatically] He *never* filled out a report.
Not one.
I did *all* the agendas.
We discussed what was but *I* did I was responsible for the *agenda*.
I was responsible for the *budget*.
I was the district *treasurer.* . . .
So he was you know he *really* had it made.
Consequently I *always really* worked with him before he went
    into a board meeting on Monday

I spent the *day with him going tutoring* him on what
because I didn't want him to have to turn to me and say
you know I was still [deep sigh] [p]
trying to make him look good
and willing to take the back seat . . .
I didn't begrudge him [the high school principal] applying for
   the job.
What I *REALLY* detested was that this superintendent *knew*
and if he had stayed neutral and said
"either one of them is an *excellent* candidate"
because he knew
but he did not feel like I could handle the job the people.
But *I KNEW* I had the people skills to do it.
SC: So he didn't—you were ready but he didn't he didn't know
   you were ready or he didn't—
LS: *He* didn't *he* went with the good old boy.
He went with [p] because he was a man.

Laura Stuart's confidence in her readiness for the title and full responsibility of the superintendency comes through loud and clear. Through a series of first-person, declarative statements, she convinces us of her competence and that she had already taken on much of the superintendent's work. She also expresses outrage at her superior's blatant sexism in failing to recommend her as his successor. As listeners, we sense that this discriminatory episode was a turning point, the moment at which she decisively rejected her previous pattern of doing male superiors' work for them. At the same time, she acknowledges her collusion in the superintendent's facade, and her deep sigh indicates her understanding that something was terribly amiss in that arrangement. What remains unstated, however, is how she got herself into such a situation in the first place and how she felt about it at the time. We need more emotional details to understand the transition fully. Again, the point is not that such a situation is unimaginable; indeed, it is all too familiar in professional women's stories. Rather, the point is that Laura Stuart hints at a story that remains untold—the story about taking a back seat while working hard to make the superintendent look good. As interviewers we need to attend to submerged stories like this one and invite their telling. This story appears to be more difficult to tell than a story about growing professional confidence, which is the dominant frame Stuart uses in her work history, including in this excerpt. From my retrospective, analytic standpoint, I begin to wonder whether this submerged story is related to the earlier one about feelings of inadequacy.

Toward the end of her long work history, Laura Stuart described a situation in which a colleague in another school district had invited Stuart rather than others to apply for a certain prestigious job. She expressed genuine pleasure at being singled out in this way. At this point her feelings of inadequacy suddenly resurfaced:

LS: [sigh] I think *some*body is going to tap me on the shoulder
    one of these days and tell me to get back down where I belong
    (CB: hmmm)
you know I have those feelings sometimes
I don't know if you all ever experience it or not
and my daughter sent me a book titled *The Imposter* ||*Feeling*||
CB: ||hm hmmm||
so that's ||what you're thinking about||
LS: ||and I read it|| you know I get it out every once in a while
    and go back and read a chapter or two because [p]
I didn't have any self-confidence uh for a number of years.
But now I feel like I can do it
you know I feel in*adequate* sometimes
I feel like Ruth and they are are so much *smarter* than I am
but I *still* feel like I can hold my own
I'm running this school system too
maybe not as *big* as what they are doing but I still
I'm making things work for me. (CB: hm hmm)
I I'm proud of myself I really am.
SC: What changed there?
You said you used to not have self-confidence and now you do
    even though sometimes—
LS: I I went back to school.
I went back to college and made straight As.
My first report card my first grades I could not *believe* it
I was so amazed.
I thought "*I* can do *this*."

CB: So actually doing things

LS: I guess

CB: you've convinced ||yourself||

LS: ||yeah|| and along about that time after I got out of college
I lost some weight
and um it made a difference in my appearance.
I'm not beautiful but I like myself better now.
And I don't know just all of it added together maybe.

Here my coresearcher and I finally attend to Laura Stuart's feelings of inadequacy, perhaps because she dwells on the topic for a while, or because feeling like an impostor is more extreme than feeling inadequate, or because she includes us as professional women who may have felt similarly. Notice that once again she counters these negative feelings with her confidence and even pride in her accomplishments. When I ask "What changed there?" I am finally trying to bring the submerged story to the surface. Although my question asks for her process of self-development on this issue, my interrupted phrase "even though sometimes—" only hints at the more problematic feature of her narrative: Her lack of self-confidence *recurs* even now that she has achieved a prominent leadership position. The nagging persistence of these feelings needs more illumination. The best way to tap that would have been to ask about specific recent incidents when she felt inadequate or like an impostor.[12]

In sum, Laura Stuart experienced our request for her work history as an invitation to tell her story about her upward mobility from secretary to superintendent, and about her hard work, determination, and growing confidence in confronting obstacles—including sex discrimination—that she encountered along the way. In taking up that invitation, she eagerly embraced responsibility for the import of her talk. However, the excerpts I have examined from her work history reveal narrative difficulties in the form of hinted at but unarticulated aspects of her experience, narrative difficulties that call for reiteration of the invitation to tell her story. Our task as interviewers, then, includes listening for gaps, silences, or contradictions, and reiterating the invitation through questions that encourage fuller narration of the complexities of her story. By reiterating the invitation, we work at continually shifting narrative responsibility to the other.

Narrative Analysis: Studying the Relation Between the General and the Particular

Many researchers who study narratives produced during interviews assert that we learn about general social processes through analysis of specific narratives.[13] From this standpoint, narrative analysis is grounded in a particular theoretical commitment: Understanding general social processes *requires* a focus on their embodiment in actual practices, that is, in actual narratives. In other words, life stories themselves embody what we need to study: the relation between *this* instance of social action (*this* particular life story) and the social world the narrator shares with others; the ways in which culture marks, shapes, and/or constrains this narrative; and the ways in which *this* narrator makes use of cultural resources and struggles with cultural constraints. By analyzing the complex process of narration in specific instances, we learn about the kinds of narratives that are possible for certain groups of people, and we learn about the cultural world that makes their particular narratives possible—and problematic—in certain ways. The significant point here is that the general (cultural and discursive resources and constraints) is not fully evident to us in advance; we know the general fully only through its embodiments.

My discussion of narrative difficulties in the previous section illustrates this theoretical commitment. By attending to the problematic content of Laura Stuart's narrative (the gap between her self-confidence and her feelings of inadequacy) as well as to disjointedness in her narrative process (the sudden surfacing and submerging of her feelings of inadequacy), we can begin to analyze the boundaries of cultural discourse about professional work. Similarly, the smoothly narrated parts of her work history—for example, about growing self-confidence through increasing responsibilities—point not only to her personal comfort with that aspect of her experience but also to the kind of cultural discourse that is readily accessible for describing one's professional development.

Laura Stuart's work history also illustrates how general social processes related to gender and social class are embedded in her narrative. She speaks directly about her working-class background and the unusual pattern of her upward mobility. Furthermore, she suggests that her background and atypical career path have enabled her to develop specific skills that are useful in her work as superintendent. She also explicitly acknowledges sexist treatment she encountered as she worked her way from secretary to educational administrator. Notice that we did not have to ask directly about gender issues to hear about them; I asked the fruitless series of questions that produced her reports about gender-related experiences *after* she gave us her work history. Her sex discrimination story, which she told as part of her work history, is much more fully developed than those reports.[14] Laura Stuart's direct references to gender and class hint at the impact of general social processes on her work experiences; more precisely, they tell us how *she* interprets the relationship between the general and the particular in her own life.

However, what is more interesting to me, and much more difficult to decipher, is how general social processes related to gender and class are embedded in Stuart's submerged stories. To address this question, we would need to identify all of the places where submerged stories surface, such as those about inadequacy, impostorship, and taking a back seat to men while doing their work for them. Then we would need to examine the relationship between those submerged stories and her larger, more fully developed narrative about growing self-confidence. Are there any patterns in the way she mentions and then drops the subject of inadequacy? What aspects of her work experience does she use to push these feelings aside? What is it about these submerged experiences and feelings that inhibits their fuller expression in her work history? By contrast, what is it about her larger story of hard work, determination, and growing self-confidence that makes those aspects of experience easy to narrate?

It is reasonable to consider that there might be gender and class underpinnings to the narrative difficulties in Laura Stuart's work history. After all, women from working backgrounds receive little cultural encouragement to be ambitious and plenty of encouragement to work selflessly for others and to think of themselves as inadequate. But the task of narrative analysis is to find out *how* she embeds those general social processes in her narrative. We might continue our analysis by examining the places where she easily acknowledges how class and gender shape her experiences and comparing them to the places where she could have pointed to gender and class influences but didn't. What in the submerged stories keeps her from making similar connections? Could it be that she attaches shame or self-blame to the experiences hinted at in those stories? For example, might she be ashamed of herself for colluding with a man's exploitation of her, thinking that as a professional woman she should have known better? If so, a sense of responsibility for her own predicament may make it difficult for her to identify gender and class influences in the experiences described in these submerged stories. By contrast, it might be easier to identify blatant sex discrimination and material obstacles related to her working-class background (such as having to work full-time while pursuing her education) as problems not of her own making.

The excerpts I have examined from Laura Stuart's work history are not sufficient to demonstrate any particular argument; I have simply suggested possibilities for further inquiry. In any case, analyzing specific narratives to answer questions like these allows us to develop fuller knowledge about how cultural discourses simultaneously provide us with resources for articulating experience and constrain us when we do so. Such analysis also educates us about the range of ways in which narrators reproduce those discourses and struggle with those constraints as they make sense of their life experiences. However, this kind of narrative analysis depends on our ability to invite others to recount their life stories in rich detail and on our sensitivity to narrative difficulties that signal our need to reiterate the invitation again and again throughout our interviews. The more fully *particular* are the stories we hear, the stronger our analyses will be of the relationship between the general and the particular. We serve our theoretical interest in general social processes when we take seriously the idea that people make sense of life experiences by narrating them.

Notes

1. See, for example, Blum and McHugh (1984), Brown (1987), Bruner (1986), Hunter (1990), Maines and Ulmer (1993), Martin (1986), Mishler (1986), Mitchell (1980), Richardson (1990), and Rosenwald and Ochberg (1992).

2. See also Riessman (1990), especially the appendix, "A Narrative about Methods."

3. The idea of studying the general through the particular continues to be more widely accepted in anthropology and psychology than in sociology. Nonetheless, several sociological traditions—symbolic interaction, phenomenology, ethnomethodology—advance the idea that individuals' practices embody what is general to the group or society of which they are members. For full discussions see Blum and McHugh (1984), Garfinkel (1967), and Chase (1995), especially chapter 1. Rosenwald (1986) articulates similar ideas from the standpoint of psychology.

4. For discussions of the influence of feminism on research methods see Cancian (1992), Harding (1987), and Reinharz (1992).

5. "Laura Stuart" is a pseudonym as are all of the names of people and places mentioned in the interview excerpts. I have also given a pseudonym to "Rose Jones," the student who interviewed me, as discussed in the next section.

6. Sociologists and others who base their research on interviews typically edit interview talk when they present excerpts. They exclude what appears to be extraneous, distracting material: stutters, repetitions, asides, pauses, the interviewer's questions, interruptions, and nonlexical responses such as "hm hmm." The intention of such editing, of course, is to provide readers with the content of speech. Yet as many others have argued, such editing ignores that meaning is communicated through the complex practices of speech as well as through words (Mishler, 1986; Stromberg, 1993). Thus my interview transcripts include material that some deem distracting. By listening carefully to how speakers express themselves, I can interpret more fully what they are saying. My transcribing procedures highlight the flow and intensity of speech. Each line of a transcript represents what Chafe (1980, pp. 14-15) calls a "spurt of language." I determine the boundaries of a "spurt" by listening to intonation, a rise or fall in pitch. When a "spurt" is longer than a line of text, I indent the subsequent lines to show that speech is continuous. Italics indicate emphasis; capital letters signify extra emphasis or loudness; and dashes show a break-off of speech or interruption. When speakers talk simultaneously, their overlapping words are placed within double lines. Noticeable pauses of less than 3 seconds are identified by [p] and pauses of more than three seconds by [P]. Laughter and other nonlexicals are noted in brackets. I use punctuation sparingly, only when intonation clearly indicates a full stop or question. Quotation marks show that a speaker is reporting someone else's (or her own) speech. Ellipses (. . .) mark places where I have deleted material. My method of transcription is closest to that developed by Riessman (1990). For a discussion of how theories of language are embodied in transcribing practices, see Mishler (1991) and Ochs (1979).

7. For an analysis of awkward moments produced by these questions in one of our earliest interviews, see Chase and Bell (1994).

8. This may be a gendered story. See Aisenberg and Harrington (1988), especially chapter 2, "Transformation."

9. During the interview Rose Jones agreed to give me a copy of the interview tape; unfortunately, she accidentally erased the tape after making a rough transcript. I quote here from the transcript she gave me.

10. I develop this idea in chapters 1 and 2 of Chase (1995).

11. Stuart's statement of her inadequacy could also be interpreted as a marker, "a passing reference . . . to an important event or feeling state," a hint thrown out for the interviewer to pick up on (Weiss, 1994, p. 77).

12. Weiss (1994) provides the best discussion I have read of how to elicit full, detailed stories from interviewees (especially pp. 71-73). Interestingly, he does not relate his discussion specifically to narrative research.

13. Within this general idea of narration as a complex social process, narrative analysts have various interests and purposes. For example, some focus on how narratives embody, reproduce, and/or alter cultural scripts or disjunctive discursive realms (Chase, 1995; Walkover, 1992). Others examine the ways that narratives push at the boundaries of what is unsayable and untellable in particular contexts (Greenspan, 1992; Stromberg, 1993). And some are interested in how narration shapes identity and in the formative and deformative effects of narration (Rosenwald & Ochberg, 1992).

14. Some women superintendents did not talk about discrimination as they narrated their work histories. In those cases we asked a direct question about sex and/or race discrimination at the end of her work history. Unlike the series of questions we asked Laura Stuart and a few other women at the beginning of the study, this question was intended to reiterate the invitation to tell her story. In other words, we were asking about what we assumed was being left out. Indeed, all of the women acknowledged that they are subject to some form of gender and/or racial inequality. If we wanted to hear the full story of women's work experiences, then, sometimes we needed to ask directly about those experiences of inequality that the professional world discourages them from talking about. See Chase (1995), especially chapters 3, 4, and 5.

References

Aisenberg, N., & Harrington, M. (1988). *Women of academe: Outsiders in the sacred grove.* Amherst, MA: University of Massachusetts Press.

Bell, C., & Chase, S. (1993). The underrepresentation of women in school leadership. In C. Marshall (Ed.), *The new politics of race and gender* (pp. 144-154). London: Falmer Press.

Blum, A., & McHugh, P. (1984). *Self-reflection in the arts and sciences.* Atlantic Highlands, NJ: Humanities Press.

Brown, R. H. (1987). *Society as text: Essays on rhetoric, reason, and reality.* Chicago: University of Chicago Press.

Bruner, E. M. (1986). Ethnography as narrative. In V. W. Turner & E. M. Bruner (Eds.), *The anthropology of experience.* Urbana, IL: University of Chicago Press.

Cancian, F. M. (1992). Feminist science: Methodologies that challenge inequality. *Gender & Society, 6,* 623-642.

Chafe, W. L. (1980). The deployment of consciousness in the production of a narrative. In W. L. Chafe (Ed.), *The pear stories: Cognitive, cultural, and linguistic aspects of narrative production* (pp. 9-50). Norwood, NJ: Ablex.

Chase, S. E. (1995). *Ambiguous empowerment: The work narratives of women school superintendents.* Amherst, MA: University of Massachusetts Press.

Chase, S. E., & Bell, C. S. (1994). Interpreting the complexity of women's subjectivity. In E. M. McMahan & K. L. Rogers (Eds.), *Interactive oral history interviewing* (pp. 63-81). Hillsdale, NJ: Lawrence Erlbaum.

Garfinkel, H. (1967). *Studies in ethnomethodology.* Englewood Cliffs, NJ: Prentice Hall.

Greenspan, H. (1992). Lives as texts: Symptoms as modes of recounting in the life histories of holocaust survivors. In G. C. Rosenwald & R. L. Ochberg (Eds.), *Storied lives: The cultural politics of self-understanding* (pp. 145-164). New Haven, CT: Yale University Press.

Harding, S. (Ed.). (1987). *Feminism and methodology: Social science issues.* Bloomington: Indiana University Press.

Hunter, A. (Ed.). (1990). *The rhetoric of social science research: Understood and believed.* New Brunswick, NJ: Rutgers University Press.

Maines, D. R., & Ulmer, J. T. (1993). The relevance of narrative for interactionist thought. *Studies in Symbolic Interaction, 14,* 109-124.

Martin, W. (1986). *Recent theories of narrative.* Ithaca, NY: Cornell University Press.

Mishler, E. G. (1986). *Research interviewing: Context and narrative.* Cambridge, MA: Harvard University Press.

Mishler, E. G. (1991). Representing discourse: The rhetoric of transcription. *Journal of Narrative and Life History, 1,* 255-280.

Mitchell, W. J. T. (Ed.). (1980). *On narrative.* Chicago: University of Chicago Press.

Ochs, E. (1979). Transcription as theory. In E. Ochs & B. B. Schieffelin (Eds.), *Developmental pragmatics* (pp. 43-72). New York: Academic Press.

Polanyi, L. (1985). *Telling the American story: A structural and cultural analysis of conversational storytelling.* Norwood, NJ: Ablex.

Reinharz, S. (1992). *Feminist methods in social research.* New York: Oxford University Press.

Richardson, L. (1990). Narrative and sociology. *Journal of Contemporary Ethnography, 19,* 116-135.

Riessman, C. K. (1990). *Divorce talk: Women and men make sense of personal relationships.* New Brunswick, NJ: Rutgers University Press.

Rosenwald, G. C. (1986). A theory of multiple-case research. *Journal of Personality, 56,* 239-264.

Rosenwald, G. C., & Ochberg, R. L. (Eds.). (1992). *Storied lives: The cultural politics of self-understanding.* New Haven, CT: Yale University Press.

Sacks, K. B. (1988). *Caring by the hour: Women, work, and organizing at Duke Medical Center.* Urbana: University of Illinois Press.

Sacks, K. B. (1989). What's a life story got to do with it? In Personal Narratives Group (Ed.), *Interpreting women's lives: Feminist theory and personal narratives* (pp. 85-95). Bloomington: Indiana University Press.

Stromberg, P. G. (1993). *Language and self-transformation: A study of the Christian conversion narrative.* Cambridge, NY: Cambridge University Press.

Walkover, B. C. (1992). The family as an overwrought object of desire. In G. C. Rosenwald & R. L. Ochberg (Eds.), *Storied lives: The cultural politics of self-understanding* (pp. 178-191). New Haven, CT: Yale University Press.

Weiss, R. S. (1994). *Learning from strangers: The art and method of qualitative interview studies.* New York: Free Press.

❦ 2 ❦

Imagining the Real

Empathy, Narrative, and the Dialogic Self

Ruthellen Josselson

*W*hen I was a freshman in college, taking introductory psychology, I was required to participate in a psychological experiment. On a dark, snowy night in February, I trudged through the snow drifts to a University of Michigan lecture hall where I was asked to write stories in response to brief descriptions of situations—like "at the end of the first year, Anne is at the top of her medical school class." I was not in a good mood. I was angry about being dragged out in the cold and snow and I wrote stories as absurd and bizarre as I could make them. Satisfied with my revenge, I went home and forgot all about it.

Two years later, I took a course in motivation with a well-known professor. I learned then that this "experiment" I had participated in was designed to assess "fear of success." For my final paper in this course, I was assigned to write about some aspect of the study of motivation, and I decided to reflect on my own experience being a subject

AUTHOR'S NOTE: A modified version of this paper was delivered as an invited address in receipt of The Henry A. Murray Award at the American Psychological Association meeting, Los Angeles, August 1994.

in such a study. I began my paper describing the dark and snowy night, still parodying, now Hemingway. I was an impetuous student. The thrust of my argument was that a study that purported to be studying my motivation wasn't tapping it at all. Indeed, as a young woman in 1967, I knew about the fear of success. I knew about it deeply and pervasively. That was the central issue on which my life was poised at the time. The only problem was that no one was asking me what I knew or what I experienced. My responses to the stories reflected my resentment at being called out on a miserable night, not my deep struggles with what it meant to me to succeed.

My professor took the argument in my paper to heart. To his credit, he felt I was worth arguing with. Point by point, he picked my position apart—he wrote nearly as much as I had. And at the end of his response, he wrote, "I think, Ruthellen, you should reconsider your plan to become a psychologist. I think you have an emotional resistance to the scientific study of man."

I was taken aback, but I became a psychologist anyway. And I still believe in the truth that lies in experience and still hold to a conviction that a psychology that does not take as its enterprise the study of whole human beings, in context, in time, is no psychology at all. Since the time that I was an undergraduate in psychology, our understanding of what comprises "the scientific study of man" has changed. At least it is now more multiform and there are no longer universally acknowledged paths to truth. Many have advocated the ideological position that psychology is, or ought to be, the study of how experience—conscious and unconscious—is organized, interpreted, and reshaped throughout the life cycle, and others have provided the epistemology for a different approach to psychological understanding.

New philosophical ideas rooted in hermeneutics are undergirding a return to the study of experience,[1] a return shepherded by a revival of narrative and empathy as standpoints within psychological research. I take my title from Martin Buber, whose idea of imagining the real is that of making the other present in their wholeness, imagining "what another . . . is wishing, feeling, perceiving and thinking" (1965, p. 70) not in a detached way, not as a set of variables, but as part of a process of a living Other. We cannot know the real without recognizing our own role as knowers, and that is why I am taken with Buber's idea of imagining it, for this is, I believe, an accurate word for what we do. We take whatever observations we have made of the external world and, making them part of ourselves, interpret them and tell a story about what we believe we know. Empathy and narrative are an inevitable part of all research, whether quantitative or qualitative in design, but these are processes that have been relegated to the shadows in psychology, disowned, disavowed but, like all that is repressed, ever-present.

Interest in the study of whole people, beginning with Murray's seminal work in 1938, has sputtered throughout the past 55 years. Despite intermittent critiques of psychology for abandoning this idea, the study of the whole person has never been part of the mainstream of academic psychological endeavor. In recent years, however, it has been enjoying something of a renaissance, largely in the wake of interest in hermeneutics and postmodern epistemologies.

To study whole persons, we cannot rely on logical positivist methods that isolate simple factors and trace their effects through statistical analysis. Such analysis aims for elucidating universals but effaces the intending individual. Whole human beings cannot be objectively described as though they are molecules. To approach this topic we need a metaphysics that embraces relativity and an epistemology that is simultaneously empirical, intersubjective, and process-oriented (Flax, 1990). I propose that empathy and narrative are routes to imagining what is real in whole people in their world.

I want first to challenge the idea that empathy and narrative are salient only for research approaches that are qualitative in design. I think that qualitative methods highlight these processes in their epistemology, but that they are present in quantitative approaches as well. Data, after all, do not speak for themselves. They presuppose certain ways of asking questions and certain ways of interpreting results. The results of our experiments are never self-evident in their import. They are merely the occasion for us to try to weave a narrative in which obtaining a certain set of "significant" results makes sense—sense in the context of ongoing narratives both of epistemology and of a developing communal tale of human experience. And "sense" is a product of interpretation, grounded in the social conditions in which we live, formed by inescapable ideology, and spoken in a consensual language.

In quantitative work, we still must become empathic with our subjects, but at a greater distance.

The Empathic Stance

Empathy has been undervalued and rarely taught in its own right in the social sciences, except perhaps by a few remaining followers of Carl Rogers. It has not been privileged as a means of understanding. Within psychoanalysis, Heinz Kohut (1977) caused a furor by advocating an "empathic stance" in relation to analytic material. He argued that the idea of an inner life is unthinkable without our ability to know via "vicarious introspection" (p. 306), his definition of empathy. I might similarly advocate an "empathic stance" within research, a way of approaching data that allows for discovery rather than seeks confirmation of hypotheses and that fosters more exhaustive quests for explanation rather than the illusion of finding a preexisting truth. If we listen well, we will unearth what we did not expect. This becomes the paradigm for discovery.

I take as a premise that we cannot know the real—we can only create an image of it—that is, collectively imagine it. In her analysis of the history of science, Evelyn Fox Keller (1985) distinguishes between the traditions based in Platonic knowing—a knowing that is metaphorically based in eros, union, transcendence, and love—and the Baconian model, based on power, control, and domination.

Heir to the Baconian legacy, modern natural science has taken prediction as its main goal. To this extent, it has been interested only in those aspects of the real world that are amenable to control. Hypothesis-testing models in psychology consider only part-aspects of people, titrating out bits that might be changeable given one intervention or another. With this goal in mind, this form of attention obliterates concern for the whole being and the dynamic tension by which the parts are integrated. What is often considered error variance in psychology is exactly that wholeness of person that we work so hard to factor out of our science.

The Platonic ideal of knowing, by contrast, knowledge as transcendence, involves the creation of, in Winnicott's (1971) phrase, a "potential space" in which the boundaries between self as knower and other as known are relaxed. In this space, aspects of the known are allowed to permeate the knower, and this is the essence of empathy. Research then becomes a process of overcoming distance rather than creating it, moving what was Other, through our understanding of their independent selfhood and experience, into relation with us. In that sense, in Buber's terms, we make the other present and know them better. The very indeterminacy between subject and object thus becomes a resource rather than a threat. Empathy is recruited into understanding precisely because its continuity and receptivity allows for a clearer perception of others. We aim to reach the internal array of an Other's experience, bounded always by our shared participation in a matrix of signification. As both a tool and a goal of psychological research, empathy is premised on continuity, recognizing that kinship between self and other offers an opportunity for a deeper and more articulated understanding. Empathy becomes an attitude of attention to the real world based in an effort to connect ourselves to it rather than to distance ourselves from it.

The empathic stance takes hermeneutics as its epistemological ground. When we study whole human beings, we are aiming to interpret others who are themselves engaged in the process of interpreting themselves. This was the essence of my undergraduate quarrel with my professor. I was deeply engaged in making sense of my own understanding of ambition and intellectual desire in the context of a world that made these suspect in women. I was wary of anyone who presumed that their understanding of my experience could be known without an empathic awareness of my own meaning-making efforts. The prevailing assumption at the time was that science could learn more about me by abstracting me out of my context than by studying me within it.

Narrative as a Form of Knowing

We have, however, entered a new age, the age of narrative, an interest that is sweeping a range of academic disciplines. The historians, grappling with narrative frames of reference, are wondering about the relationship between history and literature and between history and autobiography. Are autobiographies history? How do the stories that people tell reflect the dominant assumptions of their age? And people in literature are wondering about how to distinguish what has usually been thought to be literature from autobiography. Just as within psychology, the question of how to treat people's lived experiences embarrasses our more technical understandings of intellectual conceptualizations.

Within contemporary psychology, Jerome Bruner (1986) has most championed the legitimization of what he calls "narrative modes of knowing." This mode privileges the particulars of lived experience rather than logical positivist constructs about variables and classes. It is an effort to approach the understanding of lives in context rather than through a prefigured and narrowing lens. Meaning is not inherent in an act or experience, but is constructed through social discourse. Meaning is generated by the linkages the participant makes between aspects of her or his life as lived and by the explicit linkages the researcher makes between this understanding and interpretation, which is meaning constructed at another level of analysis.

The empathic stance orients us as researchers to other people's experience and meaning-making, which is communicated to us through narrative. To understand another within the empathic stance means being able to understand their stories. In Clifford Geertz's (1973) way of thinking, it involves looking over someone's shoulder at the text they are reading and writing.

Narrative is the means by which we, both as participants and as researchers, shape our understandings and make sense of them. The question is not whether narrative approaches are science, but how we can bring autobiographical awareness into scholarly conversation with our understanding of science. The truths inherent in personal narrative issue from real positions in the world—the passions, desires, ideas, and conceptual systems that underlie life as lived. People's personal narratives are efforts to grapple with the confusion and complexity of the human condition. Our intellectual task as psychologists is to write a superordinate narrative that encompasses them.

When we aggregate people, treating diversity as error variance, in search of what is common to all, we often learn about what is true of no one in particular. Narrative approaches allow us to witness the individual in her or his complexity and recognize that although some phenomena will be common to all, some will remain unique.

I have just finished an analysis of a 20-year follow-up of 30 women whom I have been following since they were seniors in college. My project has been to trace the development of their identity over time. In analyzing these interviews, I set myself the task of working with all the data, not just the women who fell neatly together in common patterns. The challenge was to try to understand the ones who didn't fit my emerging understandings as well as those who did. I found it an immensely humbling experience. For some women, I simply have to say that, try as I might, I simply cannot understand why their life course took one direction rather than another. Nor, in many cases, can they. This places our understanding in perspective. It treats diversity as the unknown, as either the not-yet-known or the unknowable. It is inherent in the work. It is not error.

Narrative approaches also force us to supersede dichotomies. People are not *either* introverted or extraverted, field-dependent or field-independent, or this or that. Dichotomous thinking eliminates the inner contradiction that is intrinsic to human personality. Because people are composed of a dialectic of opposites, the self is inherently dialogic. But I will take this up in greater detail later.

Narrative is the representation of process, of a self in conversation with itself and with its world over time. Narratives are not records of facts, of how things actually were, but of a meaning-making system that makes sense out of the chaotic mass of perceptions and experiences of a life. This is the revolutionary idea that Donald Spence brought to us in his book *Narrative Truth and Historical Truth* (1982). Even study of the most closely observed lives, those of people in psychoanalysis, is not an archaeological excavation but an excursion into reframing a story in search of life plots that better serve the individual in the present.

My own research on the same participants over time has taught me a great deal about how narrative is reshaped and rebalanced as the life course progresses. Events that loom large at one life stage may be underground at another, only to recur. Amanda, for example, as a senior in college, was staking her adolescent independence on a relationship. Raised in a tight-knit, highly traditional Italian Catholic family, growing up on the same street as her grandmother and three aunts, Amanda found it difficult to conceive that her future life could be other than life as she had always known it. But in high school, she became involved with an African American boyfriend, to the chagrin of all around her. Their reaction caused her to question all that she had previously believed. "With religion talking about love thy neighbor and all men are equal, and it was all right until he asked me out," she said. But after 6 years, she triumphed by forcing her family to accept him. As she told her story at the end of college, she was certain of her future plans. She would become a social worker, marry her boyfriend, and fight the prejudice. She was ready to pioneer, to struggle, to live her values with the man she loved.

When I reinterviewed Amanda when she was 33, this boyfriend had simply vanished from the narrative. Now married to another man, with two children and working full-time, Amanda's understanding of her present and past life was focused on her dream to realize a self that could be both occupationally engaged and a mother at the same time. Her past was rewritten to lead inevitably to the end at which she found herself. Only when I asked directly about her former boyfriend did she tell me of the growing distance that had emerged between them when he dropped out of college. She recounted how she eventually realized that she could not have the life she dreamed of with him. He had become a footnote to her life.

But at age 43, he was back as an important internal character in Amanda's life. The catalyst here was Amanda's struggle with her 15-year-old daughter, who had become intensely involved in a relationship with a boy. It was not that Amanda didn't like the boy—he was perfectly acceptable. What was hard to accept was her daughter's exclusive investment in him, an investment that was beginning to interfere with her academic success and with her other interests in life. "I just don't understand why she's had that need to get so involved in such a monogamous relationship at such a young age," Amanda said. "I look back and know why I rebelled. Because my parents were so strict. But I've let her do almost everything. I feel like I've done just the opposite of my parents in bringing her up and here she's doing the same thing. I didn't expect it from her."

Through her daughter's experience, Amanda is now remembering intensely her own adolescence, a time that was relegated to the shadows just 10 years earlier. Only now her understanding of her adolescent involvement is cast as rebellion, not as love or principle, but as part of a disowned and outgrown dependent and rebellious self that she hoped would not appear in her daughter.

As the literary critic Peter Brooks says, the narrator always knows the ending. Narratives select the elements of the telling to confer meaning on prior events—events that may not have had such meaning at the time. This is a narrative transposition of Kierkegaard's famous statement that we live life forwards but understand it backwards. In understanding ourselves, we choose those facets of our experience that lead to the present and render our life story coherent. Only from a hermeneutic position are we poised to study the genesis and revision of people making sense of themselves.

Narrative models of knowing are models of process *in process.* When we record people's narratives over time, we can observe the evolution of the life story rather than see it as a text in a fixed and temporal state. As a novel leads inevitably to its end, personal narrative describes the road to the present and points the way to the future. But the as-yet-unwritten future cannot be identical with the emerging plot and so the narrative is revised. The future expressed in narratives contains the loose ends, the beginnings that expire, the desires that fade or fall by the wayside. Continuity and change are emplotted in narrative form. A "good-enough" narrative contains the past in terms of the present and points to a future that cannot be predicted, although it contains the elements out of which the future will be created.

The Dialogic Self

Most narratives include a multitude of discourses, and it is this multiplicity of discourse that resists being reduced to a single voice. When my students come back from the field, as it were, having completed an intensive interview, they are usually exhausted and overwhelmed. They told me too much, they complain: How will they make sense of it all? This is the problem, to be sure. But what kind of science operates better with less data? The issue is to reflectively decide on what aspects of narrative data to respond to—given that we can never contain another in their absolute wholeness. What we inevitably do is to create signposts to guide our knowledge of another.

If empathy is the road to the experiential core, how do we know when we have arrived? If narratives overwhelm us with their complexity, how do we focus them or summarize them so that we can learn from them? I have found some clues to these riddles in the work of Mikhail Bakhtin, the recently rediscovered Russian literary critic and philosophical anthropologist.

Bakhtin's critique of prenovelistic visions of the individual mirrors current postmodern critiques of academic psychology's view of the individual. In Bakhtin's view, before the genre of the novel, the individual was represented as a finished entity who "has already become everything he could become and [who] could become only that which he has already become. . . . His internal world and all his external characteristics lie on a single plane" (1981, p. 34). The emergence of the novel made possible the representation of the individual in greater complexity, as existing on multiple planes, all in dialogue with each other. Bakhtin's view of the self is relativistic. The self can exist only in relationship to some other, whether that other be another person, other parts of the self, or the individual's society, or her or his culture. In this view, the individual is always in process. "A dynamic authenticity was introduced into the image of man, dynamics of inconsistency and tension between various factors of this image; man ceased to coincide with himself and consequently men ceased to be exhausted entirely by the plots that contain them" (Bakhtin, 1981, p. 35).

Bakhtin's theory of the novel is intimately tied to a theory of language, language being the medium in which reality is represented. His ideas offer much to inform the theory of narrative analysis, but here I wish simply to make the point that without the availability of our participant's language—and here I refer to what de Saussure calls *parole*, that is, the signified—we as psychologists are locked into our own language systems and cannot represent another's worldview. Language connects experience to understanding. Only by listening to what our participants tell us of their experience can we enter into dialogue with their meaning system—and this is the value of narrative forms of investigation. In Bakhtin's world, reality is always too contradictory and heteroglot to be fit into a straightforward genre. Thus he wrestles in literature with the same problems that contemporary psychology debates—the movement into a relativistic rather than a dualistic universe, a universe of human beings always in process, existing on multiple planes of present experience, poised in complex relation to the past and to the future.[3]

If we wish to trace the growth of whole people, we must cease to regard people as finished entities and, somewhat paradoxically, we must find those places within narrative where the self is most clearly in dialogue with itself. These moments of crisis represent nodes of change in which the individual becomes other than he or she was. As Bakhtin points out, we cannot really represent evolution in literature. Rather we refer to it through depicting crises and rebirth. In these dialogic moments, where the planes of self meet, the challenge to empathy and to our capacity to narrate is greatest and is also where our learning about the other is maximized. In contrast to a mere recitation of events (which are themselves also dialogic), we might conceive of dialogic moments expressed in narrative that are personal keys to meaning-making, the place where a person's self-understanding is put to a self-imposed test. By witnessing the working-through of internal contradiction, we are at the heartbeat of psychological organization, the point where the tectonic plates of experience move into contact with one another, and herein, I think, lies the key to psychological entry into another.

I can best illustrate these points with a narrative of a segment of an individual life story. In this final section, I present Fern, one of the women I have been following in my 20-year longitudinal study. In presenting her I wish to highlight the themes I have discussed in more abstract terms—empathy, narrative, and the dialogic self. My aim in this study was to track the unfolding of identity in women and, in particular, to document moments and processes of revision.

I choose Fern because she has been, in many ways among my participants, the most deceptively easy for me to understand on one level, and the hardest to understand on another. She leads me to my own internal dialogue. Over the years that I have been talking about her at conferences, she has also most aroused passionate censure among psychologists. She typified a form of identity formation classified as Identity Foreclosure, which bypasses exploration and holds to childhood-based goals, values, and personality organization (Marcia, 1980). I will describe Fern in a highly abbreviated form, my aim being to arrive at describing what I term a dialogic moment—a moment that allowed me access to what I think are the deepest processes of her identity revision and also to a greater understanding of the dialogic in psychological organization.

Fern was difficult for me to resonate with partly because her interview was a "press release" of her certainty about things rather than an exploration of herself and her world. At the same time, among all the people I interviewed, Fern was easiest to label with psychological concepts. In both her interview and on psychometric measures, she was rigid, introverted, authoritarian, socially isolated, dependent on her mother for structure, insecure but highly field-independent. Attending a state university majoring in physical therapy, Fern's identity was most structured around an intense and concrete investment in the Catholicism of her childhood. When she was 11, her father died after a long illness and it had been a family project, led by her mother, to persuade him to convert to Catholicism before his death. Their success in this wedded Fern to her faith, and all matters of belief and action were phrased in terms of religious dictates. Fern, at age 21, was perplexed by and scornful of her agemates' forays into drugs and politics in the turmoil of the late 1960s. "I don't understand people getting high on drugs," she said, "I can get high on life."

Her image of herself was as a saint. She formed her occupational dream when, as a young girl, she had been the only one in the neighborhood willing to play with a younger neighbor who had cerebral palsy. Right then she determined that her life mission was to help such people and she had never wavered in her goal.

At the time of this first interview, Fern seemed to see herself, as Bakhtin might say, in epic terms, one-dimensional and finished. She felt she had become who she had to become and, having become so, could only continue to be as she always had been. And my psychological standpoint presented convenient labels; she fit nicely into the ready-made categories of personality theory. Perhaps in part because of the way I presented her in speeches later, psychologists were quick to prophesy dire outcomes for Fern. She will get depressed, my psycho-analytic colleagues especially said. She will have a breakdown before she's 40. The developmental psychology literature was no less pessimistic. Foreclosures, people like Fern, are generally discussed in highly pejorative terms.[2]

But I discovered when I met Fern again when she was 34, that dire things did not befall her. On the other hand, she hadn't changed much. She became a physical therapist and married a man who allowed her to convert him to Catholicism and to all her rules for living. She had two children and still understood everything in terms of religious teaching. She resisted the liberalization that the Church was undergoing in the '70s and clung to the more traditional views. Her life was filled with missions, callings; she was still unwavering in her conviction about what was right and wrong and still maintained that she never strayed from the true path. She was clearly still a Foreclosure, but she had adjusted to life and was contributing to society not only through her work but through numerous charitable involvements. If there were other inner voices beside the epic one that still permeated the narrative of this time, they were too muffled for me to be able to hear. Her interview, her narrative, was a recitation of achievements and ideological stances, and I, in response, still could only label her. I couldn't learn from her much about the inner workings of the self.

Now, in that we are all steeped in the same narrative tradition, it is undoubtedly apparent to you that this story will change at the next observation moment. Narrative convention, how we tell stories, is mediated by our culture. And as psychologists, we are more responsive to change than to continuity. Plot of story, like plot of lives, involves progress toward meaning.

If Fern hadn't changed, I probably would never have chosen her to present. Yet I couldn't know that when I went to interview her 10 years later. I was, indeed, surprised at the revisions she had made in herself and her understanding of her world. Fern at 43 had changed, and with this change in her came a change in my ability to know her empathically. What made her accessible to me was her narrating what I now think of as a dialogic moment in her life.

Not long after I saw her when she was 34, Fern decided to speak to her priest about a growing feeling of disappointment she had in her marriage. She felt that her husband wasn't as affectionate as she wished he would be, and she felt guilty about harboring resentment toward him. Her priest suggested that they participate in marriage encounter workshops through the church. In this process, Fern discovered that it wasn't just he who had to change, that she, too, had to revise her understanding of their relationship. This opened for her the world of others, of recognizing and tolerating their difference, of locating herself in a more shifting but, at the same time, more sure place in the world. This change Fern told me about at age 43. I could hear her ruefulness at her prior self, one narrative superseding and encompassing another. Fern's sense of self was becoming more layered.

In the intervening 10 years, Fern has also been through a crisis at work. As the director of physical therapy at a large urban hospital in a time of worsening economic conditions, her department was dealt yet one more budget cut. Now the uncompromising Fern reared up once again. This was beyond her ethical sense of what it meant to do her work. Her department couldn't adequately serve their patients with the funds the hospital administration was willing to allot them. But Fern's salary was the lion's share of the family's income. Nevertheless she resigned. She mortgaged their house and emptied their savings to establish a private service that would serve disadvantaged clients who were being turned away under the hospital's system. Fern was frightened: She was putting her family's welfare in the service of her scruples, but it was something she felt she had to do.

Fern prayed. But the reality was more turbulent than she had envisioned. Business partners reneged on their commitments. People she shared an office with left without paying the rent. For the first time, Fern had to be careful about what food she put in her grocery cart. But she managed to keep afloat.

At the center of Fern's life, though, was not her work, but her wish to provide for her children. When her 16-year-old son came home with news of a class trip to France, Fern was determined that, despite the money struggles, he should go. She took out a loan. Now here, in Fern's report of her experience of her son's trip, is what I term the dialogic moment. And here we must listen to Fern:

> So he went on that trip to Paris and I was so angry at him because he came home and the main thing he wanted to talk about was leaning out the hotel windows and hollering up to the girls above and talking about other experiences that I could have arranged in the seedier parts of town here for much less money. He wasn't talking about seeing the Mona Lisa. His first recounts were of adolescent experiences and I was furious . . . I wanted to say, "I didn't work for the last 6 months for you to come home and talk about this stuff." So I just didn't say anything. I know my expectations were different than his, but I still have a hard time letting go of mine. Because that was my dream too that went and what came back was not the dream that I sent.

And here, with the poignancy of that statement, she laughed.

Now—in this brief vignette are multiple aspects of Fern in dialogue with each other. The narrative is not one of action, but of tension between self-experience and inner resolution. "I was so angry at him . . . . So I just didn't say anything. . . . Because that was my dream too that went." In this statement is a signifier of the massive internal change that Fern has undergone. But her statement, if we listen dialogically, invites our empathic knowing rather than an impulse to label. The text that Fern is creating of her life now includes multiple points of view—so different from how she was in college when she couldn't understand the rebellion of her agemates. And she can honor that awareness even when it is most painful to her, when it represents her difference from her much-loved son. Yet she still holds to her own morality-based stance, a condemning self that retains its continuity with an older dominant self and abhors what seems to her to be a sin-filled world. And these are poised in relation to her mothering self that is determined to let her son learn from his own experience. Fern's awareness and choice, then, exists in relation to her son, to her understanding of the ethical context she carries and to her knowledge of contemporary adolescent culture as well as in relation to her representation of her own past and future selves. The planes of self are in motion, and we see them organized in dynamic relation to each other—this, in Bakhtin's terms, is the dialogic self.

The essence of the novel, in Bakhtin's analysis, is its capacity to put different orders of experience into dialogue with each other. Similarly, when we analyze an interview, we can track this dialogue between different orders of individual experience or the dialogue of the individual with the social world of others. People tell us about their awareness of their own multiplicity, different self-experiences, often with different usages of language.

In addition, human consciousness exists always in relation to other consciousness. All expression is oriented to a response from some Other and shaped by the context in which it occurs. "To be means to communicate," says Bakhtin (1984, p. 287).

Beyond representing people in their situation in the world, an adequate psychology must depict people as poised for change. Existing dialogue points toward a new discourse that we cannot predict. We observe the immense inner growth in Fern as she becomes more cognizant of—and communicates—her inner dialogue, but there will be continuing alternations in her consciousness. Perhaps tomorrow she will decide to "say something" to her son and the narrative will require further rewriting. Bakhtin stresses that human beings are defined by their "unfinalizedness." We retain always the capacity to surprise ourselves and others (Morson, 1986). Context, to Bakhtin, encompasses "infinite dialogue in which there is neither a first nor a last word" (1986, pp. 167-168).

Only through an empathic stance toward people's narration of their life experiences can we uncover the dialogic nature of the self—the dialogue both within the self and the dialogue with the world that is the center of process in development and in living. Only by observing the tensions and flow in this dialogue can we construct a metanarrative of whole people, not by reducing people to their parts, but by recognizing in the interplay of parts the essence of wholeness. Only then are we positioned to imagine the real.

I am proposing, then, that an empathically grounded narrative psychology take as its aim the explication of the architectonics of the self—the ways in which parts are held in dynamic relation to one another and maintain themselves in unending dialogue. This is what I feel was missed when I was a subject in a psychological experiment. At the time, my wish to succeed was held in dynamic tension with my wish to be other things as well—feminine, well liked, acceptable— and my fear that the social world in which I found myself would not allow me all my parts. In psychology, we must have room for people to have all their parts—for Fern's struggle to bring her moralism and her humanism, her religious traditions and her existence in an ethically complex world into relation. The essential message of hermeneutics is that to be human is to *mean,* and only by investigating the multifaceted nature of human meaning can we approach the understanding of people.

Notes

1. For elaboration of the relationship between hermeneutics and modern psychology, see especially Messer, Sass, and Woolfolk (1988) and Kvale (1992).
2. James Marcia, however, has stressed that Foreclosures are most likely to experience difficulty when the context changes.
3. Both Gregg (1991) and Hermans and Kempen (1993) extensively and brilliantly develop similar ideas.

References

Bakhtin, M. M. (1981). *The dialogic imagination.* Austin: University of Texas Press.
Bakhtin, M. M. (1984). *Problems of Dostoyevsky's poetics.* Manchester, UK: Manchester University Press.
Bakhtin, M. M. (1986). *Speech genres and other late essays.* Austin: University of Texas Press.
Bruner, J. (1986). *Actual minds, possible worlds.* Cambridge, MA: Harvard University Press.
Buber, M. (1965). *The knowledge of man.* New York: HarperCollins.
Flax, J. (1990). *Thinking fragments.* Berkeley: University of California Press.
Geertz, C. (1973). *The interpretation of cultures.* New York: Basic Books.
Gregg, G. (1991). *Self-representation: Life narrative studies in identity and ideology.* Westport, CT: Greenwood Press.
Hermans, H. M. J., & Kempen, H. J. G. (1993). *The dialogical self: Meaning as movement.* San Diego, CA: Academic Press.

Keller, E. F. (1985). *Reflections on gender and science.* New Haven, CT: Yale University Press.

Kohut, H. (1977). *The restoration of the self.* New York: International Universities Press.

Kvale, S. (1992). *Psychology and postmodernism.* London: Sage.

Marcia, J. (1980). Identity in adolescence. In J. Adelson (Ed.), *Handbook of adolescent psychology.* New York: John Wiley.

Messer, S. B., Sass, L. A., & Woolfolk, R. L. (Eds.). (1988). *Hermeneutics and psychological theory.* New Brunswick, NJ: Rutgers University Press.

Morson, G. S. (1986). Bakhtin: Essays and dialogues on his work. Chicago: University of Chicago Press.

Spence, D. (1982). *Narrative truth and historical truth.* New York: Norton.

Winnicott, D. W. (1971). *Playing and reality.* London: Tavistock.

❦ 3 ❦

Biographical Work
and New Ethnography

Jaber F. Gubrium
James A. Holstein

*T*he social sciences are witnessing a radical reorientation to the study of lives. Ethnography, for example, was once viewed as the systematic observation of a social setting, the discovery of patterns of interaction and meaning, and the description of indigenous ways of life. Field-work combined looking, listening, asking questions, taking notes, and managing social relations with informants in a wide variety of settings, including nonliterate societies, urban communities, formal organizations, gangs, and social movements (Bogdan & Taylor, 1975; Filstead, 1970; Glaser & Strauss, 1967; McCall & Simmons, 1969; Schwartz & Jacobs, 1979; Shaffir, Stebbins, & Turowetz, 1980; Spradley, 1979; Wax, 1971). Reporting ethnographic findings was mainly a matter of sifting the information gathered and writing a systematic and objective description. In this approach, there was little sense that participants of a setting might have authoritative stories of their own to tell, or that their accounts and descriptions actively constituted rather than just reflected the realities of their worlds. There was relatively minor interest in how participants' stories accorded with each other or what discrepancies might mean, beyond traditional concerns with reliability, validity, and truthfulness. Questions concerning the relationship between participants' stories and the ethnographer's account were not seriously considered.

"New ethnography" has come a long way. We no longer limit our analytic concerns to issues of objective or naturalistic representation. Indeed, much new ethnography is concerned with multivocality, centering on the question of how to deal with participants' own representations of their worlds, with objectivity being only one of several related issues (Atkinson, 1990; Clifford & Marcus, 1986; Clough, 1992; Geertz, 1988; Marcus & Fischer, 1986; Spencer, 1989; Strathern, 1987; Van Maanen, 1988). Where the older ethnography cast its subjects as mere components of social worlds, new ethnography treats them as active interpreters who construct their realities through talk and interaction, stories, and narrative (see, e.g., Behar, 1993; Burgos-Debray, 1984). What is "new" about this is the sense that participants are ethnographers in their own right.

Methodologically, the emphasis now is as much on documenting the interpretive practices through which the realities of social settings are assembled, as on observing and describing social life in detail (Emerson, 1983; Gubrium, 1988a; Heritage, 1984; Holstein & Gubrium, 1994b; Silverman, 1993). Recent empirical studies have shown how the taken-for-granted world of everyday life is interactionally constituted. The studies demonstrate how diverse forms of reality, such as family (Gubrium & Holstein, 1990, 1992; Holstein & Gubrium, 1994a), community (Hazan, 1990), mental illness (Holstein, 1993), the life course (Buckholdt & Gubrium, 1979; Gubrium, Holstein, & Buckholdt, 1994), labor markets (Miller, 1991), battered women (Loseke, 1992), and even the stars in the sky (Garfinkel, Lynch, & Livingston, 1981) and the world under the sea (Goodwin, 1993), are socially constructed.

This chapter shows how new ethnography can shed light on the social construction of individual lives. We refer to this constitutive process as *biographical work* to underscore participants' active, creative involvement. At the same time, we must emphasize that lives are not constructed arbitrarily in a contextual vacuum. Whether it is the personal past, the present, the future, a combination of them, or the life course as a whole, participants work at characterizing their lives in relation to the interpretive horizons of social settings, using available interpretive resources. The nursing home resident who speaks of life and, in the process, produces a sense of its quality, takes account of the conditions of nursing home living in relation to his or her sense of life as a whole (Gubrium, 1993). The legal and mental health agents who participate in involuntary mental hospitalization hearings, define and consider a candidate patient's dangerousness or so-called grave disability in terms of professional and organizational interests and agendas (Holstein, 1993). Biographical work thus reflects locally promoted ways of interpreting experience and identity so that what is constructed is distinctively crafted, yet assembled from the meaningful categories and vocabularies of settings.

In the following sections, we illustrate biographical work from ethnographic and narrative material gathered in nursing homes, family therapy, and community mental health agencies, paying special attention to the interpretive horizons that mediate the construction process. The presentation centers on three analytic terms that have guided our studies of interpretive practice: narrative linkages, local culture, and organizational embeddedness.

Narrative Linkages

How are we to understand what participants of social settings tell us about their lives? Answers to this question distinguish new from older ethnographic approaches. If we treat talk and interaction as the means through which lives are constructed, we direct our attention to what participants actively "do with words" to structure and give social form to experience. Interpretive practice—the activities through which persons understand, organize, and represent experience (Holstein, 1993; Holstein & Gubrium, 1994b)—becomes our focus. Empirical research, then, might center on how participants articulate the stories they tell about themselves so as to construct biographies pertinent to matters under consideration (Gubrium, Holstein, & Buckholdt, 1994). In this approach, narratives are not simply more or less accurate reports of individual experience through time. Rather they are artfully and situationally constructed communications, offering a complex sense of biographical patterning (Bruner, 1986; Cohler, 1993; Gergen & Gergen, 1993; Mitchell, 1981; Rosenthal, 1993).

We can illustrate the complexities of narrative production by comparing "life story" interviews to conventional assessments of nursing home residents' quality of life. Health care professionals and social gerontologists have become increasingly interested in the "quality of life" and the "quality of care" experienced by the frail elderly. Their analytic concerns and methodologies have been the subject of considerable controversy, however. Some of the debate centers on the relations between so-called objective measures on the one hand and more subjective accounts on the other (see Svenssön, 1991). If recipients of care are consulted in the typical "objective" assessment process, they are asked to convey the qualities of their care and lives in nursing facilities in terms of the response categories of precoded, fixed-choice survey instruments. Typically, they are not directly consulted; standardized assessment protocols do not allow them to characterize quality of life and care in their own terms, through their own stories (e.g., see Morris et al., 1990). In objective assessment, care recipients are mainly passive objects of measurement, if they participate at all. Measures of their care and life pertain mainly to such matters as physical and psychosocial functioning. A controversial question is whether this method adequately represents the care recipient's nursing home experience.

When residents are given the opportunity to discuss the qualities of their care and lives in their own words, the accounts can be strikingly different. In a recent study of narratives of nursing home experience (Gubrium, 1993), for example, residents were asked to tell their life stories, following Bruner's (1986) procedure for eliciting subjectively relevant accounts of life. The residents were encouraged to speak of the qualities of their care and life in relation to lifelong experiences and to common public concerns such as the personal consequences of institutionalization. The analytic focus of the study oriented to the following question: If residents were asked to be ethnographers of their own lives in the nursing home, how would the quality of those lives be construed?

In analyzing the interview data, the term *narrative linkages* was used to refer to the experiences that residents linked together to specify the subjective meaning of the qualities of care and nursing home living. Consider the responses of two residents who made contrasting narrative linkages with life experiences. (All names have been fictionalized.) Resident Bea Lindstrom's life story is told in terms of a personal ethic of distributive justice. According to Lindstrom, life has centered on the expectation that others will treat her fairly and that she, in turn, will never take undue advantage. She assiduously respects others' dignity and property and expects the same from them. Details of Lindstrom's childhood experiences, her marriage, her earlier adult life, and, now, her interpersonal relations in the nursing home are conveyed in similar terms.

Like other residents who narratively link their stories with this ethic, Lindstrom is enduringly vigilant. Her narrative is a tale of being on constant guard, lest other residents or staff members invade her personal space or treat her badly, a watchfulness she claims to have maintained her whole life. She notes that she is careful not to intrude into other residents' affairs nor to infringe on staff members' work. Taken together, the narrative linkages show a direct and continuous preoccupation with such matters, engrossing Lindstrom in the ongoing qualities of care and life in the nursing home. In speaking of her life, Lindstrom narratively appropriates the care and living qualities of the present to the core of her biography.

Compare this with resident Julia McCall, who constructs the qualities of life and care in her facility in terms that marginalize the quality of her experience in the nursing home. In her words, she "loves the Lord" and thinks mainly of God's kingdom, not this world. Like some other nursing home residents, her story is suffused with references to religious beliefs and church-going. As she speaks of her life, McCall links each fact of her past and the present, from childhood to old age, with what she believes God intends for her in His grand design, and she looks ahead to heavenly bliss. Hers is a story narratively centered in the afterlife, mundane matters taking second place to otherworldly concerns.

Against a horizon of otherworldly narrative linkages, McCall's interest in the quality of care and life in the nursing home is relatively minor. She is not oblivious to how the staff treat her, how clean the premises are, or to whether other residents are friendly. But as far as "lovin' the Lord" is concerned, the qualities of care and of life in the nursing home are at worst a source of daily irritations and at best a gamut of mere comforts.

Taken together, residents' narratives have clear implications for quality assessment. As far as our knowledge of care and life quality is concerned, the narratives show that traditional assessment systems provide a very narrow view of quality, albeit a significant and useful one. When residents are asked to tell their stories and speak of the quality of care and of life in their own terms as biographically active subjects, the meaning of quality is revealed to be diverse, linked with, and given meaning in relation to lifelong experience (see Holstein & Gubrium, 1995). We need to begin to understand the qualities of care and life for nursing home residents in terms of the variable experiential contexts within which meaning is assigned. The contexts extend well into accounts of the past lives of their subjects.

Equally important is the implication for intervention. We cannot simply design intervention to improve the lot of *the* nursing home resident. To do so would be to formulate expensive and time-consuming window dressing that reflects very few residents' experiences, even though standard quality assessment does inform us of the "objective" conditions of nursing facilities. That there are horizons of meaning for nursing home residents does not suggest that standardized quality assessment is irrelevant. Such assessment is useful for helping to maintain minimum levels of care. But we need to remind ourselves, too, that residents live in subjective worlds as much as they are affected by objective conditions, and intervention should take this into account.

Local Culture

Another analytic term guiding our studies of interpretive practice and biographical work is *local culture*. The term refers to the locally shared meanings and interpretive vocabularies that participants in relatively circumscribed communities or settings use to construct the content and shape of their lives (Gubrium, 1989; Gubrium & Holstein, 1990; Holstein & Gubrium, 1994b). Local cultures are diverse and setting-based and contrast with culture writ large, which is more socially encompassing. In our view, local culture does not so much determine participants' biographical work as it provides circumstantially recognizable and accountable interpretive resources for constructing an understanding of lives.

Small groups have local cultures. Gary Fine (1983), for instance, describes the cultures of adolescent and young-adult gaming groups, which offer members a shared basis for constructing recreational fantasy. Gubrium (1988b) shows how participants in Alzheimer's disease caregiver support groups use local understandings of family responsibility to set the personal limits of home care and to construct rationales for institutionalization. Formal organizations, too, have local cultures (Frost, Moore, Louis, Lundberg, & Martin, 1985). There are corporate cultures, institutional therapeutic cultures, and professional cultures among a host of setting-based ways of viewing and interpreting experience.

We can see how local culture mediates biographical work in two family therapy programs with contrasting understandings of domestic order (Gubrium, 1992). One program, based at an outpatient clinic called Westside House, centers on the view that the family is an authority structure. A family with a clearly defined hierarchy of decision making, with no cross-cutting lines of authority, is considered functional. Dysfunctional families and domestic disorder stem from children who act like parents or parents whose actions are divided against each other. Needless to say, Westside staffers view the families that come to treatment as having ineffective authority structures, typically stemming from absent fathers, indecisive mothers, and out-of-control children.

The other therapy program, based at an inpatient psychiatric facility called Fairview Hospital, centers on the view that the family is a configuration of emotional bonds. All family members have feelings, even the youngest child. A parent who does not listen to the feelings expressed by his or her children risks never realizing a common source of domestic troubles. A child who refuses to acknowledge that parents also are emotional beings builds a wall between them. Addictive, self-absorbed fathers and denying, "codependent" mothers, unconcerned with their children, add to the communicative barriers. Feelings must be acknowledged, lest they become explosive and tear the family apart. Accordingly, staff members emphasize the effective communication of emotions, stressing "active listening" and "asser-tive" (not aggressive or passive) communication. Just as dysfunction-ality derives from problems of communication, a family whose mem-bers know how to talk and listen to each other behaves functionally.

As salient as they are, the contrasting local cultures of domestic disorder do not strictly determine the interpretation of family mem-bers' conduct in therapy. Instead, they provide a set of understandings that participants regularly take into account in assigning meaning to life experiences. Therapists at both facilities engage in considerable biographical work to concretely locate evidence of dysfunctionality in what family members present. In both facilities, a system of mundane signs conveys domestic disorder, embodied in family members' seat-ing arrangement, postures, and verbalization in therapy. The signs inform the therapists that what they have observed and heard is evi-dence of domestic disorder or developing order, as the case might be, which is a concrete basis for intervention.

Take therapists' biographical work at Westside House. In the local cultural scheme of things, parents in functional families are viewed as presenting more vocally than their children. The father who sits too quietly behind other family members at the back of a consulting room signals a family in trouble. Children who seat themselves promi-nently between parents and talk incessantly, interrupting the parents, convey domestic disorder. Assigning meaning to these mundane signs in accordance with the local culture of dysfunctionality, Westside therapists construct biographies for family members that reveal long-standing, personal histories of "weak, ineffective parenting" and children engaged in incessant "power trips."

Comparable biographical work at Fairview Hospital produces contrasting lives. The father or mother who sits quietly and does not monopolize a family's conversation is viewed as listening effectively. A child who "opens up," rather than keeping opinions to himself, at least tries to communicate feelings, which is the bedrock of domestic order, according to the local wisdom. In the context of Fairview Hospi-tal's program, few parents act this way, and few children present in this manner, which serves to explain their families' troubles. Parents' longstanding inattention to their children's feelings, for example, is seen as leading to children being out of control.

Each local culture thus provides particular interpretive resources for assigning meaning to family members' experience. The biographical work connects cultural particulars with concrete signs, bridging between the abstract and the concrete or commonplace. Local culture and biographical work combine to diversely constitute definitions of dysfunctional domestic lives. Family members' experiences and domestic order are not so much objective entities and conditions as they are mundane ontological projects, so to speak, of the biographically active participants of these particular settings (Gubrium, 1988c).

Organizational Embeddedness

Biographical work can be further mediated by differential adaptations and applications of local culture within a social setting. The structure of interpersonal relations, specialized mandates and missions, and professional or occupational outlooks and orientations that make up an organization, for example, provide members with distinctive tools for interpretive and biographical work. Although, as Mary Douglas (1986) suggests, organizations and institutions supply typical and routine ways of representing reality, biographical work's *organizational embeddedness* also reflects institutionally salient priorities and agendas.

The diversity of organizationally and professionally mediated biographical constructions is vividly illustrated in a case observed at a multidisciplinary child guidance clinic (Gubrium, Holstein, & Buckholdt, 1994, pp. 152-154). The clinic had several departments and programs, offering many outpatient therapies and services for children reporting emotional and related problems. Although a shared culture of childhood troubles centered on therapeutic intervention and recovery from illness, different professional outlooks modified what were ostensibly shared orientations so that distinctly different understandings of troubled lives emerged.

One 12-year-old client, Charles Grady, was originally referred to the clinic when he got into trouble with the police. Charles had a history of minor disruptive behavior in school and other public settings. When he was finally apprehended, along with a "rowdy" group of teenaged boys, for causing a disturbance in a fast-food restaurant, a police juvenile officer told Charles and his parents that Charles would either have to enroll in the clinic's delinquency-prevention program or face charges in juvenile court.

One of the program's professional guidelines was that juveniles engaging in deviant and disruptive activities were often responding to peer-group influence. A goal of the clinic was to provide positive alternatives to "gang pressures," so Charles was assigned to a peer group led by a counselor named Mr. Burke. Under Burke's guidance, Charles was integrated into adult-supervised, peer-oriented activities that removed him from his normal afterschool routines. Burke explained that the problem with boys like Charles was they were extremely susceptible to the bad influences of friends and others of their own age whom they often mistakenly admired. Charles, and others like him, would gravitate toward gang membership because, as Burke put it, "Preadolescence is a time when kids are looking for acceptance, approval, anything to prove that they belong." According to Burke, Charles's misbehavior in school, his brushes with the law, and his tendency to get into fights and skirmishes were proof that Charles was trying to impress a crowd of "undesirables" and become one of them. This reflected Burke's organizationally and professionally informed outlook on delinquency.

Three weeks later, Charles was again picked up by the police, this time for minor vandalism on school property. When he was returned to the clinic, Charles was taken to the youth program's supervisor and one of the staff therapists, Mr. Miller. In a meeting of staff members, Miller commented on the results of the cognitive and emotional development tests Charles had taken when he first arrived at the clinic. Miller suggested that perhaps he should "take a look at Charles," and, following a 2-hour interview, he offered an alternative perspective on Charles's problem. In Charles's case file, Miller noted that Charles's "antisocial outbursts" were due to "misdirected frustration and energy." Shifting the therapeutic language for biographical work from the social to the psychosocial, Miller wrote that Charles was "going through a difficult adolescence. He has difficulty adjusting to newly developed sexuality and physical maturity. . . . He vents his feelings and frustrations in aggressive outbursts and senseless acts of hostility and destruction." Miller recommended that Charles begin weekly therapy sessions, explaining to the supervisor that "Charles's psychosocial development and social skills haven't caught up with his hormones."

Charles continued with clinic activities for another month without major incident, but there still were occasional reports from school and clinic personnel that he had been involved in fights and disruptions. Entirely coincidentally, Charles saw a physician for a general physical examination in anticipation of enrolling in summer camp. During the examination, Charles's mother apparently mentioned some of Charles's recent troubles. She later told the clinic supervisor that the physician, Dr. Cook, had spoken of the possibility that her son was "hyperactive." Cook apparently had done some tests and written a prescription for Ritalin, the current pharmacological treatment of choice for hyperactivity (cf. Conrad, 1975). Mrs. Grady quoted the doctor as saying, "Charles acts so immature because he probably has some sort of medical disorder."

Contrasting applications of local therapeutic culture, deriving from Burke's and Miller's different organizational and professional outlooks, initially provided alternate ways of interpreting Charles's life and problems. The physician's medical "gaze" (Foucault, 1975) further altered the significant parameters of Charles's troubles. As the case moved between these organizational and professional outlooks, its interpretive jurisdiction changed. In the process, Charles's life was alternatively characterized in related biographical vocabularies.

Conclusion

By foregrounding the biographically active participant, new ethnography takes us in directions virtually absent in older ethnography. It allows for the possibility that the concrete realities of a social setting are constitutively diverse. Settings and perspectives may mediate quite distinct understandings of social entities, such as quality of life, personal family history, and adolescent troubles. Although older ethnography may have taken the diversity of interpretation to be rather random variations on common cultural themes, new ethnography sees qualitative experiential differences in the reality of lives as a function of the active mediation of contrasting local perspectives, resources, and applications.

Although new ethnography theorizes and documents the social construction of lives, it also retains an interest in traditional topics, such as the social organization of self and life history. In pursuing that interest, however, new ethnography holds that if self and life history, for example, are treated as real in the everyday routines of a setting, they are realities actively articulated, assigned, and managed. New ethnography offers an appreciation of participants' indigenous accounts, descriptions, and theories of their own lives that is absent from more traditional approaches.

Methodologically, then, new ethnography orients to the ethnographic behavior of participants themselves. We observe traditional ethnographic subjects in different and important ways, "listening in order to see" how they interpret and construct their lives and worlds (Gubrium & Holstein, 1990, pp. 8-10). As far as biographical work is concerned, their voices are now heard to circumstantially create the reality and patterns of their experience, rather than merely report them. New ethnographers listen to, and take account of, the reality-constituting voices of subjects as much as they attend to their own analyses as participant observers.

References

Atkinson, P. (1990). *The ethnographic imagination: Textual constructions of reality.* London: Routledge.

Behar, R. (1993). *Translated woman: Crossing the border with Esperanza's story.* Boston: Beacon.

Bogdan, R., & Taylor, S. (1975). *Introduction to qualitative research methods.* New York: John Wiley.

Bruner, J. (1986). *Actual minds, possible worlds.* Cambridge, MA: Harvard University Press.

Buckholdt, D. R., & Gubrium, J. F. (1979). Caretakers: Treating emotionally disturbed children. Beverly Hills, CA: Sage.

Burgos-Debray, E. (Ed.). (1984). *I, Rigoberta Menchu.* London: Verso.

Clifford, J., & Marcus, G. E. (1986). *Writing culture.* Berkeley: University of California Press.

Clough, P. (1992). *The end(s) of ethnography.* Newbury Park, CA: Sage.

Cohler, B. (1993). *Aging, morale, and meaning: The nexus of narrative.* In T. R. Cole, W. A. Achenbaum, P. L. Jakobi, & R. Kastenbaum (Eds.), *Voices and visions of aging* (pp. 107-133). New York: Springer.

Conrad, P. (1975). The discovery of hyperkinesis. *Social Problems, 23,* 12-21.

Douglas, M. (1986). *How institutions think.* Syracuse, NY: Syracuse University Press.

Emerson, R. M. (1983). *Contemporary field research.* Prospect Heights, IL: Waveland.

Filstead, W. J. (1970). *Qualitative methodology.* Chicago: Markham.

Fine, G. A. (1983). *Shared fantasy.* Chicago: University of Chicago Press.

Foucault, M. (1975). *The birth of the clinic.* New York: Vintage.

Frost, P. J., Moore, L. F., Louis, M. R., Lundberg, C. C., & Martin, J. (Eds.). (1985). *Organizational culture.* Newbury Park, CA: Sage.

Garfinkel, H., Lynch, M., & Livingston, E. (1981). The work of a discovering science construed with materials from the optically discovered pulsar. *Philosophy of Social Sciences, 11,* 131-158.

Geertz, C. (1988). *Works and lives.* Stanford, CA: Stanford University Press.

Gergen, M. M., & Gergen, K. J. (1993). Narratives of the gendered body in popular autobiography. In R. Josselson & A. Lieblich (Eds.), *The narrative study of lives* (Vol. 1, pp. 191-218). Newbury Park, CA: Sage.

Glaser, B., & Strauss, A. (1967). *The discovery of grounded theory.* Chicago: Aldine.

Goodwin, C. (1993). *Perception, technology and interaction on a scientific research vessel.* Unpublished manuscript, University of South Carolina.

Gubrium, J. F. (1988a). *Analyzing field reality.* Newbury Park, CA: Sage.

Gubrium, J. F. (1988b). Family responsibility and caregiving in the qualitative analysis of the Alzheimer's disease experience. *Journal of Marriage and the Family, 50,* 197-207.

Gubrium, J. F. (1988c). The family as project. *Sociological Review, 36,* 273-295.

Gubrium, J. F. (1989). Local cultures and service policy. In J. F. Gubrium & D. Silverman (Eds.), *The politics of field research.* London: Sage.

Gubrium, J. F. (1992). *Out of control: Family therapy and domestic disorder.* Newbury Park, CA: Sage.

Gubrium, J. F. (1993). *Speaking of life: Horizons of meaning for nursing home residents.* Hawthorne, NY: Aldine.

Gubrium, J. F., & Holstein, J. A. (1990). *What is family?* Mountain View, CA: Mayfield.

Gubrium, J. F., & Holstein, J. A. (1992). Phenomenology, ethnomethodology and family discourse. In P. G. Boss, W. J. Doherty, R. LaRossa, W. R. Schuum, & S. K. Steinmetz (Eds.), *Sourcebook of family theories and methods* (pp. 649-670). New York: Plenum.

Gubrium, J. F., Holstein, J. A., & Buckholdt, D. R. (1994). *Constructing the life course.* Dix Hills, NY: General Hall.

Hazan, H. (1990). *The paradoxical community.* Greenwich, CT: JAI.

Heritage, J. (1984). *Garfinkel and ethnomethodology.* Cambridge, UK: Polity.

Holstein, J. A. (1993). *Court-ordered insanity: Interpretive practice and involuntary commitment.* Hawthorne, NY: Aldine.

Holstein, J. A., & Gubrium, J. F. (1994a). Constructing family: Descriptive practice and domestic order. In T. Sarbin & J. Kitsuse (Eds.), *Constructing the social* (pp. 262-272). London: Sage.

Holstein, J. A., & Gubrium, J. F. (1994b). Phenomenology, ethnomethodology, and interpretive practice. In N. Denzin & Y. Lincoln (Eds.), *Handbook of qualitative research* (pp. 262-272). Thousand Oaks, CA: Sage.

Holstein, J. A., Gubrium, J. F. (1995). *The active interview.* Thousand Oaks, CA: Sage.

Loseke, D. (1992). *The battered woman and shelters.* Albany, NY: SUNY.

Marcus, G., & Fischer, M. (1986). *Anthropology as cultural critique.* Chicago: University of Chicago Press.

McCall, G., & Simmons, J. L. (Eds.). (1969). *Issues in participant observation.* Reading, MA: Addison-Wesley.

Miller, G. (1991). *Enforcing the work ethic.* Albany, NY: SUNY.

Mitchell, W. J. T. (Ed.). (1981). *On narrative.* Chicago: University of Chicago Press.

Morris, J. N., Hawes, C., Fries, B. E., Phillips, C. D., Mor, V., Katz, S., Murphy, K., Drugovich, M. L., & Friedlob, A. S. (1990). Designing the national resident assessment instrument for nursing homes. *The Gerontologist, 30,* 293-307.

Rosenthal, G. (1993). Reconstruction of life stories. In R. Josselson & A. Lieblich (Eds.), *The narrative study of lives* (Vol. 1, pp. 59-91). Newbury Park, CA: Sage.

Schwartz, H., & Jacobs, J. (1979). *Qualitative sociology.* New York: Free Press.

Shaffir, W., Stebbins, R., & Turowetz, A. (Eds.). (1980). *Fieldwork experience.* New York: St. Martin's.

Shotter, J. (1993). *Conversational realities: Constructing life through language.* London: Sage.

Silverman, D. (1993). *Interpreting qualitative data.* London: Sage.

Spencer, J. (1989). Anthropology as a kind of writing. *Man, 24,* 145-164.

Spradley, J. P. (1979). *The ethnographic interview.* New York: Holt, Rinehart & Winston.

Strathern, M. (1987). Out of context: The persuasive fiction of anthropology. *Current Anthropology, 28,* 251-281.

Svensson, T. (1991). Intellectual exercise and quality of life in the frail elderly. In J. E. Birren, J. E. Lubben, J. C. Rowe, & D. E. Deutchman (Eds.), *The concept and measurement of quality of life in the frail elderly.* New York: Academic Press.

Van Maanen, J. (1988). *Tales of the field.* Chicago: University of Chicago Press.

Wax, R. (Ed.). (1971). *Doing fieldwork.* Chicago: University of Chicago Press.

❦ 4 ❦

Life History and Academic Work

The Career of Professor G

Steven Weiland

Social and behavioral scientists have made narrative one of their objects of inquiry and have adopted the narrative perspective, or the disposition to find storytelling, in many forms of human experience and discourse (e.g., for economics, McCloskey, 1990; for psychology, Sarbin, 1986). But conventional storytellers themselves remain valuable guides to why tales are worth telling, providing (in contrast to scholarly interpreters) the simplest of reasons to pay attention to them. At the outset of Josephine Humphreys's novel *Rich in Love* (1987), the young narrator asserts her right to an audience because she has had "the kind of life that can be told as a story—that is, one in which the events appear to have meaning." All lives have meaning to the people living them. Finding or supplying meaning to lives so that others can observe, take pleasure in, and perhaps even learn from them is the aspiration of narrators. So it is also of scholars who find in narrative fresh perspectives on experience.

Searching for suitable written forms for representing lives is not a new interest in scholarship. The famed Harvard psychologists Henry Murray and Gordon Allport and sociology in the Chicago tradition have been important contributors (see Bulmer, 1984; Craik, Hogan, & Wolfe, 1993; Rabin, Zucker, Emmons, & Frank, 1990). And the maverick sociologist C. Wright Mills made narrative central in his program of intellectual innovation. Mills asked for more narrative inquiry by directing the social and behavioral sciences toward the humanities: "No social study that does not come back to the problems of biography, of history, and their intersections within a society has completed its intellectual journey" (1959, p. 6). But biography can mean many things, as is revealed in the forms of life history writing in anthropology, psychology, politics, sociology, literary studies, and the history of science.

The narrative study of lives inevitably reflects the conditions of particular domains of human activity. In what follows I offer a biographical profile of a single professor as a form of inquiry into academic work. The narrative is framed by a brief discussion of academic life history and then a longer one addressing practical and theoretical problems in understanding faculty careers. Academic biography and autobiography are the subjects of a previous essay (Weiland, 1994). My purposes, in extending work by scholars of academic life (Becher, 1989, as treated below; and others, e.g., Baldwin & Blackburn, 1981; Clark, 1987; Lawrence & Blackburn, 1985) are first, to demonstrate the utility of highly localized study of the academic professions, chiefly by subject matter but also by site, and second, to identify a form of "intellectual journey," the writing of career biography missing from inquiry into higher education if not, for example, from the study of teachers or physicians (Goodson, 1992; Kaufman, 1993).

The chief source for my study is a series of interviews with Professor G during the summer of 1993 as he was preparing to spend the following academic year teaching at a foreign university, a favored activity in his career. We discussed (similarities in our professional backgrounds prompted more than the standard question and answer format) the origins, circumstances, achievements, disappointments, prospects, and other features of his professional life. The interview procedure reflected the principles elaborated by Elliot Mishler (1986).

In the matter of context, I identify both institution-specific and general matters in the area of higher education as well as recent work on English as a discipline. The social and intellectual history of the post-World War II period is also part of this tale even if the report can only suggest the presence of such background. Context is a complex idea whose meanings are sometimes simplified—under- or overstated—in trying to explain the activities of the self in the world (Dannefer, 1992). My approach relies on attention to variability in examining the nature and effects of contexts, trying to find out where some contextual influences are weak where others may be strong, and how these may change over time (e.g., the role of the academic department or disciplinary association in the lives of professors).

Inevitably, this chapter also addresses, explicitly and implicitly, themes in postmodern epistemology. One is the problem of the human subject, or the relation of individual experience and consciousness to its social or historical construction. Within the scope of the "intellectual journey," as named by Mills, the problem of what can be known and how we come to know is present for the subject and the history writer. Writing about a career requires first of all a scientific or scholarly *investigation* of experiences, events, ideas, relationships, and other essentials of the subject's professional life. Because all of the material is in language—and it is investigated jointly by the person who has lived the experience and the one seeking to give it written form—it carries many levels of signification.

Biography is also *interpretive* because its goal is to find meaning in human experience. Hence well-known problems in method—completeness, reliability, and generalizability—must be seen in light of the biographer's quest to bring forward the qualities of lived experience, mindful of how discourse conventions both give form to and constrain the activity of writing a life. The perspective of the subject must be given priority and the pace of moving through standard experiences maintained. A place must be found for "nonnormative" experiences (as explained later) without under- or overestimating their impact. And what cannot be told to an interviewer must be recognized if nowhere recorded—sealed over in the order and the flow of the narrative—even beyond the breaking of some taboos as part of the joint reconstruction of a life. For Professor G, academic tenure yields a "secret sin."

Finally, giving form to lives is *interactive*—one person faces another—and to the degree that writers are self-conscious about it, the work can show how important themes in the careers and growing self-knowledge of authors are revealed in such encounters. My interest in Professor G's midcareer situation reflects the closeness of our ages and backgrounds.

As sociologist Norman Denzin (1989) shows, biography in the social and behavioral sciences entails a struggle for form even as it is a contribution to the history of a particular kind of living or working or to psychological or sociological theory. I employ the form of the biographical career profile, reflective of life history methods in the social and behavioral sciences but independent of them, too, given the special purposes of this inquiry. The focus on the career and neglect of childhood is the primary special purpose. As an experiment in genre, the profile is part of an essay, but it employs many of the techniques and exhibits several of the characteristic problems of more complex biographical forms. It is selective and interpretive in the manner, for example, of extended essay-length accounts of the careers of American scientists (Hilts, 1982), but having as its subject a typical professor, the narrative is intended as a novel contribution to the study of academic work.

Representing the Academic
Self: The "Plain" and "Average"

What do we know about professors' lives and how do we come to know them? The *New York Times Magazine* (e.g., Atlas, 1988) now regularly features scholars and their campus controversies. Recent volumes of academic autobiography in sociology, psychology, ethnography, and philosophy, and of biographical interviews in physics have other purposes than making news out of intellectual and curricular disputes (Berger, 1990; Brannigan & Merrens, 1993; Fowler & Hardesty, 1994; Karnos & Shoemaker, 1993; Lightman & Brawer, 1990; Riley, 1988). Reticence has been a scholarly convention, institutionalized in the habits and strenuous justifications of objectivity marking many disciplines (e.g., Novick, 1988). Scholars speaking now more frequently in their own voices illuminate the origins and personal meanings of academic work. Predictably there is great variety not only in perceptions of disciplinary norms and practices but in the individual patterns they illustrate for academic achievement.

Consider the cases of two sociologists. Alice Rossi, now over 70 and reflecting the burdens of women of her generation in academic work, began her career late and succeeded by applying her worldliness and sense of human differences, including the cause of feminism, to the regularities of age- and stage-structured theories of adult development (Rossi, 1990). Gary Marx, 20 years younger than Rossi and favored with the advantages of his academic cohort (e.g., an expanding job market and high-status consulting opportunities), appeared to succeed at once but then lost a prestigious appointment only to recognize the value of failure (Marx, 1990). These autobiographies carry hints of allegory, invitations by professors themselves to understand the academic life as in reality many different academic lives. But are Rossi and Marx typical sociologists? In collecting sociological autobiographies, Bennett Berger (1990) had as his main goal serving graduate students and young professors by taking some of the mystery out of scholarship, by demonstrating the "presence of the theorist in the text." However different they are from other sociologists (and from one another) Rossi and Marx are certainly well-known ones, if perhaps in separate sectors of their discipline. Why else would Berger have invited them to contribute to his volume? One is rarely renowned and representative, as any dictionary definition of either term will reveal.

That is the reason, I assume, why in one of his path-making studies of the cultures of the university, British sociologist of higher education Tony Becher asserts the virtues and limits of his ethnographic approach:

> The province of inquiries into academic culture is by definition sectional and localized; their impact on the system as a whole is muted at best. They lack the obvious relevance, the broad authoritative sweep, of organizational, political, or policy-centered research. Dealing as they do with the mundane and everyday—*the plain takes of average academics*—they are low on glamour and high on hard grind. (Becher, 1984, p. 195, emphasis added)

But despite the authority in his work (e.g., Becher, 1989) deriving from attention to disciplines and of specializations in the spirit of

Clifford Geertz's formulation of "local knowledge," Becher himself does not employ narrative. Nor does Burton Clark (1987), whose study of *The Academic Life* is, I think, the best account we have of the work of teaching and scholarship in the United States. Clark focuses on how the motivations and activities of academic careers are fitted to the circumstances of the different sectors of higher education. We get revealing glimpses of individual professors, but it was Clark's purpose to present group portraits as part of the historical development of higher education, not academic lives in depth.

The increasingly popular habit of professors to tell their own stories has not provided an actual case literature. The problem remains of representing academic work in the form of "plain tales of average academics." In other words, Becher (like Mills) urges a project in biography. But as a biographical research program, Becher's terms are not altogether self-explanatory. "Plain" is as misleadingly simple as a description of the form of such work, partly because it reflects individual taste in matters of representation. We may ask: *How* plain? Does a "plain" tale ignore the character problems of academic specialties, at least partially expressed in their distinctive vocabularies? Becher, an advocate of the need to focus more on specialization, would hardly endorse that. Moreover, no tale is plain to its subject. It is the responsibility of biography to represent internal complexity in accessible if not simple form. "Average" has similar problems, especially in so far as it is meant to convey representativeness. We can understand average without an arithmetical formula but be cautious in assigning examples to it, not least because (in the developmental vocabulary) cohorts may respond quite differently to historical effects. I will consider this matter in more detail later.

Finally, a "tale" can be fact or fiction. Becher does not endorse the latter, though the academic novel is a revealing form for contemplating faculty careers otherwise unknown, as in the interwoven lives of the young Russian scholar and late-career botanist in Saul Bellow's *More Die of Heartbreak* (1987). Academic lives presented as "tales" will have form and meaning, purposeful narratives of human events and ideas. They may be "plain" in the sense that they are well-focused on their "average" subjects, but they must contain enough to provide insight into scientific and intellectual work in their contexts.

The Subject

The subject being presented is Professor G. He is a white male member of the English department at a large public research university in the Midwest. Now in his mid-50s, he is married with three adult children. He was educated at public and private institutions. Since leaving graduate school in the mid-1960s, Professor G has taught at the same university, where he now has the option of early retirement, an important matter for his academic cohort having so little mobility. There is demographic interest in Professor G's career even if it is not fully revealed in this chapter (see National Research Council, 1991; Robinson & Lee, 1993). More than half of all American professors are now over 50 years old, most having entered academic life at about the same time as Professor G, a period of rapid expansion of colleges and universities, of general public and institutional confidence in higher education, and of consensus about goals. They are aging together (in two senses, given the general lack of mobility) in an environment having many of the features they anticipated but also one filled with dispute over the curriculum and uncertainty about the future of higher education.

Professor G has taught many courses at all levels of the curriculum. He is a specialist in modern American literature but his interests and beliefs have changed as his career has evolved, including those regarding teaching and learning. Professor G has published more than 30 essays in scholarly journals and in magazines of opinion and commentary, many of them early in his career when he also published a textbook of essays by well-known novelists. He has held administrative posts, departmental and university-wide. In addition to his teaching and writing he now directs a small multidisciplinary program that does not offer degrees but coordinates and supplements regular undergraduate and graduate offerings in the liberal arts. He has taught abroad frequently and in off-campus programs serving nontraditional students.

Early in his career, in a period of public volatility, Professor G served on the local school board. And he is now an active member of his religious community. Widely recognized as a good citizen of his university, he is not uncritical about it. Most important for purposes of this study he is naturally reflective about his own career and discipline, his role in his institution, and his and its place in the recent history of higher education generally. As a teacher of literature, Professor G may be said to be disposed to the form and meaning of the personal narrative, but in the structure of the interviews I rely on his complementary habits of critical reflection and detachment to tell this "plain tale," in so far as that is possible, as anyone else might tell theirs. His self-consciousness about the process is part of the structure of such research, as is the biographer's awareness of the peculiarities of background and interest he brings to the biographical text.

The Career of Professor G

Asked why he became a teacher and scholar in literature, Professor G says simply that "the only things I've ever been good at" are reading and studying books. He majored in English as an undergraduate at a public urban university with plans to become (in the parlance of the 1950s) a "schoolteacher." His actual career was to depend on some casual advice in the form of a question. "One of my professors said to me—and this was all it took—'Have you thought of being a college teacher?' " Initially incredulous, he remembers thinking that "you had to be called" to such work, if in fact it was work at all. In contrast to many of today's more career-oriented students with academic aspirations, Professor G confesses that he really didn't know what his professors did when not conducting the classes he was in. "I thought that they sat at home and read books and then came into class and talked about them."

In college (he graduated in 1959), few of Professor G's teachers were productive scholars. But they were dedicated to teaching. He interprets their professional stance as partly derived from and justified by the practices of the famous method of literary studies called the "New Criticism," although of course many professors who were affiliated with this theory and method published steadily. The New Criticism—whose key manifestos and critical works were published in the 1940s and early 1950s—stressed close reading of texts, focus on their internal structure, and neglect of historical, biographical, and other external matters (Graff, 1987; Leitch, 1988). "We were encouraged to read the books and respond. I was taught to stay within the text and not do much else." It was a view of textual and intellectual activity Professor G welcomed and has nurtured throughout his career. He has not rejected other features of the work, but the image of *the reader*—for its private and its collaborative or classroom pleasures— has from the beginning been essential to his identity. Although reading has been problematized by literary theory—a phenomenon of the 1980s Professor G accepts with ambivalence—it retains for him its status from his earliest experience of literature in higher education (or even before). For English majors in the 1950s, "It was you and the book. You wrote about the book, not about how some critics might read the book."

Despite having written many essays himself, Professor G's commitment to criticism and scholarship has always been fragile, shaped by his college years and the pleasure in teaching that has come to dominate his career in midlife. His career was built on a set of assumptions about the academic literary vocation, primarily that one pursued it because of the pleasure of reading and, at least initially, the limits of potential literary meaning and applications outside the text: "I thought that being an English major and teacher meant being a proponent or advocate [not a critic or scholar]. It never occurred to me that I might teach a book I didn't like in order to illustrate something." When he modified this view later in his career, it was not due to a new theoretical commitment but was in the service of adaptive ideals for teaching and the work of universities in guiding the young adult development of students.

Professor G spent his first 2 years in graduate school as a master's degree student at a highly regarded private university in the East with a strong program in literature. He began with only a very vague idea about how it was that one actually prepared for being a professor, especially the kind typically produced by the institution he had chosen (it was both close enough to and far enough from his home). "I didn't know what a secondary source was or how to use the library or what the Modern Language Association was." He was slow to impress his teachers—many of them well-known literary historians and critics— one reason, perhaps, that he could proceed with more enthusiasm for the academic life than with realistic knowledge of it. "It was only in my last year at [another graduate school] that I had any formal advice about the structure of academic careers." With his guiding image of the reader as teacher (and occasional scholar) and the expanding job market, there was seemingly little need for it.

Although he had a manifest love of literature, Professor G felt that when he arrived in graduate school immediately after college he was "badly prepared." He had anticipated that graduate study was merely the next educational step rather than a profoundly different activity. But his willingness to read closely and participate in class discussions was not enough. "The professors weren't interested in my opinion about John Donne!" Nonetheless he enjoyed the new (to him at least) form of student inquiry with more emphasis on what would later be recognizable as professional parts of the vocation. And he absorbed the academic ethos of this traditional institution in a peculiarly lasting way. Even 30 years later he sees himself as, in a sense, "in exile" from the university where he began but did not complete his graduate education. Interested since adolescence in the novels of F. Scott Fitzgerald, Professor G remembers that his lasting impression of the university was like Gatsby's when he saw with astonishment Daisy's imposing family home. Perhaps this is why, enrolled in a master's degree program with no guarantee of staying on for the Ph.D., he deferred to his graduate school professors' judgment of his academic abilities: "When they decided not to keep me I knew they were correct."

The influential anthropologist Clifford Geertz (1983) has proposed that almost all academic careers have the form of "downward mobility," that is, a portion of disappointment in the fact of having to make a life at an institution with less prestige than the one in which one was prepared. Professor G partakes of this syndrome in an unusual way, via a transitional if nonetheless powerful experience. He often thinks, as Geertz predicts, in the vocabulary of exile from academic Eden. In any case, Professor G's reaction to his academic failure came to define in part his later success, which was built on considerable powers of self-assessment and gratitude for the opportunities and pleasures he has had.

When Professor G moved on to a Ph.D. program in literature, it was at a large public university, an institution lower in status than the one he had left but still highly regarded for its scholarly traditions in the arts and sciences as well as in engineering and agriculture. Even with his admissions of feeling "in exile" he does not appear to have been very status-conscious at any time in his professional life. There was never any question about what prompted him to continue his training to become a professor: "It was still the love of books. It is what motivates me today. That that has never changed." He began teaching freshman composition at once (it was the fall of 1962) in a highly structured program typical of that time. There was thoughtful supervision but he appreciated especially the egalitarian atmosphere of his department and institution. He "learned to be a professional," at least in the sense that it was necessary to teach, do his coursework, and begin planning, however vaguely, for a career.

Professor G's increasing sense of competency in literary studies reflected his generally outstanding performance and the interest his professors took in his future. The latter meant that although he understood himself to be identified with the American literature wing of his department, he was informally recruited to medieval studies by a well-known professor in that field. He remembers this misdirected effort because it was at the time an indispensable sign that "someone was interested enough in me or my potential as a teacher and scholar to take me out to lunch." Indeed, his choice of an academic specialty was hardly a choice at all, more an expression of his earliest literary preferences and his belief in the natural limits of intellectual aspiration. "I have never understood how an American can choose to become an expert on Dickens or Shakespeare or on anything not American. The idea that you can presume to know enough about another culture to be a specialist in it staggers me. I went into American literature because I am an American. I have always felt myself to be American in very positive ways. How can you become an expert in 18th-century British culture? It seems so remote, so far away, so much work."

After more than a year in his Ph.D. program, Professor G also better understood the research role and the demands it places on those wishing for success in all areas of academic life. "I was teaching, and whether I knew it or not, I was learning how to balance being a teacher with being a graduate student, which if it is not the same thing as being a scholar is something like it. I was writing papers while I was trying to teach. So early on I understood that professional life was some kind of balance. I didn't know I was learning a lesson. It was a practical thing I had to do." At that stage in the history of the academic profession, many graduate students could safely assume that their prospects would not be defined almost exclusively by their scholarly interests, their "field," and their potential to rapidly make a mark in it. Looking ahead to his search for a job as an assistant professor, Professor G remembers thinking the Modern Language Association ads were going to say, "WANTED: TEACHER." In fact, this turned out to be close to the truth because he ultimately accepted a position (in 1966) that did not exist until a department chair, in the days before search committees, hired him after deciding that he would be a valuable colleague whatever his specialty. Professor G recognizes how different his situation was from the pattern that emerged only a decade later, with its focus on specialization, the commitment of new Ph.D.s to major theoretical or interpretive projects, and the departmental problem of "slots" to be filled.

Looking back from the point of view of today's intellectual (as opposed to employment) opportunities for graduate students in the humanities—with the proliferation of critical methods and theories—it might appear that the early 1960s was a time lacking in interest or promise. Some historians of literary study see things this way, with the immediate postwar years as a time for the playing out of the New Criticism with its peculiar mix of intellectual ambition and resistance to capitalizing on literature's relations with other domains of art and inquiry, and with politics, history, and biography. Professor G has a different view, finding instead a better environment for apprentice professors: "Because of the total absence of theory there were no constraints. You didn't have to take sides on your author or on anything else." His way was eased not only by the absence of theory but by the good fortune of winning a generous award to complete his dissertation. A Kent Fellowship (a program of the Danforth Foundation) "shaped me as much as my formal education." The 30 or so Kent Fellows from institutions across the country, all in the humanities, attended an annual week-long conference in which the focus was on values in higher education. "No one at the institutions I knew talked that way. At the time it was a real eye opener." Professor G attended the conferences for a few years after finishing his degree, giving his departmental apprenticeship an unusual but durable accent.

Recent attacks on academic "professionalism" (e.g., Wilshire, 1990) have traced the problems of the universities to the faculty's neglect of moral dimensions of teaching and learning. And indeed, the first half of Professor G's career can be understood within an emerging contest between the putative "values" of education and what the academic professions have come to value: specialized research, the commitment to disciplinary rather than institutional tasks, modest teaching loads, and resistance to teaching undergraduates. Professor G has not been a vocal partisan in the battle, except to form his own career out of some skepticism of the professionalizing tendencies of his field.

That is not to say, however, that the attractions of a *career* were not part of his wish to teach literature. What brought Professor G (at age 27) to the institution at which he has taught since leaving graduate school? Professors in his cohort have powerful, often guilt-ridden images of their easy entry into the profession. He began the search for his first job by "drawing a circle on the map" and then pursuing a desirable position in a seller's market. With an offer in hand he visited the campus and his future colleagues not quite knowing what to expect. But it was not the curriculum, the library, the teaching schedule, or research opportunities that confirmed his interest in an academic career at this particular institution. "I'll never forget this," he says now, recalling that when he entered the home of a future colleague there were books lining the paneled living room walls and a fire in the fireplace. "This is how I want to spend my life!" was his immediate reaction. He quickly established a strong personal relationship with the department chair who recruited him. What he confirmed from his side of the relationship was "not so much a professional career but the sense of a lived life. This is how you do it, this is the kind of house you live in, this is how you do things." What did he know about the institution, about the opportunities it might offer for satisfaction as a scholar and teacher, about his chances for tenure or for taking the first steps in a career that might lead to future appointments, perhaps at more prestigious institutions (i.e., a return from exile)? "Almost nothing," he says now.

Today's professors are part of a dense and often tense (in particular departments) and acrimonious debate about academic ideals and responsibilities. As late as the mid-1960s, it was probable that young professors could be socialized into their fields less painfully, often with the example of senior colleagues. Professor G describes a famous scholar associated for many years with his department:

> He was the most important man in this department. He had been chair for 15 years. He had won a Pulitzer Prize for one of his scholarly books. And he was the most modest, kind, and egalitarian man. He would teach at eight in the morning. He would teach introductory courses. It was very healthy for the department. Because he never pulled any prima donna stuff nobody else would try to. He could have had anything he wanted but he never asked for anything beyond what everyone else had. His teaching load was the same as everybody else's. He would show up for everything. He had an enormous sense of responsibility. He was the senior man in my specialty. I came to regard him [and another senior member of the department] as being the most positive thing about what institutional culture there was. I identified the way they did things as the university's way of doing things. I identified them with the best that there was here. What they were was what the place was.

Such models helped to confirm Professor G's belief that English professors led a different kind of academic life from other faculty members. "I've always felt that people in literature are on a different plane. That sounds arrogant. I think literature as a field is on a much higher level than sociology or even history." In its attention to values it is closer to religion or philosophy. "But it is not unworldly. I've always thought of being an English professor as conferring a kind of special status. I see this as coming out of the 1950s—my own teachers' attitudes and those even of the New Critics who were moralistic and pietistic."

In the matter of politics itself, Professor G says, in apparent confirmation of the fears of today's conservative critics of higher education, "I have never known anyone who was not a liberal." Even so, he felt himself to be more of an observer than a participant in the campus upheavals of the late 1960s and early 1970s. Love of books still defined his relation to the profession and the kinds of relations he sought with students. "I feel that in a sense I lost contact with a cohort of students who 10 years earlier would have been our natural students— what I had been as an undergraduate, deeply in love with literature, wanting to talk about books—but these kids were caught up in politics and drugs, and since I had no contact with either I never connected with these students and I regret that."

However, Professor G's ambivalence about the role of politics and social change in higher education must be understood against his acceptance of an invitation from the department chair in the early 1970s to offer a new course in black literature. There was no promise of released time to do so, just the implication that the course was important to the department and the duty of a young teacher of American literature, especially an untenured one (although in a department that rarely failed to grant tenure to its assistant professors). The result was a fresh view of his subject:

> I gave myself an education in "Negro literature" as it was called then. That opened my eyes. It changed the way I thought about literature. I had never thought about literature before as being about real life, as dealing with problems. It never occurred to me that novels could be what Richard Wright [author of *Black Boy* and other powerful works of fiction] called "weapons" or that I would be interested in books because I could learn from them things that I could not learn from life. It gave me a whole new notion of what literature could do, not political in the ideological sense but politics as an opening into a world I would ordinarily have no access to. I read things that flabbergasted me. I was over 30 years old and had a Ph.D. but I was amazed that [black] people had to live this way.

The former Kent Fellow knew that the burden of good intentions in higher education was especially heavy in the increasingly volatile curricular area of race. Now well past his graduate school and apprenticeship years, he finds a hint of professional self-consciousness if not self-interest among new converts to black literature. "There was a kind of smugness on my part and other whites who did this. We thought of ourselves as people who had good values."

Professor G tells a complementary if contrasting story about being asked in the 1970s also to participate in his chair's initiative in writing and composition, subjects of increasing neglect (paradoxically enough given the student rebellions of the period) in many English departments keen on advancing their research and theoretical interests if not to avoid the presumably low-status activity of teaching freshmen. "The chair had a struggle on his hands to convince those of us in literature that this was appropriate. He succeeded not with me but did with some colleagues." They in turn made teaching a theme of more significant interest in the department.

But Professor G's reluctance to join this sector of the department's work did not signify indifference to thinking about pedagogy. His effort in black literature made him a better teacher, including the reflective habits it prompted about himself and his classroom responsibilities. Throughout his career he has responded to opportunities to approach his teaching with greater and greater care as a function first of his intellectual life—the unfolding of new subjects and the opportunities they present—and then of his private life, in his case, the circumstances of the "postparental years." Never an enthusiast for institutional faculty development programs, he nonetheless has been dedicated to their goals all along, though in discipline-specific and private forms. When he reflects on the debate over the canon it is not as an ideological matter but part of his mature and still evolving identity as a classroom teacher with a responsible role in the university curriculum.

As is suggested below, Professor G is concerned about the generation gap in his field and its meaning for the second half of his career. But the kinds of questions his younger colleagues raise have also made him, he thinks, a better teacher, more self-conscious about his goals, more modest in his claims for the priorities he was in the habit of giving to his subject.

> I have never thought of myself as a [literary] canon former
> but when I put together a book list I am shaping and defining

a canon as far as my students are concerned. It has made me think very hard about what texts to teach. I have consciously inserted texts that I didn't think were so terrific because I thought that this should be represented or that should be. It has made me think more than I ever did about what a course is—what am I trying to accomplish in a course in 20th-century American fiction—what should such a course accomplish? In the old days it was very clear to me: Fitzgerald, Hemingway, and Faulkner—that was it. I don't feel threatened, even as someone who has made a career with these writers, by the idea that they must step aside for others.

He has learned from his younger colleagues, but the differences between the academic generations go deeper than disagreements about what to teach and how.

Surely the most profound cohort or historical effect defining Professor G's career was the nature of the job market at the time he entered the profession. In his own view he was marked by gaining tenure early, in his case at age 30 after just 3 years in his department. Mindful of the historical changes that have made his case (typical at the time) the source of resentment to succeeding cohorts and of public attitudes regarding the psychology of tenure and the job security it offers, Professor G is remarkably candid. "Tenure made me less ambitious and less interested in writing books," if not, it is apparent, in reading and talking about them. "Many in my cohort were tenured early. The way to expand the department was to keep moving people up quickly into tenure in order to create more untenured lines. It had a very strong effect on me." The consequences were private and professional. "I spent an enormous amount of time with my kids and wife. When I confess as much I feel I am confessing to some kind of secret sin. I never worked at night and I never worked on weekends. I never brought home anything. I did everything during the day. That was it. I never thought to do anything differently. I haven't been lazy but tenure allowed me to do all kinds of other things like serve on the local school board or teach abroad." In his case, simply gaining tenure and then maintaining a pattern of professional dedication meant more than sufficient opportunities on campus and in attractive overseas appointments. "It isn't as if I have gotten these things because I am some star. They are there to be had by most people in the profession. They are not a reward for being terrific."

Estimating how possibilities and achievements have been fitted to aspirations is at the center of anyone's thinking about the form of a career. For Professor G (again thinking of the effects of tenure) there is not only guilt but some regret. "I have never been all that careerist," Professor G asserts, but that doesn't mean he has not contemplated the "costs" of his choices even if they mean less than others may assume. "I think that in my case tenure has discouraged productivity. Those in my department who earn more do it strictly on the basis of publishing. It is not because they are better teachers. I know that. Or because they do more of anything else. It's because they publish books. And I accept that. On the other hand the financial difference isn't so big. So the money isn't that much of an incentive."

But to Professor G, whatever might be justified (or, as someone else might suggest, even rationalized) must also be understood as part of a career that was lost. "I think that I am one of those people who may have written more, written better, written more interestingly, kept up more in my field." The problem is traceable to his own choices and to his entry into a profession at a time when there was much less explicit or even implicit attention to a structured format for academic success, especially in the area of research. Asked about whether early in his career he had some idea of where he was headed beyond the gratifications offered by teaching and the modest amount of scholarship needed for success in his particular department, he says: "No. That was probably a mistake. If I had had a schedule. If I had had a keener sense of what I should have been doing in terms of stature and status in the profession. If a [scholarly] book had been part of the expectation I would have done that. I wish that I had done more and I've always wished that I was better thought of by colleagues in the profession, that I was famous, but not enough for me to do anything about it."

As is widely recognized, at all but the leading institutions the problem of status in a discipline is generally understood to mean having a reputation and widespread professional relations with colleagues at *other* universities. By revealing his interest in renown, in external recognition, Professor G is also expressing what might be called his sense of internal isolation at his own institution. He has spent his whole career in a department in which there have been few battles over tenure, ideology, or other matters. But that does not mean that it has always been a satisfying place to work. In his view, the department never exhibited or encouraged a nourishing academic environment. "My closest intellectual relationships have been with students. But I would have liked to have had more of a collegial sense. I have lots of gaps in knowledge and ways of thinking. I think I would have been stimulated by more opportunities for team teaching [and other strategies for bringing colleagues together]. I think my views are fairly typical here. There are some self-contained groups in the department, especially in small enough specialties like the medieval period or even the Renaissance. The Americanists don't have that much in common." Professor G proposes a distinction revealing an awkward dissonance: "I don't think my career has suffered but I have suffered professionally."

The fault is his, he knows, and also his colleagues' for accepting habits of departmental administration that favor their professional autonomy without always giving it meaning. "The tendency in my department is not to do anything about anything much. Most of us—and I am as guilty of this as anybody else—want to be left alone to do our teaching and to do our research, and as long as the department lets that happen then you reckon the administration successful even though more things should happen. We should be made to do more things than we are made to do. There isn't much collegiality, no sitting around and talking about books, none of that, zero." Admittedly ambivalent about the role of academic administrators, Professor G nonetheless has wished for the reorientation of departmental leadership around the field's manifest conflicts. "If it doesn't come from the chair, where will it come from?" And without a taste for organizational reform or demanding group initiatives, he notes that if he had been chair (he had in fact lost an election for the post in the early '80s), "I would have moved the coffee machine from the department office—anything to force faculty members to find themselves in the same place during the day."

But there are, of course, more considerable problems of academic leadership. For more than a decade—one of the most volatile in

American academic and intellectual life—the chairs of his department have generally not had identifiable intellectual or ideological interests they hoped to make visible in an institutional format. Of this neglect Professor G says, "I think we have suffered for that. Someone with a vision can be very dangerous but also very exciting. He or she can motivate and make things happen. We have had chairs who were pragmatic, who had no particular agenda to fulfill, and consequently our department has not been participating in the battles and struggles [of English and the humanities] in any real way. The atmosphere just hasn't been very interesting." In effect Professor G endorses the developmental benefits for professors of the curricular strategy, proposed by Gerald Graff (1992), of making the faculty's intellectual disagreements more visible to students. But he is not by nature a contentious person, and, in an apparent paradox revealed below, he takes more and more pleasure in relying on his own resources to fortify the priority he gives to students and teaching.

Even if Professor G's departmental relations have not been particularly satisfying, the cohort entering the academic profession in the 1960s could count on a general consensus about literary methods. But with the late 1970s and the 1980s came a breach reflecting the commitments of younger colleagues to "theory," a form of professional or intellectual shorthand in English designating a preference for demanding forms of literary criticism (as opposed to just "reading"), the implications of literature's relations with other fields (especially philosophy and the study of language), and for international interpretations of the sociology and politics of the arts and scholarship. As Professor G reports ruefully, "A colleague of mine recently gave a course on Henry James. Much of the course was given over to reading criticism of James. That is totally different from what I was trained to do in graduate school. My education included no theory, none, zero. I'm out of it, just out of it." He traces this circumstance, predictably perhaps, to what for many years seemed to be the advantage of his earliest training and his loyalty to it even as he became more professional.

Professor G is also willing to say now that "I think this approach [the unmediated focus on the literary text] has handicapped me because I am not comfortable with theoretical material and I may be making a mistake in conveying to my students that it is not terribly important because now it may be much more important than it used to be." Nonetheless, it turns out, as Professor G explains changes in his teaching style, that students stand to gain more from him precisely for his having maintained his indifference to criticism and theory. He teaches as his first teachers taught him. Classroom time belongs to students' views, not to their professors', much less to the critics and theorists favored by those who keep current in the field. If Professor G and his younger colleagues "don't speak the same language," that is something to regret but not correct.

Now in midcareer, Professor G is both narrowing and expanding his horizons. He has, for example, virtually stopped giving papers at scholarly conferences, which he had attended with pleasure and profit as a younger faculty member. His reasons will bring a wry smile from many scholars, even those enthusiastic about annual disciplinary gatherings.

> I reached a point where I stopped enjoying it and I stopped feeling that anybody was paying much attention. I knew that I wasn't paying much attention to anybody else's paper and I didn't have a sense that anybody was paying much attention to mine. I didn't resent it. I just identified that as the way it is. It began to feel like I was going through the motions. So you can get on a program, or get your way paid to New Orleans. All of which is very nice. And the price of that is that you often have to show up at eight in the morning and sit on a panel with three other people. And maybe there are six other people in the room. You read your paper and the other panelists aren't that much interested because they are busy thinking about how much time they have left for themselves. And the six people in the room aren't much interested because they have hangovers or would rather be somewhere else or because they are worrying about the paper they are giving 2 hours later. I have lately begun to get much more satisfaction out of teaching, which has nothing to do with rewards in this profession. And since I am not looking for rewards it doesn't matter now.

Professor G notes that the example of several of his colleagues tells him that diffidence about scholarship is not an inevitable result of many years of experience in the profession. The decision to slow down has been his, not a departmental or professional norm conveniently adopted and rationalized as the product of seemingly self-defeating circumstances (i.e., the structure of the academic reward system).

After nearly 30 years in academic life, Professor G feels that the satisfactions of inquiry—including textual discoveries and even the reconceptualization of one's intellectual point of view—can now be safely husbanded for the purposes of one's own classes, and in his case, new institutional efforts. An old friend who might notice Professor G's absence from scholarly meetings and assume that he had run out of things to say about literature would have had no knowledge of how he feels powerful new intellectual stirrings. These he describes in tones similar to the ones used to account for his response to black literature. This time it is a new undergraduate course on the literary response to the Holocaust. "I have never felt so excited in my life about a body of literature. I felt like I was teaching for the first time because the material made me rethink in serious ways the argument that literary texts are inconsequential or that literature is evasive [the latter a byproduct of some forms of "theory"]. Nobody who has read [Jerzy Kozinski's] *The Painted Bird* could make that claim."

Surprisingly, Professor G believes that his experience is age-related, proposing that had the same opportunity been available 10 years before he would not have been so open to it. But one cannot plan for such revisions of professional life. "It's all accidental isn't it? I think I have done very little long-range thinking. I have tended to respond to things as they have come up, which means going in directions I hadn't necessarily planned for or predicted." Despite the presence of ranks, and the built-in repetition in the work (in teaching), and one may add today the decline in mobility, any individual faculty career path is quite contingent. Professor G recalls being asked when he was looking for a job, "What do you expect to be teaching and writing about 10 years from now? And I remember as a faculty member asking candidates that crazy question. What would I think of somebody who really thought he knew?"

Even if the form of a career cannot be anticipated, a professor building and maintaining one does get older. Indeed, age consciousness now amounts to a critical arena for Professor G's professional life, especially in the matter of teaching. The problem of collegial relations has been adapted to a new frame of mind. "It has always been very important to me to be thought well of by my elders, by colleagues, by people in the profession. It didn't used to be important to me to be thought well of by my students, but now that is much more important to me." Accordingly, Professor G has nearly abandoned the lecture style and in effect recovered the lessons of his own undergraduate education by making the interpretations of his students the focus of his literature classes. His students, even the most ordinary, he claims, "experience the newness" of a text in ways now unavailable to him, and such fresh perspectives are critical to literary study.

But Professor G also interprets the new form of classroom success as a feature of his own adult development.

> The well-being or happiness of the student has become much more real to me as I have gotten older. At the beginning of my career I felt no paternal feelings toward my students. Then I reached a point where the 18-year-old sitting in the classroom was the age of my oldest child. And since nothing has given me more pleasure in life than being a father, when I could no longer be a father to my children [after they had careers of their own], I think I transferred some of my feelings to my students. Many of the things I used to get from being a father to my children I now get from being a teacher to my students.

We are unused to such intimacies in theorizing pedagogy in higher education. But the inner life of teaching and scholarship, including the complex human relations they entail, has human accents only perhaps understandable in a vocabulary very different from the one found in abstract schemes for describing the faculty life cycle (for an example of what such a vocabulary might look like, see Loewenberg, 1985). Professor G himself hints at the problem of fear, inevitably enclosed in self-deprecating humor: "That was a risk I wasn't willing to take [writing a book] because an article doesn't get reviewed. There is the danger that someone will say you are stupid or the book stinks. I think that might be something I have been afraid to risk. That's negative recognition. I want only positive recognition."

As Professor G surveys his inner transformations he recognizes a fundamental shift in values and orientation toward other people. Cast in the form of a speculation about the adult developmental meanings of gender, his self-analysis derives from new classroom habits. But it is directed too at explaining his acceptance of a role for educational institutions in boosting the self-esteem of its students or otherwise promoting psychological in addition to intellectual well-being. He acknowledges that "when I started and into the 1970s and 1980s I would have said that the only function of the university is to teach subjects." But just as there has been a breach between the academic generations, there is now a maturational divide reflected in his attitude toward the individual academic life.

> I think something happens to some men when they pass age 50. Perhaps it is related to the lowering of testosterone. I feel that I have grown more generous than I used to be, more tolerant, sympathetic, empathic, more interested in and sensitive to other peoples' problems and needs. I think this is a function of age. I feel myself having grown more feminine in ways I regard as positive. I feel less need than I used to to talk about myself, about what I am doing, and I've grown more critical of men who do that. My teaching is more co-operative and communal and less hierarchical. I think that may account for why I am writing and publishing less. I am less confident that what I have to say needs to be said or deserves to be published. I am not as confident as I used to be that my reading of a novel has to get out to the world. I feel less authoritative.

Many men without the unique developmental arena provided by the university classroom, with its presumptions of authority and abundant opportunities for counterpoint, apparently change in such ways as part of a reversal of gender traits in midlife (Gutmann, 1987). But in Professor G's case, such changes can be overstated when applied to his new administrative responsibilities (for a small interdisciplinary program) in which he recognizes the need to mobilize just the traits he feels himself to have abandoned. "This seems to be a contradiction," he acknowledges. For he is now facing the need to be assertive, aggressive, even demanding about program development and fundraising. But he relishes this paradox from the newly feminized side of his temperament with its more benevolent standards of success.

Professor G's interpretation of his intellectual and organizational transformation relies too on another critical feature of his story: a heart attack in his early 40s. He made a rapid recovery and the "crisis" (a term he generally rejects in characterizing adult development on behalf of "change" or "transformation") turned out to have its benefits. The event had a very large impact on every aspect of his life. It initiated his aging. "I was functioning but for some time I wasn't myself. I was filled with feelings of fragility and tenuousness." But aging for him has also been a period of dramatic change and the experience of promise. "As it turns out, the results of being ill have been positive, powerful and good," of the kind he describes above as the gradual moderation of his personality and behavior.

Professor G has contemplated taking advantage of his institution's early retirement option but not because of any decline in his classroom capacities. Quite the opposite is the case. "The wonderful thing about the academic world is that age doesn't seem to have anything to do with the ability to teach. I honestly think that every year I have become a better teacher and however good I am this year I will be better next year. I don't see any reasons why I should reach a point of decline. I don't see any reason why I shouldn't be able to teach well when I am 80." He acknowledges that this aging effect—the accumulated knowledge of texts and of the means for exploring them—has not been transferred to his scholarship but adds, "I haven't lost the hope that I might eventually do something wonderful. I don't see why I should. On the other hand, if I don't I won't be very disappointed."

Temperament is the best stay against disappointment in Professor G's career. Critiques of contemporary academic life and more restrained—if equally pessimistic—research on professors have found them to be generally alienated, dispirited, even "imperiled" (Bowen

& Schuster, 1986; Wilshire, 1990). Professor G's generally sunny view of his career—especially unending improvement in teaching—derives from having the prerogatives of academic work at a large research university. In his view, the calling of English may be unique, but it does not supply particular resources for aging in the profession even if "the study of literature does sensitize you to human problems and aging should be one of them." Still, a well-known literary image of aging—Arthur Miller's play *Death of a Salesman*—is a vehicle for posing the problem of his professional self image:

> When I first read that play I identified with [the young adult] Biff. Obviously the older I get the more I identify with Willy. I don't flatter myself that I have been any more of a success as an academic than Willy has been as a salesman. He was never much of a salesman so we are not seeing some terrible decline here. He is assessing himself accurately and fairly when he comes to end of his life and asks, "What have I done?"

The ability to determine the timing of his own retirement is certainly "not a Willy Loman situation" as Professor G sees it. Nor does he feel disadvantaged by the academic reward system. "I have to admit that even though I am on the low end of my cohort I don't feel underpaid. Maybe I have been lucky. I can't complain about my salary even though it would have been nice to make more and not to go into debt at different points in my life. I am not sure I can tell you what it is I feel deprived of." Is he satisfied with his career? "Oh yes! Oh my yes! More than satisfied. I feel privileged, absolutely privileged to be earning my living this way."

Academic Life History: Categories of Inquiry

A genre experiment, as I suggested earlier, is a way to gain a new perspective on a subject, but it should also yield a report on the problems, meanings, and uses of the inquiry. Thus I return here to the activity of doing academic life history, especially in the form represented above. In what follows I name four categories of inquiry in the life history method as it may be applied to the study of faculty careers, to identify (in the manner of sociologists Faraday & Plummer, 1979) the uses of the biographical form in a particular domain of experience. Each category is itself a site for multiplying the theories and findings of behavioral and social scientists, as well as the ideas and interpretations of literary critics, historians, and others interested in biography and other forms of life history. The facts of an individual life, presuming they are discoverable as actual facts and not interpretations or even distortions of them as part of memory, are not identified here as a special methodological category. In this matter I would paraphrase Clifford Geertz's objection to the assumption that the primary work of ethnography is to describe what did or did not happen in a particular place: *It is the task of life history writing to demonstrate what a piece of biographic interpretation consists of: tracing the curve of a life; fixing it into an inspectable form* (based on Geertz, 1973, p. 19).

Academic Work and the Life Span Perspective in Human Development. At the very least, the tale that can be told of a faculty career is an implicit comment on conceptions of the academic life cycle, on stage-structured theories of human development (on which the specialized theories of careers typically depend), and on work deriving from what is generally called the "life span perspective" in the behavioral and social sciences (Featherman, 1983). Ironically, despite its name, life span oriented research is often hostile to the stage-structured approach, a paradox whose meaning would be valuable to explore for purposes of understanding faculty careers because virtually all life span researchers are professors. There is much to recommend in the efforts to give academic careers stage- and age-specific form (e.g., Baldwin, 1990; Baldwin & Blackburn, 1981; Newton, 1983), including the codification of both professional aspirations and constraints, although the want of discipline-specific discriminations limits their application, as it does in the case of otherwise revealing work on the "changing consciousness" of professors in midlife (Karp, 1986).

With these theory-guided projects we now have a growing number of accounts of individual careers, in personal academic narratives of several kinds and in biography (Weiland, 1994). The two complement one another, the one helping to define developmental patterns, the other individual differences. Professor G's career must be understood in terms of the interwoven effects of having matured in a particular intellectual environment at the same time that his adulthood reflects common developmental themes. Hence his devotion to the New Criticism and resistance to recent theoretical initiatives in literature study are made part of what is desirable in teaching for anyone of his age whose children are grown. His dedication to students and rejection of the norms of contemporary literary scholarship make sense to him in the developmental logic supplied by being a middle-aged parent in a faculty and disciplinary cohort.

In the vocabulary of life span inquiry, individual differences are often the product of "nonnormative" influences on development. There are, for example, Professor G's initial graduate school failure, his illness, even perhaps his chance to study and teach a new subject well into his career. "Nonnormative" influences work with those that are "age-graded" and "history-graded" as a "system," however that term may be understood when at least some of its key elements are unexpected (Baltes, 1983). Describing individual lives with due regard for their complexity and accounting for the causes of change or development are "converging" activities in life span research. "This is plausible because diversity and discontinuity in the patterning of influences (in terms of content, sequencing, duration, etc.) are prerequisites for diversity in developmental outcomes" (Baltes, 1983, p. 95). Life span oriented approaches can be brought to the study of academic life from the point of the "self" (e.g., Freeman, 1992; Ryff, 1986), or of more external formats for inquiry aimed at integrating psychological and sociological perspectives (e.g., Dannefer & Perlmutter, 1990; Lerner, 1991). As resources for evaluating narrative studies of lives, they help to identify diversity across and within the disciplines.

As the profile of Professor G is meant to suggest, a case may force the adaptation of familiar developmental theories or make new ones possible. Professor G's explanation of the sources and consequences of his instructional paternalism, especially in the value-laden domain of literary study, is a developmental question that, given the size of his academic cohort, makes the theme of the postparental years a timely one. It is apt to call teaching and research (in Erik Erikson's widely used vocabulary) "generative" work. So also may Professor G's account of what behavioral scientists recognize as midlife androgyny (e.g., Gutmann, 1987) be of interest with its surprising reversal of presumably gendered personality traits. In a domain as self-conscious as is academic life about the meanings of sex and gender, the prospects for a developmental role for androgyny (and with the lengthening life span and, again, with the end of mandatory retirement) should prompt unexpected kinds of inquiry into late academic life. Is such a form of academic development "nonnormative," or will recognition of some measure of mid- and late-career androgyny, with the aging of the increasingly larger number of faculty women, alter our images of professional gender and its impact on scholarship, teaching, and administrative roles? The road not taken in Professor G's career—that is, his increasing indifference to academic scholarship—means more than is understandable in the conventional vocabulary of the academic reward system.

Academic Cultures and Faculty Lives. When Lawrence Veysey (1982) asked for the addition of the internal histories of the disciplines to the study of higher education, in general he could not have anticipated today's interest in also adding the personal dimension, or what amounts to a redefinition of "internal." What can be learned about academic work from an account of an academic life that cannot be learned from other forms of inquiry? Or, what constitutes the unique epistemology and authority of narrative? The simplest and best answer, I think, is that it provides the opportunity to penetrate academic work in terms of the organization of experience and the assignment of meanings that make sense to the individual directly in personal narratives like autobiography and with the aid of a mediating discourse in biography. The search for narrative understanding, reflecting as it does the indispensability to the self of a coherent story, collapses the distinction between a life or career and the form of its representation.

In a bold essay, cognitive psychologist Jerome Bruner registers his belief that narrative functions as the chief mental instrument in an individual's construction of reality:

> Eventually it becomes a vain enterprise to say which is
> the more basic—the mental process or the discourse form
> that expresses it—for, just as our experience of the natural
> world tends to imitate the categories of familiar science,
> so our experience of human affairs comes to take the form
> of the narratives we use in telling about them. (Bruner,
> 1991, p. 5)

Bruner's inventory of the elements of narrative invites their adaptation for the seemingly specialized purpose of contemplating the meaning of academic careers. "Seemingly" because the very idea of *career*
is itself a form of narrative understanding, used by individuals and
societies to represent a major segment of experience (though in history
largely male experience). For although the term is used to signify "a
profession for which one trains and which is undertaken as a permanent calling," a career is also a course or passage over time, the "pursuit
of consecutive professional achievement" (*Webster's Tenth Collegiate
Dictionary*). Most important, with its several overlapping roles, a
career is a human activity with particular motives, expectations,
troubles, and rewards (Super, 1980).

Higher education has its characteristic narratives. Burton Clark
(1972) identifies institutional models in his widely cited essay on
"The Organizational Saga in Higher Education." With his adaptation
of the idea of the saga, Clark demonstrates the meaning of narrative
self-images for administrators and the faculty working together at
historically "distinctive" colleges. In the lives of individual professors
across the many sectors of higher education, self-images are given
form by the period of educational apprenticeship, the tenure system,
the academic ranks, and the standard record of activities and achievements. Although the professional curriculum vitae is a narrative of a
kind (Miller & Morgan, 1993), it does not convey what meanings
inhere in a discipline from the story of how its forms of research and
teaching have been absorbed by practitioners. Internally narrativized
accounts of academic life (Bruner and others would say there are no
other kind) can reflect a "personal myth" of professional experience
as a life-long psychological defense (Kris, 1956) or a discipline's ways

of explaining its historical purposes and institutional role. These overlap and share meanings, joining life history and social history.

In apparent recognition of the autonomy of academic work and of the power of rhetorical identity especially for mature scholars, Bennett Berger (1990) refers to the sociologists who contributed to his collection as "Authors of Their Own Lives." But their narratives also amount to a set of disciplinary precedents, norms, and meanings. Together they signify one of the many kinds of academic culture even as many variations on it are displayed. Culture is the name we give to the cumulative meanings of similar narratives by members of any group. Bruner calls this process "narrative accrual" and names it the least studied of all the aspects of the subject, although, as he recognizes, historians and critics of the disciplines are in the early stages of constructing critical accounts of intellectual and scientific work, revealing how professionalization protects career prerogatives, combats institutional pressures, and supplies useful public images (e.g., in literary studies, Graff, 1987; for the humanities generally, see Robbins, 1993).

Academic life is prized for its autonomy, but professionalization is a group phenomenon signifying how membership is an important part of professors' lives. Accordingly, the "culture concept," as it used to be called in anthropology, is now a fixture of inquiry into academic life (e.g., Austin, 1992; Kuh & Whitt, 1988). Context does matter, but as Professor G's case shows, in quite variable ratios of individual desire and value to disciplinary formations or to departmental and institutional obligations. To be sure, the rhetoric of life history writing is part of such variability, for example, as reflected in the selection of incident and the incidental comments woven into the profile of Professor G and in a consideration of the "biographical encounter."

Academic individuality—including the "average" faculty career—is the territory of life history attempting to document academic culture with attention to the smallest but indispensable unit of analysis. Bruner (1991, p. 20) views the advantage of narrative accrual this way: "It is a sense of belonging to [the] canonical past that permits us to form our own narratives of deviation while maintaining complicity with the canon." Geertz supplies a similar addendum to the rhetorical problem of life, writing: "Understanding a people's culture exposes their normalness without reducing their particularity" (1973, p. 14).

As his tale unfolds, Professor G relies on the history and culture of literary studies to explain the form of his career. Initially guided by a set of assumptions about what constitutes the field—its texts, methods of inquiry and teaching, and collegial and institutional routines—he discovers points of departure in the discipline (e.g., "black literature") fitted to his experience if not to the expectations of succeeding generations. By telling his story he justifies his career while exploring long-held beliefs, resistances, and potential anomalies. Appropriately enough for an English professor, professional identity is a rhetorical achievement. To younger, theoretically oriented colleagues with different understandings of the curriculum, course design, and teaching, Professor G's career appears to have the form of one that must be surpassed if the discipline is to fulfill its newest ideals. Professor G himself is not without an interest in innovation, having selected adaptations in keeping with his experience, judgment, and locale. But as he asserts, the habits of autonomy make it difficult to make his preferences and regrets into a professional (i.e., departmental) conversation.

The Biographical Encounter: Forms of Colleagueship. Life history writing must, though not uncritically, take the perspective of the subject even as it inevitably represents the perspective of the writer. Biographers have not been diffident about their intellectual and emotional relations with their subjects. Indeed, what some call the biographical transference (Edel, 1984), based of course on the psychoanalytic version, is a frequent theme of introspection by biographers (e.g., Baron & Pletsch, 1985). Most biographers are content to present the encounter of subject and life history writer as a separate object of inquiry. But in a rare textual intervention, Erik Erikson interrupted his life of Gandhi (1969) with a long "letter" to his subject questioning his motives and integrity. In activating the relations between subjects and life history, writers this way the benefits of candor may sometimes be worth the risk of sacrificing the detachment putatively required of biographical authority. Erikson's special tools of analysis, and his stature as a biographer, prompted and perhaps even legitimized his outburst and gave unique form to the text, Gandhi's midcareer ethical triumphs in effect standing as a rebuke to his skeptical Western critic. Erikson, without question a partisan of Gandhi's ideology and methods, used his reactions to some features of his subject's behavior as a young adult to force recognition of what as a biographer he admired. Unlike the psychoanalytic situation, the process did not have the subject as its "audience" but readers of Erikson's text, observers of the relations between biographer and subject.

What of academic biography in which the biographer shares a vocation with the subject and is certain to have opinions about teaching, scholarship, academic administration, and other matters? After all, the most likely writer of a life history of an "average" professor is another "average" professor with a research interest in narrative, adult development, and academic careers. This means perhaps easier access to the subject and the apparent advantage of an insider's insight. But for this work, comembership in academic culture has its dangers, particularly the biographer's own views about the activities he or she shares with a subject. My own attitudes toward teaching methods and the value of maintaining an active scholarly life (in publication) differ from Professor G's, a fact that is, I think, subordinated to my interest in his pleasure in academic work, however defined. Neither of us believes that being a professor is burdensome work with inadequate rewards. Still, his manifest regret about writing less and less is not, to me, a reflection of the movement in higher education to revise the idea of a scholarly career (e.g., Boyer, 1990; Edgerton, 1993). It is, in my view, an unwelcome feature of mature development in academic life, supplying an explanation (unremarked on by Professor G) for a disappointing element of an otherwise satisfying career.

The interactive form of the biographical encounter itself—having some features of a mutual elaboration of shared ideas and experiences—can yield a productive accent to an academic life history and reveal choices *not* made. The written form, representing the biographical interaction but now focused on the life history writer's encounter with readers, presents fresh problems of recognition, emphasis, and judgment, or responsibility in the matter of capitalizing on the advantages of biography over autobiography. In the brief form of the career profile, it exhibits what I would name thematic bias—that is, the use of the life history materials in the direction of particular themes: teaching, keeping up with scholarship in one's field, or colleagueship. Each is important in an academic career but each has meaning in relation to the others as determined by the practices and values the subject and biographer hold in common and sometimes disagree about (to invoke here with modesty the example of Erikson).

Academic colleagueship, for example, is part of the structure of the biographical encounter itself and it supplies an unavoidable life history theme. It is a matter that is rarely explored, perhaps due to the difficulty of defining its parameters (Neumann, 1993). One of the few sources of dissatisfaction in Professor G's career is his want of colleagueship. As present in the career profile it stands, I think, in poignant relation to Professor G's love of teaching and ambivalence about scholarship, which is (with humor if not complete fairness) caricatured in his account of why he no longer writes papers for academic meetings. But print, or even manuscript, is a stable and transportable medium of intellectual exchange far exceeding the benefits available in casual academic conversation or routine colleagueship. Is the rejection of traditional scholarship—with what such work brings of relations with other scholars (including the give and take about important curricular and theoretical matters Professor G wants)—to risk losing opportunities for colleagueship of the kind that experienced professors might make a crucial part of their mature vocations? Are professors who write little isolated in their classrooms? Do they make a virtue of necessity in their (admirable if nearly exclusive) dedication to teaching? These questions imply judgments of Professor G's career deriving from our colleagueship, as well as our independent relations with colleagues at our own and other institutions, but reflecting mutual regard for choices made and still to be made.

Is N = 1 Too Little and Too Much? Small samples or even the single case, for the specificity and depth they offer, are the great temptation of qualitative inquiry in the social and behavioral sciences. And they are, according to critics, the greatest threat to the value of such work. Is Professor G, because he is white and male, of limited interest or significance in the study of higher education? Some in the field no doubt will believe as much, preferring to focus on the increasing gender and racial diversity of the faculty and what that means to individuals and to the academic professions generally. Others might say that Professor G is right—English professors *are* different, and hence his tale has little relation to the lives of colleagues in, say, history or sociology, much less engineering or agriculture. Still others might argue that Professor G's age means he is of less general or institutional interest than younger faculty members, who reflect the changing character of higher education and have been, justifiably, a major subject of attention in the literature of faculty development (e.g., Boice, 1992).

Professors in the second half of their careers generally appear in investigations of scholarly productivity or theories of the academic life cycle. Lacking major longitudinal projects, the study of faculty careers must rely, often productively, on conventional techniques in the behavioral sciences. But the limits of such work, when it obscures individual differences and understanding of the whole life, has prompted an equally vigorous scholarly convention having the advantage of rebellious statements in the heyday of academic positivism (e.g., White, 1952 and later editions) and of many recent justifications of "qualitative" research, in which biographical methods are housed in psychology, education, and other fields. These often rely on the legitimacy of the case as a form of postmodern inquiry in which researchers are acutely aware of problematic relations between ideas and evidence (Ragin & Becker, 1992). Disputes about generalizability will continue in the behavioral and social sciences even as the study of the individual gains in meaning, whether recast in the spirit of Murray or Allport (e.g., Alexander, 1993; McAdams, 1993), or in forms reflecting new initiatives in the study of adult cognition, particularly scholarly, scientific, or creative work (e.g., Gardner, 1994; Wallace & Gruber, 1989). In either case, the life history narrative will help to unify projects in the "human sciences" (Cohler, 1988).

Even so, perhaps Erikson (1940/1987, p. 162) was right when he said, "Illustrations can only convince him who already believes that those selected are representative." If Professor G's career can be said to be representative, is it representative of any more than of English professors in his academic cohort at similar institutions? To address this theme we must be mindful of first, the significance of disciplinary specialization and how it makes professors so different from one another (as Becher, 1989 insists), and second, the force for difference inherent in working in one of the several sectors of higher education (as Clark, 1987 reminds us). There are events in Professor G's career, and the ways in which he conceptualizes and carries out his academic work, that bind him to many others doing the same thing in different places. But he is different from all other professors also, even those working down the hall in his own department. Life history narratives should be poised between these two ways of understanding his experience.

We can gain a concrete sense of this possibility from a lapse, I think, in Gerald Graff's authoritative history of literary studies. Near the end he objects to well-known critic Helen Vendler's proposal (in her 1980 presidential address to the Modern Language Association) that we never abandon the essence of literary inquiry, the "taste on the tongue" for our favorite texts, in favor of the many "secondary discourses" [i.e., those competing for research and curricular attention]. Graff (1987, pp. 254-255) calls the distinction misleading and rejects Vendler's position as a "primordial" wish for the "pre-critical" reader. In his view, Vendler simply accepts the cultural resources she brings to reading—those that fortify the "taste"—without considering how they are wanting among today's students, presumably those not at Harvard where Vendler now teaches. As Professor G's career shows, although he is ambivalent in the matter of "theory," he relies on the durability of the "taste on the tongue" to sustain the continuity in his work, or his personal narrative of the academic life. We can understand such a circumstance concretely and recognize that he is not resistant to change but selective in which domains he welcomes new texts, themes, and approaches to teaching.

"The Career of Professor G" is meant to illustrate such habits of selection, the differences they reflect, and what they may tell us about our colleagues. From one familiar point of view in the social and behavioral sciences, a single case tells us too little about an object of inquiry as large and diverse as the academic profession. But from another point of view, one representing the nature of biography itself (as proposed by Mills and illustrated more recently by many scholars of personal narrative [e.g., Josselson & Lieblich, 1993]), a single case may also offer too much: by making itself accountable to many complex matters of context and meaning that are difficult to incorporate into conventional studies in the social and behavioral sciences. Becher knew that there would not likely be an audience for "plain," full-length studies of the "average" professor, so the pressure for briefer narrative form is significant, especially with regard to the problem of representativeness.

Allowing for differences of institutions and fields, Professor G understands his situation in many if not all respects to be quite typical of his cohort. Does the difference between "many" and "all" make the individual case insignificant? As Geertz asserts, from the point of view of his increasingly "local" studies of culture, "It is not necessary to know everything in order to understand something" (1973, p. 20). How much must be known to make a claim on knowledge in social inquiry? Enough to signify how meaning is made by individuals and made into interpretable form by scholars, including biographers. Responsible life history writing does not propose the replacement of all other forms of inquiry with biography. Nor does life history solve the problem of relations between individuals and contexts. But in the domain of higher education research, the counterpoint it offers to conventional studies of the faculty (typically as large groups) can guide us to a more concrete idea of how academic lives are fashioned from what is common in academic careers and what is contingent.

References

Alexander, I. (1993). Science and the single case. In K. H. Craik, R. Hogan, & R. N. Wolfe (Eds.), *Fifty years of personality psychology*. New York: Plenum.

Atlas, J. (1988, June 5). Battle of the books. *New York Times Magazine*, pp. 24-26, 72-76, 94-96.

Austin, A. (1992). Faculty cultures. In B. R. Clark & G. Naeve (Eds.), *Encyclopedia of higher education*. Oxford, UK: Pergamon.

Baldwin, R. (1990). Faculty career stages and implications for faculty development. In J. Schuster & D. Wheeler (Eds.), *Enhancing faculty careers*. San Francisco: Jossey-Bass.

Baldwin, R., & Blackburn, R. (1981). The academic career in developmental perspective. *Journal of Higher Education, 52,* 598-614.

Baltes, P. (1983). Life-span developmental psychology: Observations on history and theory revisited. In P. Baltes (Ed.), *Developmental psychology: Historical and philosophic perspectives*. Hillsdale, NJ: Lawrence Erlbaum.

Baron, S. H., & Pletsch, C. (1985). *Introspection in biography: The biographer's quest for self-awareness*. Hillsdale, NJ: Analytic Press.

Becher, T. (1984). The cultural view. In B. Clark (Ed.), *Perspectives on higher education: Eight disciplinary and comparative views*. Berkeley: University of California Press.

Becher, T. (1989). *Academic tribes and territories: Intellectual inquiry and the cultures of the disciplines*. Milton Keynes, UK: Open University Press.

Bellow, S. (1987). *More die of heartbreak*. New York: William Morrow.

Berger, B. (1990). *Authors of their own lives: Intellectual autobiographies by twenty American sociologists*. Berkeley: University of California Press.

Boice, R. (1992). *The new faculty member: Supporting and fostering faculty development*. San Francisco: Jossey-Bass.

Bowen, H. R., & Schuster, J. H. (1986). *American professors: A national resource imperiled*. New York: Oxford University Press.

Boyer, E. (1990). *Scholarship reconsidered: Priorities of the professoriate*. Princeton, NJ: Carnegie Foundation for the Advancement of Teaching.

Brannigan, G. G., & Merrens, M. R. (Eds.). (1993). *The undaunted psychologist: Adventures in research*. New York: McGraw-Hill.

Bruner, J. (1990). *Acts of meaning*. Cambridge, MA: Harvard University Press.

Bruner, J. (1991). The narrative construction of reality. *Critical Inquiry, 18*, 1-21.

Bulmer, M. (1984). *The Chicago school of sociology: Institutionalization, diversity, and the rise of sociological research*. Chicago: University of Chicago Press.

Clark, B. R. (1972). The organizational saga in higher education. *Administrative Science Quarterly, 17*, 178-184.

Clark, B. R. (1987). *The academic life: Small worlds, different worlds*. Princeton, NJ: Carnegie Endowment for the Advancement of Teaching.

Cohler, B. (1988). The human studies and life history. *Social Service Review, 62*(4), 552-575.

Craik, K. H., Hogan, R., & Wolfe, R. N. (Eds.). (1993). *Fifty years of personality psychology*. New York: Plenum.

Dannefer, D. (1992). On the conceptualization of context in developmental discourse. In D. L. Featherman, R. M. Lerner, & M. Perlmutter, (Eds.), *Life-span development and behavior* (Vol. 11). Hillsdale, NJ: Lawrence Erlbaum.

Dannefer, D., & Perlmutter, M. (1990). Development as a multidimensional process: Individual and social constituents. *Human Development, 33*, 108-137.

Denzin, N. (1989). *Interpretive biography*. Newbury Park, CA: Sage.

Edel, L. (1984). *Writing lives: Principia biographica*. New York: Norton.

Edgerton, R. (1993, July/August). The re-examination of faculty priorities. *Change, 24*, 10-24.

Erikson, E. H. (1969). *Gandhi's truth: On the origins of militant nonviolence*. New York: Norton.

Erikson, E. H. (1987). Studies in the interpretation of play: Clinical observation of play disruption in young children. In S. Schlein (Ed.), *A way of looking at things: Selected papers from 1930 to 1980*. New York: Norton. (Original work published 1940)

Faraday, A., & Plummer, K. (1979). Doing life histories. *Sociological Review, 27,* 773-798.

Featherman, D. (1983). Life-span perspectives in social science research. In P. B. Baltes & O. G. Brim, Jr. (Eds.), *Life-span development and behavior* (Vol. 5). New York: Academic Press.

Fowler, D. D., & Hardesty, D. L. (1994). *Others knowing others: Perspectives on ethnographic careers.* Washington, DC: Smithsonian Institution Press.

Freeman, M. (1992). Self as narrative: The place of life history in studying the life span. In T. M. Brinthaupt & R. P. Lipka (Eds.), *The self: Definitional and methodological issues.* Albany, NY: SUNY.

Gardner, H. (1994). *Creating minds: An anatomy of creativity seen through the lives of Freud, Einstein, Picasso, Stravinsky, Eliot, Graham, and Gandhi.* New York: Basic Books.

Geertz, C. (1973). Thick description: Toward an interpretive theory of culture. In C. Geertz (Ed.), *The interpretation of cultures.* New York: Basic Books.

Geertz, C. (1983). *Local knowledge: Further essays in interpretive anthropology.* New York: Basic Books.

Goodson, I. (1992). *Studying teacher's lives.* New York: Teachers College Press.

Graff, G. (1987). *Professing literature: An institutional history.* Chicago: University of Chicago Press.

Graff, G. (1992). *Beyond the culture wars: How teaching the conflicts can revitalize American education.* New York: Norton.

Gutmann, D. (1987). *Reclaimed powers: Toward a new psychology of men and women in later life.* New York: Basic Books.

Heilbrun, C. (1988). *Writing a woman's life.* New York: Norton.

Hilts, P. (1982). *Scientific temperaments: Three lives in contemporary science.* New York: Simon & Schuster.

Humphreys, J. (1987). *Rich in love.* New York: Viking.

Josselson, R., & Lieblich, A. (Eds.). (1993). *The narrative study of lives* (Vol. 1). Newbury Park, CA: Sage.

Karnos, D. D., & Shoemaker, R. G. (1993). *Falling in love with wisdom: American philosophers talk about their calling.* New York: Oxford University Press.

Karp, D. (1986). Academics beyond mid-life: Some observations on changing consciousness in the fifty to sixty year decade. *International Journal of Aging and Human Development, 22,* 81-103.

Kaufman, S. (1993). *The healer's tale.* Madison: University of Wisconsin Press.

Kris, E. (1956). The personal myth: A problem in psychoanalytic technique. *Selected papers of Ernst Kris.* New Haven, CT: Yale University Press.

Kuh, G., & Whitt, K. (1988). *The invisible tapestry: Culture in American colleges and universities.* Washington, DC: Association for the Study of Higher Education.

Lawrence, J., & Blackburn, R. (1985). Faculty careers: Maturation, demographic, and historical effects. *Research in Higher Education, 22,* 135-154.

Leitch, V. (1988). *American literary criticism: From the 30s to the 80s.* New York: Columbia University Press.

Lerner, R. (1991). Changing organism-context relations as the basic process of development: A developmental contextual perspective. *Developmental Psychology, 27,* 27-32.

Lightman, A., & Brawer, R. (1990). *Origins: The lives and worlds of modern cosmologists*. Cambridge, MA: Harvard University Press.

Loewenberg, P. (1985). Love and hate in the academy. In P. Loewenberg (Ed.), *Decoding the past: The psychohistorical approach*. Berkeley: University of California Press.

Marx, G. (1990). Reflections on academic success and failure: Making it, forsaking it, reshaping it. In B. M. Berger (Ed.), *Authors of their own lives*. Berkeley: University of California Press.

McAdams, D. (1993). *Stories we live by: Personal myths and the making of the self*. New York: William Morrow.

McCloskey, D. (1990). *If you're so smart: The narrative of economic expertise*. Chicago: University of Chicago Press.

Miller, N., & Morgan, D. (1993). Called to account: The CV as an autobiographical practice. *Sociology, 27*, 133-143.

Mills, C. W. (1959). *The Sociological imagination*. New York: Oxford University Press.

Mischler, E. (1986). *Research interviewing: Context and narrative*. Cambridge, MA: Harvard University Press.

National Research Council. (1991). *Ending mandatory retirement for tenured faculty: The consequences for higher education*. Washington, DC: National Academy Press.

Neumann, A. (1993). *The ties that bind: Notes on professional colleagueship as academic context*. Paper presented at the annual meeting of the American Educational Research Association, Atlanta, GA.

Newton, P. (1983). Periods in the adult development of the faculty member. *Human Relations, 36*, 441-458.

Novick, P. (1988). *That noble dream: The "objectivity" question and the American historical profession*. New York: Cambridge University Press.

Rabin, A. I., Zucker, R. A., Emmons, R. A., & Frank, S. (Eds.). (1990). *Studying lives and persons*. New York: Springer-Verlag.

Ragin, C. C., & Becker, H. S. (1992). *What is a case? Exploring the foundations of social inquiry*. New York: Cambridge University Press.

Riley, M. W. (1988). *Sociological lives*. Newbury Park, CA: Sage.

Robbins, B. (1993). *Secular vocations: Intellectuals, professionalism, culture*. New York: Verso.

Robinson, I. E., & Lee, E. S. (1993). The aging of faculty in American colleges and universities: Demographic trends and implications. In N. Julius & H. H. Krauss (Eds.), *The aging work force: A guide for higher education administrators*. Washington, DC: College and University Personnel Association.

Rossi, A. (1990). Seasons of a woman's life. In B. M. Berger (Ed.), *Authors of their own lives*. Berkeley: University of California Press.

Runyan, W. M. (1982). *Life histories and psychobiography: Explorations in theory and method*. New York: Oxford University Press.

Ryff, C. (1986). The subjective construction of self and society: An agenda for life-span research. In V. Marshall (Ed.), *Later life: The social psychology of aging*. Beverly Hills, CA: Sage.

Sarbin, T. (Ed.). (1986). *Narrative psychology: The storied nature of human conduct*. New York: Praeger.

Super, D. E. (1980). A life-span, life-space approach to career development. *Journal of Vocational Behavior, 16,* 282-298.

Veysey, L. (1982). The history of education. *Reviews of American History, 10,* 281-291.

Wallace, D. B. (1989). Studying the individual: The case study method and other genres. In D. B. Wallace & H. Gruber (Eds.), *Creative people at work: Twelve cognitive case studies.* New York: Oxford University Press.

Wallace, D. B., & Gruber, H. (Eds.). (1989). *Creative people at work: Twelve cognitive case studies.* New York: Oxford University Press.

Weiland, S. (1994). Writing the academic life: Faculty careers in narrative perspective. *Review of Higher Education, 17*(4), 395-422.

Weiland, S. (1995). Belonging to romanticism: Discipline, specialty, and academic identity. *Review of Higher Education, 18*(3), 265-292.

White, R. (1952). *Lives in progress.* New York: Holt, Rinehart & Winston.

Wilshire, B. (1990). *The moral collapse of the university: Professionalism, purity, and alienation.* Albany, NY: SUNY.

❧ 5 ❧

Developmental Patterns of Mathematically Gifted Individuals as Viewed Through Their Narratives

Ada H. Zohar

Introduction

In the course of a study of the nuclear families of Israeli women mathematicians, I interviewed in depth most of the women mathematicians in Israel, as well as a few outstanding male mathematicians. Mathematicians were defined as individuals with a Ph.D. in mathematics, employed by a mathematics department in one of the five major universities in Israel. The family study was designed to test if the segregation of outstanding mathematical reasoning ability fit recessive X-linked transmission, and the in-depth interviews were intended to explore the developmental course of individuals with this unusual gift. The findings of the family study are reported elsewhere (Zohar, Guttman, & Ginsburg, 1993). The interviews, however, yielded a richness of descriptive material that cannot be easily summarized into tables and graphs.

In some ways, each narrative was different and could only be understood in the context of that individual's life and experiences.

100

However, some distinctive patterns emerged from the narratives, which were seen as significant by most of the individuals in their development as mathematicians. All women mathematicians in Israel were approached and 10 out of 12 were interviewed. The sampling of male mathematicians was more limited. Two male mathematicians were interviewed. One mathematician was included because he had just won an important international award, making him salient to other mathematicians. The other was the husband of a woman mathematician. The interview was conducted in the individual's home or office, according to his or her choice, and was semistructured, focusing on the individual's perception of his or her mathematical development. The order of questions and issues changed from narrative to narrative, because I chose to let the conversation take its course. However, every interview included the questions: "When were you first aware that you had a special gift for mathematics?" "At what stage did you decide to become a mathematician and why?"

Because I did not anticipate the patterns of relating that emerged from the interviews, I did not directly ask about the mother-child relationship or about mentoring; rather these issues arose in response to the questions I cited. Although there were only two men and 10 women, gender differences were apparent in the interpretation and significance given to life experiences. It should be possible to discuss women mathematicians without referring to gender differences in mathematical reasoning ability, and there has been valuable research along those lines (Helson, 1971). However, because women are such a minority in the field of mathematics, and being a minority seems to exert so much influence on their experience and development, I find it impossible to discuss the two issues separately.

Gender differences in school performance in mathematics are found as early as first grade, in rural and urban schools in the United States, as well as in Japan, Taiwan, and China (Stevenson, Lee, & Stigler, 1986; Stevenson, Chen, & Yee, 1993). The importance and extent of the gender differences have been subject to controversy. A comprehensive meta-analysis of gender differences in mathematics performance shows more similarity than difference between the genders, with girls performing better than boys on computational tasks, and boys doing better than girls on problem-solving tasks (Hyde, Fennema, &

Lamon, 1990). However, in the higher ranges of mathematical reasoning ability, there is a considerable gender difference favoring boys, which emerges in adolescence and grows over the college years, and may contribute to the underrepresentation of women in engineering, physics, geology, astronomy, as well as in mathematics (AAUW, 1992).

It is important to distinguish between the normal range of mathematical aptitude and the upper extreme of the distribution. The present study focuses on individuals of outstanding mathematical reasoning ability (OMRA). Mathematical reasoning ability is the ability to use mathematical concepts to solve new problems and requires long chains of reasoning. It is neither rote knowledge nor computational ability. Outstanding mathematical reasoning ability is defined as the range of ability shown by the upper 0.01 percentile of the population (Stanley & Benbow, 1986).

The gender differences in mathematics are probably multidetermined. The AAUW report (1992, p. 52) emphasizes social expectations and stereotypes, and recommends all-girl-cooperative learning environments. Hyde et al. (1990) suggest that schools are not teaching girls enough problem solving in mathematics and are overemphasizing computation, at which girls perform better anyway. It has also been hypothesized that biological factors are influential in producing and maintaining gender differences (O'Boyle, Alexander, & Benbow, 1991; Thomas, 1993; Zohar & Guttman, 1988). I believe that the underrepresentation of women with OMRA is influenced by the genetic factors that make the potential for the trait rarer for women than for men (Zohar, Guttman, & Ginsburg, 1993) and by social processes, which make it very difficult for the minority of women who do have the potential for OMRA to express it.

Regardless of the cause of the gender differences in mathematics, there is clearly a filtering process responsible for the fact that the minority of girls who show OMRA at age 12 or 13 become a smaller proportion of the mathematically gifted pool over adolescence and adulthood. At least 1 in 14 (7.1%) of the mathematically precocious youths identified by the Johns Hopkins talent search is a girl (Benbow & Stanley, 1980, 1983). In 1991, however, in 10 of the most prestigious mathematics departments in the United States, there was one woman out of 86 (1.2%) untenured faculty members, and there were only four women out of a total of 303 (1.3%) tenured faculty (Selvin, 1992). The proportion of Ph.D.s gained by women in the United States over the past 20 years has increased steadily, but the proportion of women gaining Ph.D.s in mathematics is much lower, and the pace of growth is significantly slower for mathematics than for all other subjects combined. Women with Ph.D.s in engineering, physics, geology, and other mathematics-enriched fields are even a smaller minority (United States Bureau of Statistics, 1990). As Alper (1993) puts it, "the pipeline is leaking women all along the way" (p. 409).

As a result, women mathematicians are a minority. In Israel, as in the United States, fewer than 5% of all mathematicians are women, and they are easily overlooked. When I asked two important male mathematicians about women mathematicians in Israel, one of them could not recall any. The other remembered a woman mathematician who had failed to gain tenure in Israel, but had subsequently done rather well in the United States. Neither of them mentioned any of the women whom I interviewed for this study, nor had they, in their 30 years as professors of mathematics, had a single woman doctoral student. The women mathematicians were well aware of these male mathematicians and their achievements: The women seemed to form an information network; they knew about each other's existence, and, as my study progressed, they heard of the study and anticipated my calling them to participate. The more established women mathematicians, those in their 50s, did not identify themselves as feminists and when asked directly could not recall instances in which being women had worked against them. They implied that if other women did not do as well, it was probably because they were not talented or hard-working enough. The younger women, those in their 30s and early 40s, were more open about the difficulties of being in a minority. All the women in the course of their narrative related instances of discrimination, even those who when asked directly denied sexism. Most but not all of the instances of sexual discrimination described by the women in the study took benevolent and paternalistic forms. Typical examples were questions of why these women wanted to pursue a career that is so difficult, or the statement made during a job interview that the job was too taxing for a woman because it required traveling as well as long hours. However, the main difficulties they experienced as women mathematicians did not arise from direct discrimination, but related more to the role conflicts of being academics, wives, and mothers.

Part of my motivation for undertaking this study was to understand how women could survive in such a highly competitive and male-dominated field. As academia in general is difficult and competitive, it was also interesting to compare the narratives of the women with those of the male mathematicians. I was struck by the fact that the men saw mathematics as a particularly difficult field, requiring more devotion and hard work than other fields. Although this may be true of all scientists' view of their own fields, this perception is important to keep in mind when considering the narratives of the women mathematicians.

Although much of each individual's narrative could only be understood within the context of that person's life and experiences, some overall patterns became evident. The two most salient developmental patterns to emerge from the narratives of the mathematicians interviewed related to formative relationships. The first, an early childhood dyad of unusual intensity, and the other, a mentoring relationship in adolescence. Although about one quarter of the individuals interviewed reported the early childhood dyad, 80% reported the adolescence mentoring relationship. These two relationships seemed to exert a central influence on the individual's development.

Dyad in Early Childhood

About one fourth of the individuals interviewed were the object of a focused, intensive relationship in early childhood. They were related to in a manner unsuitable for their age. In most cases the intense relationship was between mother and child. Often the motivation of the mother was boredom, loneliness, or frustration with her own life and development, which expressed itself in a compensatory investment in the child's development. These infants may have been especially precocious and elicited this highly intellectual response from their environment (Scarr & McCartney, 1983). It is also possible that the infants found themselves in this interaction and rose to the occasion.

The first excerpt is from the narrative of a middle-aged man, a distinguished mathematician.

> My parents lived with my father's parents. My mother, who had trained as a lawyer, was not expected to work, but to stay home and take care of me. The household was taken care of by her mother-in-law, so she had all the time in the world to play with me. If I got my mathematical talent from anyone, it was from her.

(I asked why he felt he got his mathematical ability from his mother. He looked uncomfortable, met my eye fleetingly, shrugged, and continued. Because maternal transmission fitted my genetic hypothesis, I was frustrated, but felt our rapport was too shaky to insist.)

> She must have been very bored, because she started at a very early age to set me challenges. When I was 2 or 3 we would spend long hours playing chess; she would pose me logical puzzles. You must understand, she had nothing else to do except play with me. I was an only child, so nothing happened to distract her from me. I think her days were very long while my father was in his office.

I interviewed all five members of this family, and it was only in his interview that the door was closed, and one of the daughters served us drinks. The dynamic of the interview suggested that this man had retained a privileged and protected family role in middle age as he had in early childhood. The other members of the family mentioned not disturbing him as an important motivation, and no one went into his study without specific invitation. Feeling special, an outgrowth of his role as an infant prodigy, seems to have been incorporated into his adult identity and relationships. This feeling is important in the development of creative people in all fields (Albert, 1980).

The second example is taken from the interview of a 22-year-old female mathematician of great promise. She was the eldest of four, three of whom were gifted mathematically. The description of the infancy dyad is taken not from her own narrative, but from that of her mother.

Her mother, herself a mathematician, saw her relationship with her eldest daughter as an important phase of her own development.

> Soon after my daughter was born, we left Israel for the States. We spent a few months at one university, where I started a Ph.D. in mathematics. Then my husband discovered a colleague in another state, with whom he was anxious to work, so we moved there. During that time, I found it impossible to continue work on my thesis from there, so I devoted myself to being a mother. From the start, I was a very anxious mother, sterilizing everything, following my mother's advice, and always feeling worried and inadequate.

(I asked if her baby had been particularly vulnerable, and she answered that the baby had been perfectly normal, and that it was she who was prone to anxiety.)

> I had hoped that the relationship with my husband would be a spiritual and intellectual partnership, like that of the Curies. I was disappointed that he wasn't interested. Although we met in graduate school and had joint interests, he preferred to pursue his work and did not feel any need to share. My relationship with my eldest daughter during the first 3 years of her life, until her brother was born, was very intense. To this day, our relationship is special and different. I had long days alone with her and was completely devoted to her. I remember pushing the supermarket wagon with her sitting in front facing me. We would have long intelligent discussions about our shopping decisions. I went wild with toys. I would buy her wonderful toys, and we would spend hours playing. At a certain stage, my husband limited the toy buying, because we were insatiable and were exceeding our budget. I felt from the very beginning that she was like a friend, like an adult.

In this narrative, it was very clear that the child-mother dyad was being fueled by the neediness and frustration of the mother, as well as by the precocity of the daughter, who was able to respond to her mother's intensity with adroitness and sophistication. In their adult relationship, the daughter clearly felt great gratitude to her mother and had a sense of needing to live up to her mother's investment in her. It was also difficult for the mother to let her go, and it required great tact and determination on my part to get time alone with the daughter. As in the previous example, the daughter was chosen, special. However, the relationship was much more enmeshing, as mother-daughter relationships tend to be (Josselson, 1992, p. 225).

The third excerpt is from the life story of a middle-aged mathematician of international fame. His story is different from the two other examples, in that the family's circumstances did not allow his mother to devote herself to him. Instead a very intense dyad was formed between the young child and his older sister. The children were left alone together for long hours. Possibly the sister found this difficult and threatening, and compensated by forming a close bond with her younger brother.

> I was born in Eastern Europe, and with the rise of the Fascist party in Germany, my parents decided to emigrate to the United States. My father died unexpectedly when I was 3 years old. My mother took my older sister and me to the States and worked very hard to support us. My sister was 5 years older than I, and was often left to mind me while our mother was at work. I liked being with my sister. She used to keep us both amused by teaching me everything she had learned in mathematics at school. When her girlfriends came over she would enjoy having me show off to her friends, by posing increasingly difficult problems for me to solve. When I was around 11 years old, I overtook her in mathematics, and we stopped this activity.

Interestingly, there was no sense of lingering guilt or uneasiness in this man's adult relationship with his sister. Although in the other cases it seemed as if the intensity of the mother-child dyad had affected their future relationship deeply, the current relationship between the brother and sister seemed close, pleasant, and mutual. This may be due to the difference between parental and sibling relationships, but may also be due to the specific individuals in this case.

Not all the mathematicians interviewed reported a dyad of this kind. It is possible that some individuals had this formative experience and others did not. Also, not all adults are aware of the nature of their early childhood relationships.

There seems to be an overrepresentation of only-children and older children among the mathematicians interviewed, which might in part account for their mothers being able to devote themselves to their children so completely. Intense relationships with mothers are fairly common in the backgrounds of musical prodigies, writers, artists, psychologists, and others. Therefore it is quite possible that this relationship allowed the child to feel special, chosen-to-achieve (Helson, 1990) and that the actual content of the achievement was mediated by other factors.

Mentor Relationships in Adolescence

More than 80% of the mathematicians interviewed, when asked how they had decided to become mathematicians, told of seeking out an older mathematician as a mentor when they were 16 or 17 years old. The relationship with the mentor was variable. In some cases it was mainly intellectual. In others the mentoring seemed to fulfill instrumental functions as well, such as securing scholarships and providing opportunities for further growth. In all cases there seems to have been an affirming function, helping in the identity formation of the adolescent, providing unspoken confirmation that the adolescent was gifted and worth investing in. The adolescent, while identifying and idealizing the older professional, also gained a sense of validation (Josselson, 1992, p. 229).

There is reason to believe that mentoring relationships in adolescence could be even more important for OMRA adolescent girls than for boys. First, identity formation of women seems to be more tightly linked to relationships (Patterson, Sochting, & Marcia, 1992). Second, women who are mathematically gifted are a smaller minority, and thus might face more difficulty in integrating their mathematical gift into their emergent identity. Not all the women mathematicians in the study had found mentors in adolescence. The first example is that of the most extensive mentoring relationship described in the study, given by an established male mathematician who answered my question about what had influenced him to enter this profession.

> My ambition since childhood was to become a rabbi. It was a great disappointment to me when the principal advised me that I was not suited to being a rabbi, because I was too much of an introvert. When I was in high school, a friend of mine showed me a journal with mathematical problems. We both worked out a problem in geometry, and submitted it to the editor. The editor invited us to discuss our proof. After that, I often solved problems in that journal. The editor, a senior mathematician, employed me to check solutions submitted to him, or to copy mathematical material. He would lend me books and discuss my work with me. He would pose problems for me and go through my proofs. After school hours I more or less lived in his office. He arranged for a scholarship, which enabled me to get through college. As I continued into graduate school, I found other mathematicians to work with, who were closer to my evolving interests. I occasionally visited my mentor, but not really to talk mathematics. It was more out of friendship and gratitude.

In this individual's life, the mentor seems to have made a decisive contribution. The mentor not only provided confirmation of his ability, but also provided some economic support and ties to the academic world. As an adult, he was very grateful to the mentor of his adolescence, and made this clear in his tone and gestures. However, there was also a sense of having gone beyond the mentor, of leaving him behind intellectually.

The next excerpt is from the narrative of a distinguished middle-aged male mathematician. He also described some of the functions played by the mentor in the first example. However, there was a sense that the mentoring experience in the first example was a comprehensive and central relationship for the adolescent, but the second was more limited in both the instrumental and the affective dimensions. From their life stories, it seems that the youth in the first example was much more needy than the second, who had a supportive and doting family.

> Initially I thought I would be a chemist. I had a cousin who was a very famous chemist. I set up a laboratory at home, and my parents paid for the materials and would buy me components that minors couldn't come by. Then when I was 16 I had a serious accident, an explosion in my lab, and my parents decided that chemistry was not a suitable career for me after all. It was at about that time that my interest began to focus on mathematics. I began going to some evening lectures in mathematics. It was a small group, not very formal, and there was a mathematician there who noticed me. In those days, mathematics books were very difficult to find in Israel. Everything in the book shops was outdated. This mathematician would lend me books. After a while he arranged that I should work in a semiprivate mathematics library, so that I could have access to more books.

There was no sense of wonder, of gratitude, or of privilege in the description of this mentoring relationship. Rather, there was an overall feeling of entitlement, of being recognized for merit, and of getting limited instrumental help. In Josselson's (1992) terms, there was implicit validation, but very little identification and idealization.

The next excerpt is from the narrative of a young female professional mathematician about to accept her first postdoctoral fellowship. Her professor suggested that she be included in the study, and the two women seemed to enjoy a warm and relaxed relationship. The professor was obviously a current mentor, the only woman mentor I observed in the course of this study. However, her mentor in adolescence had been a man.

> When I was in high school I loved mathematics, and wanted to do a project in mathematics instead of one of the matriculation exams. My high school teacher was very supportive and put me in touch with a mathematician in my hometown university. He refused to see me, saying he was too busy. I was very disappointed but would not give up. I wrote a mathematician in a much more prestigious university in another town. He invited me to come and speak to him, and gladly agreed to supervise the project for me. We worked

together for several months, and he was very supportive
and always found time for me. Subsequently he invited me
to participate in enrichment classes and also sent me problems
and corrected my solutions. I still have very warm feelings
towards him. I am going to work in his department now, in
his university, and am going to seek him out and thank him.

In this narrative, the mentoring had important instrumental value,
but the affirming element was most salient. The girl grew up in a city
that was culturally on the periphery, and she felt unappreciated. Having
a mentor from a major university who was interested in her work not
only conferred status on her, but answered her need to be part of a
larger intellectual context. She actively and persistently sought out
this mentor, against the odds, and in a discouraging atmosphere. Unlike
in the men's reports of their mentoring relationships, she marveled
at having succeeded in forging the mentoring relationship and at
having her ability recognized. It is possible that women, while needing mentoring more, have to work much harder to gain mentors.

The last excerpt is from the narrative of a young and very promising
female mathematician, who did not have a mentor in adolescence. I
found her description of her doubts and conflicts particularly poignant. I found aspects of her narrative haunting and infuriating, yet
she herself did not seem upset, except when she talked of her mother's
interrupted career. Although her tale was one of blatant discrimination, she did not seem angry about any of the incidents and did not
make any connection between her current lack of confidence and her
past experiences.

I always liked mathematics. When I was 11 I was put in a
special calculus class in school. I particularly liked working
out the volumes of three-dimensional bodies. It was very
satisfying that there could be applications of what seemed
like such abstract ideas. In high school I got into a very
accelerated class for mathematics. There was only one other
girl in the class. The [male] teacher believed that girls could
not be mathematicians and would ridicule my work. I won a
prize in a national mathematics competition, and he sneered
about it in front of the whole class. I felt humiliated and

was convinced that I had no ability. When the time came to register for university I chose other majors. There were some basic required classes in mathematics, and I found that I liked them better than any of my other classes. At the end of my freshman year, I decided that I should study what I loved, even if I was not going to be any good at it.

(I asked her how her parents, both mathematicians, had responded.)

My parents didn't want to stand in my way, but they certainly did not encourage me. They kept saying that mathematics is a very difficult career, especially for a woman. But by this point I was beyond caring; I just knew I had to give it a try. It was a surprise to all of us when I began to excel. I think when they saw how well I was doing, they began to be cautiously proud of me. I graduated by the time I was 20, and went on to graduate school in the States. I love my work, but I'm not at all sure I can be a mathematician. Maybe after I get my Ph.D. I'll be a teacher. After all, it is very difficult to be a mathematician, especially for a woman.

This young woman had received complicated messages from her environment: Mathematics is the most inspired and important human endeavor, but it is very difficult for everyone, especially women. Her teacher in high school had been openly derisive; her parents were protective in a disabling way. There was no one when she was an adolescent to validate that she had ability and should be invested in. On the contrary, it was implied that whatever ability she showed was somehow ridiculous and of no consequence. It seems that these influences made it very difficult to integrate her mathematical gift into her identity; she tried to put it aside and deny its existence, until it surfaced. It was interesting to see that she had not quite emerged as a woman; she was plump, ungroomed, colorless. She painfully lacked confidence in her ability, even though she had objective achievements to support it. It is possible that a mentor in adolescence would have made her path much smoother and less painful.

A weakness in drawing inferences about the connection between the formative relationships I have described (formative is in itself an etiologically laden word) and the expression of OMRA in this study is that no comparison group was available of other outstanding individuals in other fields. It may well be that no specific connection exists between the intense relationship of childhood, the mentoring in adolescence, and the expression of OMRA. These individuals, like other prodigies (Bloom, 1985), were heavily invested in; perhaps it was this environment that made their natural talent as mathematicians bloom. An alternate framework for understanding these narratives was suggested to me by the work of Ravenna Helson (1971, 1976, 1990; Helson & Crutchfield, 1970a, 1970b). In her study of creative women, it seems the most important single aspect of parent-child interaction is the individual's perception that in the parent's eyes, she is singled out as special. The likelihood of a girl being chosen as special, of having her parents' expectations invested in her achievement, is much higher if she has no brothers, if she is eldest, or if she is a single child. I noted before that there was an overrepresentation of eldest children and single children among the mathematicians I interviewed. There were also three women mathematicians who had brothers who were not suitable to carry their parents' achievement expectations because of learning disability or health problems. The early childhood dyads may be the basis of the psychological perception of these individuals as special. This perception might take form as a mentoring relationship in adolescence, and at other phases in life may manifest itself in other relationships.

There is evidence that creative mathematicians of both genders (Helson & Crutchfield, 1970b) are lower in assertive self-assurance than other creative scientists. Creative women mathematicians seem more emotionally troubled than noncreative women mathematicians (Helson, 1971). The environment is hardly reassuring—academic mathematics is a male-dominated field, which is hierarchical and rule-driven; therefore it is not an environment in which women view themselves as having legitimate power (Chodorow, 1984). In this difficult environment, women are bound to feel at a disadvantage. In particular, women more than men need to develop within a relational framework. "Women tend to grow and stretch themselves by seeking closeness and connection with those they admire, whereas men tend to identify at a greater emotional distance with those they idealize"

(Josselson, 1992, p. 234). Moreover, mathematics itself is a highly abstract and impersonal field, so that the need to connect cannot be supplied by the material itself. Putting all these elements together, the environment that women mathematicians inhabit is not suited to their interpersonal needs. The relationships that women mathematicians experience as formative are worthy of further investigation.

References

AAUW. (1992). *How schools shortchange girls.* Washington, DC: AAUW and NEA.

Albert, R. S. (1980). Family positions and the attainment of eminence. *Gifted Child Quarterly, 24,* 87-95.

Alper, J. (1993). The pipeline is leaking women all along the way. *Science, 260,* 409-411.

Benbow, C. P., & Stanley, J. C. (1980). Sex differences in mathematical ability: Fact or artifact? *Science, 210,* 1262-1264.

Benbow, C. P., & Stanley, J. C. (1983). Sex differences in mathematical reasoning ability: More facts. *Science, 222,* 1029-1031.

Bloom, B. S. (1985). *Developing talent in young people.* New York: Ballantine.

Chodorow, N. (1984). Psychoanalysis and early women practitioners. *Psyche, 9,* 800-831.

Helson, R. (1971). Women mathematicians and the creative personality. *Journal of Consulting and Clinical Psychology, 36,*(2), 210-220.

Helson, R. (1976). The creative woman mathematician. In L. H. Fox, L. Brody, & D. Tobin (Eds.), *Women and the mathematical mystique* (pp. 23-54). Baltimore: The Johns Hopkins University Press.

Helson, R. (1990). Creativity in women: Outer and inner views over time. In M. Runco & R. S. Albert (Eds.), *Theories of creativity.* New York: Russell Sage.

Helson, R., & Crutchfield, R. S. (1970a). Creative types in mathematics. *Journal of Personality, 38*(2), 177-197.

Helson, R., & Crutchfield, R. S. (1970b). Mathematicians: The creative researcher and the average Ph.D. *Journal of Consulting and Clinical Psychology, 34*(2), 250-257.

Hyde, J. S., Fennema, E., & Lamon, S. J. (1990). Gender differences in mathematics performances: A meta analysis. *Psychological Bulletin, 104*(2), 139-155.

Josselson, R. (1992). *The space between us: Exploring the dimensions of human relationships.* San Francisco: Jossey-Bass.

O'Boyle, M. W., Alexander, J. E., & Benbow, C. P. (1991). Enhanced right hemisphere activation in the mathematically precocious—a preliminary EEG investigation. *Brain and Cognition, 17*(2), 138-153.

Patterson, S. J., Sochting, I., & Marcia, J. E. (1992). The inner space and beyond: Women and identity. In G. R. Adams, T. P. Gullota, & R. Montmeyer (Eds.), *Adolescent identity formation.* London: Sage.

Scarr, S., & McCartney, K. (1983). How people make their own environments: A theory of genotype effects. *Child Development, 54,* 424-435.

Selvin, P. (1992). Profile of a field, mathematics. *Science, 255,* 1382-1383.

Stanley, J. C., & Benbow, C. P. (1986). Youths who reason exceptionally well mathematically. In R. J. Sternberg, & J. E. Davidson (Eds.), *Conceptions of giftedness.* Cambridge, NY: Cambridge University Press.

Stevenson, H. W., Chen, C., & Yee, S.-Y. (1993). Mathematics achievement of Chinese, Japanese, and American children: Ten years later. *Science, 259,* 53-58.

Stevenson, H. W., Lee, S.-Y. & Stigler, J. W. (1986). Mathematics and achievement of Chinese, Japanese and American children. *Science, 231,* 693-699.

Thomas, H. (1993). A theory explaining sex differences in high mathematical ability has been around for some time. *Behavioral and Brain Sciences, 16,* 187-215.

United States Bureau of Statistics. (1990). *Statistical Abstracts, 1959-1990.* Washington, DC: Author.

Zohar, A. H., & Guttman, R. (1988). The forgotten realm of genetic differences. *Behavioral and Brain Sciences, 11,* 217.

Zohar, A. H., Guttman, R. & Ginsburg, B. E. (1993). *Outstanding mathematical reasoning ability in the nuclear families of Israeli women mathematicians: A test of the X-linkage hypothesis.* Manuscript submitted for publication.

❧ 6 ❧

The Quest for Connectedness

Loneliness as Process in the Narratives of Lonely University Students

Hadas Wiseman

"*E*verybody feels loneliness sometimes, I'm interested in hearing about when you feel loneliness." I introduced this question in personal interviews with first-year university students in an attempt to get at their subjective experiences of loneliness. Some interviewees would first ask me, "But how do you define loneliness?" whereas others (usually after some contemplation) would proceed rather naturally to talk about their loneliness experiences. In telling the story of loneliness, each person may have their own definition of loneliness. Furthermore, different types of loneliness may be experienced by different people or even by the same individual at different times.

As to scholarly definitions, differing theoretical orientations offer varying definitions of loneliness (Perlman, 1987; Perlman & Peplau,

AUTHOR'S NOTE: This research was supported by a grant from the Israel Foundations Trustees. I wish to express my deepest gratitude to Orli Bar-Shalom Lavon for her efficient work as research coordinator, to Inbar Zoor for her assistance with the interview material, to Ruthellen Josselson for her invaluable suggestions, and finally, special gratitude to the students who participated in the study for sharing their narratives.

116

1982). However, they seem to share three points: First, loneliness results from deficiencies in a person's social relationships; second, loneliness is a subjective experience (not synonymous with objective social isolation); and third, the experience of loneliness is unpleasant and distressing (Peplau & Perlman, 1982). In addition, in conceptualizing the loneliness construct, researchers are divided between those who have taken a unidimensional approach, which assumes that there are common themes to all loneliness experiences, and those who have taken a multidimensional approach, which views loneliness as a multifaceted phenomenon consisting of different types of loneliness (Hojat & Crandall, 1987; Marangoni & William, 1989; Rook, 1988; Russell, 1982).

In the present work I will focus on the need to distinguish between different types of loneliness to understand loneliness as process in the experiences of young adults in their quest for connectedness. My aim is to arrive at a more differentiated view of loneliness in young adults, as it is experienced during the time of their undergraduate university years, and to explore the process of loneliness during these years. The strategy that seemed most useful to study these issues is an approach that combines phenomenological-idiographic methodology with the use of objective measures.

Before turning to describe this strategy, I will provide a summary of the major typologies of loneliness that have appeared in the literature, followed by the rationale for the need to study loneliness as process.

Typologies of Loneliness

How many kinds of loneliness are there? Three major dimensions underlying the diverse typologies of loneliness that have been identified refer to the evaluative dimension, the type of the relational deficit, and the time perspective (DeJong-Gierveld & Raadschelders, 1982). The evaluative dimension distinguishes between positive and negative aspects of solitude and loneliness and between existential loneliness and psychological loneliness (e.g., Mijuskovic, 1979). Most loneliness researchers, however, have focused on psychological loneliness, namely, the subjective reaction to relational deficits. Among relational deficit typologies, Weiss's (1973) fundamental distinction between emotional and social loneliness has received the most attention. "Emotional loneliness" is produced by the absence of a close emotional attachment, whereas "social loneliness" is associated with the absence of an accessible social network (Weiss, 1973, 1987). Empirical support for this typology has been provided in studies by Cutrona (1982) and Rubenstein and Shaver (1982).

Further refinement of the subtypes of loneliness was recently offered by Mikulincer and Segal (1990), who conducted a multidimensional analysis of lay persons' reports of loneliness episodes. Their work differentiated between four subtypes of loneliness feelings: social estrangement, paranoid loneliness, depressive loneliness, and self-focused loneliness. Although the first type parallels Weiss's social loneliness, the second and third type refer to two distinct manifestations of Weiss's emotional loneliness. The paranoid type of loneliness includes "anger toward other people and a sense of being misunderstood, rejected and a target of others' hostility" (p. 224). The depressive type of loneliness is composed of "depressive feelings blended with boredom and painful yearning for a loved person" (p. 224). Both types are associated with lack of intimate ties, however, while the paranoid blames other people, the depressive blames himself for the lack of intimate ties. The fourth type of loneliness includes "self-focused mentations and emotions, such as self-worry, self-doubt, self-devaluation, guilt feelings, shame, anxiety and anger at themselves" (p. 224). According to Mikulincer and Segal (1990), this type of loneliness resembles "adolescent loneliness," reflecting intrapsychic identity conflicts.

The time dimension of loneliness refers to the duration of loneliness, that is, distinguishing temporary from chronic loneliness (Young, 1982) or "state" versus "trait" loneliness (Hojat & Crandall, 1987; Jones, 1987; Marangoni & William, 1989). State loneliness results from immediate interpersonal deficits in a given situation, such as the transition to college (Cutrona, 1982), and is usually temporary as it dissipates with changes in the situation and the passage of time. In contrast, trait loneliness is viewed as a relatively stable feature of personality that results from chronic interpersonal failure (Jones, 1987). In the loneliness literature, what seems missing is an attempt to better understand the process of loneliness for those trait-lonely individuals who experience feelings of loneliness as a relatively un-changeable part of their life.[1]

Loneliness as Process

As so often is the case in psychology, most studies on loneliness have looked at loneliness as outcome and have studied its correlates measured at the same point in time. To study loneliness as process, there is a need to study loneliness over time in a longitudinal design. Longitudinal studies on the transition to college (Cutrona, 1982; Hazan & Hutt, 1994; Shaver, Furman, & Buhrmester, 1985) have focused on the student's adaptation throughout the first year (from summer, autumn, and spring). These studies have found that although most freshmen recover during the school year, about one fifth of the sample remain lonely throughout their first year of college. But what happens to the most lonely students at first-year university as they are close to completing their undergraduate degree (almost 3 years later)? What is the process of their loneliness? Do they remain lonely, or does their loneliness alleviate? Moreover, can we differentiate better between state loneliness and trait loneliness by following their story of lone-liness from the transition to university (which arises state loneliness) to later points in time, when the majority of students no longer feel lonely?

Combining a Phenomenological Approach and Objective Measures

To focus on the processes involved in loneliness and its meaning to different people in different circumstances, there is a need for a more individualistic, phenomenological approach to research on loneliness (Stokes, 1987)—that is, research that emphasizes personal descriptive accounts of the loneliness experience and its meaning. In this work I have combined an idiographic-phenomenological approach based on in-depth interviews with systematic measures of loneliness, attachment style, and personality drawn from a nomothetic approach. It has been argued that obtaining objective measures is the most important precondition for drawing valid inferences from case studies (Kazdin, 1981). Such an approach to gaining in-depth understanding has been suggested in psychotherapy research, referred to as "systematic case studies" (Elliot, 1983).

In this work I chose to study intensively the loneliness narratives of four cases characterized by their high-trait loneliness scores during first-year university. In other words, trait-lonely students who were identified on the basis of objective measures of loneliness were interviewed to obtain in-depth insights into their personal experiences. I followed these trait-lonely students from the point of transition to first-year university, to the completion of their undergraduate degree, in an attempt to determine whether certain types of loneliness are more changeable than others and which conditions occur for such change in loneliness. Furthermore, to better understand how the loneliness narratives may differ as a function of attachment style (Shaver & Hazan, 1987) and personality configuration (Blatt & Blass, 1992), I found it useful to include objective measures with demonstrated reliability and validity. In this way, what is known from the research literature based on these objective measures can be integrated with the information from the narratives, and this in turn may shed further light on the complex phenomena that these measures are intended to capture.

Thus I will try to show that students with similar trait loneliness scores at first-year university may tell very different stories about their loneliness, and that the process of their loneliness is different as a function of type of loneliness, possibly due to attachment style and personality factors. Before I turn to the loneliness narratives, I will first describe how I chose the cases, the method of the interview, and the loneliness measure.

Method

Choosing the Cases. The cases of this study were participants in a study on "Relatedness and Self-Definition in the Experience of Loneliness During the Transition to First-Year University" that I conducted during the academic year of 1990-1991. This study included 152 students in an aggregate repeated measures design (Wiseman, 1993). A subsample of these students ($n = 30$) signed up for a second part of the study that included in-depth interviews. When this sample of students was toward the end of completing their third year of study (in Israel the undergraduate degree is completed in 3 years), I approached once again eight of the subjects, whom I personally interviewed. These students were chosen on the basis of their high-trait loneliness scores as well as their particular attachment style and pattern of personality configuration on objective measures.[2] Finally, I ended up with the four students who were chosen for presentation here as best exemplifying different narratives of loneliness as process.

The Four Cases. The four cases that were chosen were of two women and two men, who were single and of Jewish origin. They all were Israeli-born and they completed compulsory army service after high school, the women for 2 years and the men for 3 years. When I first met them they were first-year university students. Three of them were living away from parents and one woman (Karen) was commuting and living at home with her parents. Further details on the unique features of each case are provided later. The names of the students, and all the other names that appear in the stories, are of course not the real names.

The Interviews

The format of the interviews was semistructured, consisting of open-ended questions (Wiseman & Lieblich, 1992). To facilitate the student's ability to discuss his or her relationships at different stages of his or her life, I adopted the "relational space maps" interview procedure employed by Josselson (1992) in her development of her model of the eight dimensions of relatedness. In this procedure, the interviewee is asked to draw a diagram in which he or she places himself or herself in the middle and arranges around himself or herself the people who were important to him or her at that point in his or her life. The distance between the individual and each important person reflects the degree of emotional closeness.[3]

The strategy of using the relational map to get at the issue of loneliness seemed most useful. In talking about the different relations, students naturally talked about disappointments in relationships, separations and losses, having too small a network of friends, groups that broke up, not feeling close enough to certain people, periods of loneliness, and how they would want to have the map look different (i.e., the gap between the desired and actual relationships).

The interviews during the student's first year at the university were conducted at two points of time: The first interview was conducted at the beginning of the academic year (at the third week after arrival at university), and the second interview took place 6 months later toward the end of the second term. This interview also included the interviewees' early memories in an attempt to get a flavor of their relational makeup. The third interview was conducted toward the end of the third year (about 2½ years after the first interview).

In addition to the indirect way of having the student talk about loneliness through the relational maps, about 45 minutes into the first interview I introduced the issue of loneliness and asked more direct, open-ended questions.[4] This included asking students to report retrospectively of periods in their life when they have felt loneliness. In the following two interviews, they were asked to speak of their current loneliness experiences.

In the second interview, we also focused on early memories and experiences. The instructions were to give the first memory, and then often the interviewee spontaneously gave other early memories. Recently the focus in research on early memories is on interpersonal memories (Thorne & Klohnen, 1993). The assumption is that early childhood memories are expressions of interpersonal relationship paradigms (Acklin, Bibb, Boyer, & Jain, 1991). In this work, I viewed the early memories as providing the "opening lines" for the person's story and explored how these memories may fit with the interviewee's current relatedness concerns. Hence I will begin each story with the student's early memory.

In the third interview I asked the student "to describe to me the events that occurred in your life since we last met in the spring of your first-year university as if I were watching a movie of your life from that point on to today." Toward the end of the interview I showed students their earlier maps and they often commented on the changes.

It should be noted that the students' openness in telling their stories may have been facilitated by the investigator-interviewer being female. Being interviewed by a woman may have put the female interviewees more at ease in discussing their difficulties in their relationships with men. For the male interviewees, self-disclosure to a woman, particularly about issues of relatedness, is also more natural than self-disclosure to a man (see also Josselson, 1992).

The UCLA Loneliness Scale

The UCLA Loneliness Scale (Russell, Peplau, & Cutrona, 1980) was used as an objective measure of loneliness during first-year university. It is a 20-item self-report measure that yields a single loneliness score and is the most widely used measure of loneliness (Weiss, 1987). The scale has been shown to be reliable and its concurrent and discriminant validity has been well established (Russell et al., 1980). In the present study, participants completed both a state version of the scale, referring to their feelings "in the last 2 weeks," and a trait version of the scale, referring to their feelings "during the course of their life up to today."

The Story of the Loner

David began university when he was 24½. If I would not have met him as a participant in my study of first-year university students, I might have easily mistaken him for a 17-year-old; there was a boyish quality to him. Yet he was clearly highly intelligent, had a pleasant smile, and I immediately liked him. His story is very much the story of the loner. The Oxford Dictionary defines loner as "one who prefers not to associate with others." As I traced David's loneliness narratives, I was most curious as to the nature of this "preference," and questioned whether such a preference truly exists, is it stable, or can it change?

The objective assessment of David's loneliness via the UCLA Loneliness Scale showed that his scores both on state and trait loneliness were the highest ones of the larger sample ($n = 152$) at the point of the transition to university. Six months later, David's state loneliness had decreased somewhat, but still remained relatively high, and his trait score remained essentially unchanged. Thus David's pattern of scores was that of those who are referred to as the "chronically lonely" (Shaver et al., 1985; Young, 1982). But what can David tell us about his loneliness, and what is the picture of the process of his loneliness as we trace his story up to the end of his third year?

Relatedness in Childhood

First Memory. David's first memory is remarkable because it is a faceless one: "I remember myself . . . I think in kindergarten, age 4 or 5, I remember myself in a sandbox, something like that, I don't remember faces, I just remember myself."

Another early memory from age 5 includes other children, but it is an unpleasant memory of being separated from the group and not fitting in: "I fought with someone in the preschool, I opened up his head with a wooden brick; it was a traumatic event, as they moved me to another preschool. . . . Later on I was fine and I was friends with this boy, but it was unpleasant. It is as if I was against everybody, everybody against me. . . . He was the leader of the children, and I hit him."

In David's case, the first memory does not include an interaction with another person. The snapshot picture that David gives us in this memory is a passive one of self not-in-relation. His second picture is of an interaction with a peer, but it is a negative and malevolent interaction in which he is both victimizer and victim (see Acklin et al, 1991).

In describing his relational world as a child, David remembers himself as being "the loner type." Secluded, he kept to himself both outside the house and inside the house. Outdoors, he spent much of his time wandering around, throwing stones and observing nature, and indoors he spent much of his time reading many books. His mother would try to push him to be more of a sociable type. She would feel very bothered by his tendency to stay within himself, and she constantly would try to encourage him to come out of his shell and to go out with friends.

David's Loneliness

In response to my probe on feelings of loneliness, David clearly indicates that he thinks he is "a lonely creature." Much of what he describes of himself consists of the features of the prototype of the lonely person delineated by Leonard Horowitz and his colleagues (1982). He feels he has difficulty in creating relationships with people. He has thought of why this is so, but he says he doesn't succeed in analyzing it: "I think I had a normal childhood."

Loneliness During the Transition to University. David identifies times of transition as times of loneliness (consistent with his high state loneliness at the transition to university): "I feel loneliness every time I move to a new environment. Although I feel I am used to being lonely, this situation isn't always to my liking."

Comparing his feelings of loneliness to that of others at the point of transition to university, he feels he is more lonely, as he creates relationships with great difficulty, and even the relationships he does form he doesn't always maintain. He says usually he has relationships with only a very small circle of friends. He has two childhood friends back home, and when he is with them, he doesn't feel lonely. When I asked if he remembers a period when he felt more lonely, David answered, "No, I keep a fixed level of loneliness. Aside from these two childhood friends, I always have some friends, but they change all the time, and I don't keep the relationships."

When asked how he copes with loneliness, David responded that "I already developed mechanisms to live with it, I don't try to escape it, I simply accept it." This acceptance of loneliness that David describes is, according to Mikulincer and Segal (1990), typical of the "depressive type," who tends not to actively deal with the loneliness-creating problem.

David Toward the End of First-Year University

When I met David 6 months later he seemed more relaxed and better oriented; however, his self-description is highly self-critical and points to his interpersonal difficulties: "I have a problem with self-confidence, although it improved a bit lately, but still it is not enough. As if I lack a spinal cord. Sometimes I tend to overreact, I get stressed and depressed and tend to see the dark side of things, or on the contrary I can get too happy. A lot of the times I am confused, don't know what will be, what I'm doing, what I am, a sense of vagueness. I also get discouraged very fast, and I often lose proportions. I have problems with how to approach people, how to talk; the minute I have friends I am very relaxed with them, but until I make friends, I am very slow in this area, I usually don't initiate, I am more passive."

In general, David feels less lonely toward the end of first-year university than at the beginning of the year. "You can't compare it, a totally different world." This is also reflected in a certain decrease in his state loneliness score. When I asked him to what he attributes this change, however, his response underlies the passive aspect of his relatedness to people: "To the outside environment, I don't attribute it to myself, it is just that everything is more accessible here. I am not the initiator type; people approach me and then I start for the relationship, here it is a more pressured framework, more people, so relationships are formed." David does not see himself as an agent in the formation of relationships; rather he uses the term that they are formed.

Comparing himself to others, he differentiates between the physical and emotional and sees himself as not lonely physically but as currently the least lonely than he has ever been in his life. But emotionally/mentally he sees himself as still a loner, tending to isolate himself from others.

David seems to want to form relationships, yet seems to avoid doing so. His dialogue with himself goes this way: "Rationally I know that if I will form relationships so I will have them, both with friends, as well as with girls, I know I'm not ugly, that I am not stupid, that I am nice, when I want to be nice, and I can form relationships; but on the other hand I am very passive, and I don't do anything." It appears that David's style of avoiding close relationships is characterized by a desire for social contact that is inhibited by fears of its consequences, namely, fearful avoidance of intimacy (Bartholomew, 1990).

A time in which David's desire for social contact was more easily fulfilled was under the special circumstances of the Gulf War, which erupted in January-February, 1991 with the accompanying threat of chemical attack and the Iraqi scud missile attack on Israeli cities. During this unusual period, David was paradoxically very content and did not feel stressed. He says that when there is a real danger, he is very much controlled and shows self-confidence; this was also true of the way he functioned under stress in the army. Socially he liked the feeling of togetherness created by the sealed room. He felt the stress drew people closer and he did not feel alone. In fact, he felt less lonely during this unusual period and admits that curiously enough for him it was even a pleasant time.[5]

Relationships With Girls

When I met David the second time, one of the most marked changes was in the area of his relationships with girls. Unlike his relational map at the beginning of the year, which did not include any girls, the current map included a number of girls. University life provided him with opportunities to meet girls, and this was a new experience. It seemed that girls liked him and sought him out. The relationship would start on the initiative of the girl and he would quite happily go along with it. He enjoyed being romantically involved, but would feel guilty that he was not really in love with the girl.

Looking at the change from beginning of first-year university to end of the year, of all the interviewees, there seemed to have been a most noticeable change in David's case. However, this pattern doesn't continue to the end of third-year university.

David Toward the End of His Third Year

When we met for the third time toward the end of his degree, I was very curious as to how much change I would see in David. His self-description continues to be highly self-critical: "I am a person with many conflicts. I want very much the company of others, but I have difficulty forming relationships or maintaining them when they exist, especially with women. I have inferiority feelings that my rational side knows are not called for. I'm most of the time a withdrawn and isolated type. I am aware of my emotional difficulties and to effective ways of solving them, but I am passive and lazy in nature, and don't change out of my initiative almost nothing, which leads me many times to bad moods and despair." Hence David's self-description also includes many of the features of the prototype of a depressed person, such as feeling pessimistic, inferior, and isolated. As Horowitz et al. (1982) have found, the major features of a lonely person are a subset of those of a depressed person, whereby it is more probable for a lonely person to complain of feeling depressed than for a depressed person to complain of feeling lonely.[6]

Reflecting on Change

At age 27, David seems disappointed as to the relatively little change that has occurred in his relatedness. "Maybe I have now some insights into my behavior, but in terms of my actual social life, I am standing almost at the same point I was then. There are here and there small improvements, but all in all I don't think I have made any real progress, and again I attribute it mostly to myself and not to outside circumstances." He is not romantically involved now, and feels he has not changed much in this area. The girl he dated when we met at the spring of first year is now married. He was the one who was not interested in continuing his involvement with her. David has been talking openly with his male friends about his inhibitions with regard to meeting girls, and they have offered him phone numbers of girls to meet. Lately he decided to finally call one of them and feels a slight readiness to take the first step.

Looking at the relatedness map he drew at the beginning of first-year university, David says that then the situation was really grim. The most severe loneliness was at the beginning, and he feels it has changed. Again David does not attribute this change to himself, but rather to "the passage of time, I got to know a circle of people, some of whom have become close." Overall, he feels he himself has not changed in terms of his difficulty in forming relationships. It appears that the passage of time has helped alleviate his state loneliness, but not his trait loneliness.

The Fear of Closeness and the Desire for It

Lili's UCLA loneliness scores, like David's, were relatively high (although not as high as his). Furthermore, both trait and state scores showed an increase from the point of transition to the point at which most of the students have already made a social adjustment (in the spring). Thus Lili (age 22) was chosen to represent the case of a chronically lonely woman who remained lonely throughout the year, and whose loneliness even became more severe toward the end of the year. What can we learn from her narrative? And how much does it change by the end of third-year university?

First Memory. Lili's first memory is from about age 3: "I was playing with my girlfriend, and there were all kinds of shared experiences we remember until today, playing together, things that didn't quite work out, things like that, for example, that we planned to sleep at each other's house and we would run back and forth from house to house to ask for permission from the parents, to arrange it, and in the end nothing would come out of it . . . or that we played in the school yard and we climbed on the fence, and she hung on and didn't succeed in coming down."

I asked Lili with what kind of feeling she remembers this, and she replied that it was a good memory. Unlike David's first memory, Lili's first memory is an interpersonal one, including a sense of sharing with a good friend and a sense of mutuality (Josselson, 1992).

Transitions and Separations Earlier in Life

In talking about earlier separations from parents, she first tells me about her experience of leaving home to go into the army: "When I went to the army, I was rather apprehensive, I don't know if only from the separation, or from the whole thing of entering the army and new atmosphere and new friends, but I suspect that it was also difficult for me to leave home. In principle I know I felt uncomfortable in situations in which I had to leave home, even for a few days; in general, every time I entered a new situation, it was difficult for me, an unpleasant experience." When I asked how her parents reacted in these situations, she replies, "They didn't take it hard, didn't see it as unusual . . . but they were, of course, behind me all the way." One wonders how true that was given her sense of loneliness and anxiety about leaving. This kind of denial is typical of an avoidant attachment (see Bartholomew, 1990; Hazan & Shaver, 1990).

Lili's Loneliness

Responding to my open question about when she feels loneliness, Lili responds, "When I'm physically alone. Sometimes I like being alone, I enjoy the quietness, being with myself, but when I feel that I'm too much time alone, or not really alone, but with people that aren't really close to me, then I feel loneliness."

Loneliness During the Transition to University. Lili refers specifically to her feelings of loneliness in the dormitory: "When I sit in my room in the dormitory for hours doing my school work and there is no one I can really talk to and tell what I feel, and I don't have anyone who is really close that I can turn to." Lili says she always has a kind of picture in her head of having a close friend (boyfriend) who she could talk to and they would share with each other everything and would feel a real joy of being together.

Comparing herself to her peers in the university in the beginning of the year, Lili feels she is more introverted than others and comes out less to make connections with others, "so that leads to my greater loneliness." Yet she says there are situations in which she speaks to others, exchanges experiences and so forth, then she doesn't feel lonely. When she feels lonely at the university, she usually calls home to speak to someone who she is close to, or doesn't do anything, and just goes on with the feeling.

Lili Toward the End of First-Year University

Like David, Lili refers in her self-description to her interpersonal difficulties: "What bothers me about myself is being so introverted and shy, and difficulty with forming relationships with others, and I am very much within myself, and I keep everything to myself, and hardly tell others anything . . . aside from that I have a great need to succeed, especially in my studies, almost like a compulsive need."

Toward the end of first year, she stills feels lonely from time to time. "I have a real tendency for mood swings, I can suddenly get into a bad mood and then after 2 days be in a good mood. It appears to happen without a visible reason. But there are a lot of times that I'm in a bad mood or I feel loneliness." Specifically, she talked about her feelings of loneliness during the Passover break. She came back to the dorms to work on a paper and decided to stay there until she finished the paper. She closed herself in her room and stayed there without any contact with anyone, and "to tell you the truth I felt I was going crazy, really, because I was totally alone. I chose to work that way on my paper, but it wasn't that pleasant to be alone."

About Her Need to Achieve Academic Excellence. "I always try to succeed, it is a kind of drive from within. I've always felt pressured to achieve the highest marks. I don't know where it comes from because my family doesn't put the pressure on me; on the contrary, they always tell me that I don't need to be the best and that I don't have to get the highest mark. I'm very much of a perfectionist, and I need to be at the very top; it bothers me and scares me."

Reflecting Over Changes From the Beginning of the Year to the Spring. In some respects Lili feels that a lot has changed in comparison to her feelings during the transition to university: "When I came to the university during the first 2 to 3 weeks, I was really in shock, and I was upset all the time because I simply didn't know what university was all about, and I felt that I won't be able to cope, but now I truly know what is expected of me, I got into the swing of things."

In other respects, Lili feels that perhaps not enough has changed: "There has not been really much change, no news really, I continue to study, and continue to live in the dorms, my need to succeed is meanwhile succeeding, with a lot of hard work." When asked what she would have liked to change if she could, she replies that she would like to have a boyfriend, really a close one, and would like to expand a bit her circle of friends. Although she has been academically successful, in the interpersonal realm she has not achieved her desires and feels far from being able to obtain them: "If I look at things realistically I imagine my situation will be the same in a year. I would like to be able to suddenly be open and feel good with other people, and to find someone I want and enjoy being with, and he would enjoy being with me, but it seems like it would take a miracle for this to happen, because I don't see how it would happen otherwise, unless I do something drastic to change this."

Lili Toward the End of Her Third Year

At the third interview Lili is now 24½, and her first statement is that it is hard to believe that almost 3 years have gone by. Her appearance has definitely changed and she looks like she pays more attention to her appearance, as she is a beautiful girl.

In her self-description she now stresses more her wish for closeness: "I am very closed, very shy, although unlike the way I was at first year, I am a bit more open and a bit more sociable; then I was completely immersed and absorbed by my studies, now I socialize more and put less effort into studying. I very much want a close connection with people and I miss that, I do have it with certain people, but I still feel that I lack it. I am self-critical, my self-esteem is a bit low, I find it hard to make decisions, I find it hard to make changes. I am pessimistic, I don't plan for the far future."

Lili Seeks Counseling. At the beginning of second year, Lili went through a crisis that was triggered by a family crisis. She became depressed and felt unable to cope. She decided to get professional help and she began counseling once a week for a period of a year. In talking about her counseling experience, Lili says that "at the beginning it was very hard for me to open up, but slowly I did open up and felt secure in this relationship. In looking back now, I feel I changed quite a lot since then. Yet, I don't know if it is related to the sessions, or to things that happened to me outside. Most sessions I would talk about my family, and my difficulties in forming relationships, and we would try to understand." The counseling agreement was time-limited, and when it ended Lili felt much better and felt ready to be on her own. Now she thinks about going into therapy some time in the future to continue the work she began and "to really go deeper."

Her Connection to Her Family. During the family crisis and while she was in counseling, Lili very much distanced herself from her parents. She views her parents very differently now and questions the nice picture she drew of her relationship with them: "I didn't see other things, we were all very closed and we didn't share deep things, and that was what I was used to and I thought it was OK, I felt I had close and good relationships with my parents, but now I feel it could have been better."

Lili's Friendships. Lili became very close to her roommate. She describes her roommate as a person who is able to create intimate and close friendships and who easily self-discloses. For Lili this was a totally new experience of friendship. Although she has always had a close childhood girlfriend (that appears on her map from age 5), they never self-disclosed to that degree. Lili attributes this new experience mostly to her roommate's personality.

Opposite-Sex Relationships. During the university years Lili gets to know a number of boys, but in most cases the relationship is of a friendly and not of a romantic nature. She seems to be struggling with how much to get close to them and how much to keep her distance and is never sure how much they want to get close to her. "I feel that a lot of the times the getting close and getting away are in my own head." In listening to her describe these relationships, she seems like someone who is dancing toward and away from these men, but never really dancing together with them.

Finally, in reflecting back on her experiences of loneliness since first-year university, Lili says she feels less lonely. But still there are times, she doesn't know what triggers them, when she feels that "I very, very much want someone that will be close to me and I don't have."

The Quest for Attachment and Belonging

Michael, unlike David, looked his age—25—and was manly look-ing, yet there was a soft look to his eyes. Despite a similar pattern of high loneliness scores, his story of loneliness is a very different one.

Relatedness in Childhood

Early Memory. "This is a strong memory from the Six Day War, I was 2 years old, I remember my father standing near my bed, he was holding a gun, he told me there is a war, I remember that I asked him why are there red bullets, so he explained to me that red bullets are for red trees, and green bullets are for green trees, that's the answer he gave me. . . . I guess he didn't want to tell me what war was, now I know of course more than I want about war, but this is my memory, I can really see me and him." In this relational memory, father is trying to protect Michael the toddler from knowing about the harsh reality of war.

Michael's early memory is told with a pleasant affect. Given the notion of "mood-dependent recall" in autobiographical memory (Acklin et al., 1991), this underscores the salience of this memory that was told to me in the context of Michael's sense of loneliness in the university and his current lack of connection to his father. Perhaps in this memory Michael is telling the story of a promise not delivered. His parents divorced when he was 11 years old and he witnessed their war, which as we shall see is very much tied to Michael's story of loneliness.

Michael's Loneliness

Michael was one of the interviewees who responded to my questions about loneliness with the most elaborated responses. Other interviewees talked about their interpersonal difficulties, yet they did not always label them loneliness. Moreover, they seemed unsure whether what they felt was loneliness. For Michael there was no such question; he was painfully aware of his feelings of loneliness.

In response to my first question about when he does feel loneliness, Michael responded that actually it would be true to say that he usually feels loneliness. "I feel as if I am alone in the world." He has a wide range of interpersonal relationships, yet he longs for a romantic partner, one with whom he will build a family, a home. "I feel a constant inner pressure. Like I am always searching, searching for a close relationship. I feel I am searching for something that will help me relax." This inner pressure in the search for intimacy was referred to in Sullivan's (1953) writings on loneliness: "Loneliness . . . is the exceedingly unpleasant and driving experience connected with an inadequate discharge of the need for human intimacy, for interpersonal intimacy" (p. 290).

At the transition to university, Michael at first did not form new friendships. He viewed his loneliness as leading him to keep away from people, yet labeled it himself as a vicious circle, whereby his inner loneliness contributed to further loneliness and lack of connection to the students around him. Similar to Lili, he puts his academic aspirations in first priority and says he is sort of postponing making new relationships so they do not interfere with his studies, yet is aware that this is not very sensible on his part.

When Michael feels lonely, he calls a close friend; he searches for closeness. Yet a lot of the times he just stays with it, he knows that doing something might help, but feels it will help alleviate his loneliness just for the moment; after a minute it will return. He is looking for something to feel belonging to: "I have a very big problem of belonging. . . . It is because of the family, the divorce and all that."

I asked Michael from what age he remembers himself feeling alone in the world. He clearly located this feeling from the period of his parents' divorce. "Since the period of the divorce I became very dependent on my group of friends." His friends became an outlet for his quest for belonging and feeling part of something. Research on childhood experiences and loneliness in adulthood has shown that respondents whose parents divorced before they were 18 years of age were more lonely as adults, especially if the divorce occurred before the respondent was 6 years old (Shaver & Rubenstein, 1980). In Michael's case he remembers marital conflicts as early as age 6. Jones (1992) found that it was the experience of high levels of family conflict, rather than parental divorce itself, that heightened loneliness. As Block (1993) has argued on the basis of the Berkeley longitudinal study:

> [A] finding previously said to be a consequence of divorce was found to exist prior to the fact of divorce. . . . Indeed, the family discord often characterizing the period before parental separation may well have serious consequences for the children involved. (p. 29)

In talking about his core sense of loneliness, Michael gave the metaphor of living in a cage of glass: "It is as if I live in a cage of glass, I am seen, I see, but I don't feel . . . I don't let others touch me. There is a barrier in the sense of coming out, it is not in the sense of entering. The glass is thick from the side of the exit. It is clear to me that I am not open so there is no chance that it will resolve. To solve things you need to be open, to accept things. I admit I have a problem, I'm not sure what can help me, if therapy can help."

Michael Toward the End of First-Year University

Michael had great difficulty describing himself at first-year university. It appeared that my request "describe yourself" arose his anxiety: "It is hard for me to say my characteristics. . . . Credibility is an important asset with others, that is why I am credible, I am more the Pope than the Pope, I want very much that the people who are close to me will think highly of me, not that I look for respect, but for feedback, and for people to be sincere, truthful, and objective, not hypocritical. But this doesn't really portray me. I guess other people would say that I am a good guy, a good egg."

At the middle of first-year university, Michael says he still feels alone. However, now his feelings of loneliness have been put aside as he gets to know students in his courses and is very much engaged in his studies and is task-oriented. Forecasting the future, he finds it hard to picture himself not alone, with a family and children of his own, and sees himself devoting himself to working with children.

Michael Toward the End of His Third Year

At the third interview Michael is now 27½, and he tells me that so many things changed for him, especially in terms of his inner self. In his self-description he now refers mostly to this strong sense of change: "I think that now I'm much more focused on myself, it is much less important to me what others think. I concentrate on my own needs, and I'm much less pressured and more able to think of what is good for me. I'm much more open and generally more relaxed in terms of my quality of life. I used to be so stressed, so I can't really talk of myself without saying what changed since the last time. I have serious thoughts about the future, including plans for marriage and children, what to do and where to live. I still have the desire to work with children—that hasn't changed, but at least I'm more aware of my needs and where it comes from."

Reflecting back on first-year university, he remembers himself as a "really frightened creature, terrified from all the pressure and the things I had to cope with." He feels he was very much helpless at the time. Like Lili, Michael also decided to start therapy, and he is in ongoing therapy as we meet for the third time. He refers to some of his perceptions of himself as emerging from his work in therapy, particularly in terms of the way he perceives the impact of his past experiences in the family on his current experiences in relationships.

Until Michael met his girlfriend toward the end of second-year university, he felt he was a lonely creature and felt a sense of weakness. For a long time he avoided dating: "I got into this aloneness. I felt sorry for myself and probably it would be most true to say that I simply put up a lot of barriers from everybody, and that was also what prevented me from altogether getting close to people. Then I took the dog."

Michael's Connection to His Dog. Michael's friends saw his loneliness, so they convinced him to take a puppy. At the time he was living alone and having the dog was having someone to come home to. She put light into his home and he formed an intense attachment to her: "She is very smart, and there is a kind of chemistry. I have empathy for her, and a very strong identification with her. I feel bad when I need to leave her alone, as if she was my child. I know I project a lot of things on to her." Having the dog helped a lot, but he was aware he needed something deeper.

Michael Starts Therapy. Michael thought of the possibility of going for psychotherapy during first-year university, but he kept sending others for therapy and didn't go himself. He attributes this to his need not to show weakness and not to surrender to difficulties. But at the middle of second-year university, he felt that he was not enjoying life and decided to start therapy. In talking about his relationship to his therapist, he feels somewhat ambivalent because he would like to feel closer to her and not feel the distance he feels with her, yet he knows it is a therapeutic relationship and that it has to be different. A month after Michael started therapy he met his partner Tamar.

Michael Meets Tamar. Toward the end of second-year university Michael was introduced to Tamar. For a long time he refused to meet girls and kept saying no to his friends' attempts to persuade him to give it a try. Until, as he puts it, after always saying no, one day he said yes. He thinks there was a certain emotional readiness to open up: "Because I really wanted love, I always said that was what I was missing. . . . This is what I always wanted, because my mother left me at an early age, and a sense of family is what I always missed, so I want to have a family of my own and children."

From the very beginning he met Tamar, there was a strong click between them. They immediately became very close, as she also was looking for love, warmth, and closeness. With Tamar the barrier was broken, and he has been extremely open with her and can tell her things he dare not tell anyone (not even his therapist). Having this emotional attachment has made him much more relaxed; life is more peaceful and he is much less pressured.

Despite his love of Tamar and the security it gives him, Michael fears abandonment. He says openly (and Tamar knows this as well), that he feels that only his dog is really totally his, and that with the dog he doesn't have to fear betrayal and abandonment. He knows that Tamar is faithful to him and that his fears are irrational, yet these fears are deeply rooted in his childhood experiences.

Reflecting on Change

I asked Michael to reflect on his feelings of loneliness that were so much part of his life before he met Tamar. Recently, he suddenly became aware that he was not feeling alone anymore, "It was a strange feeling, as I was so used to feeling alone." Reflecting on the change he went through since I met him at the beginning of first-year university, he says, "It is a combination of things, I think I went through a process, that if I would have met Tamar at another time it wouldn't have happened like today. . . . Still, until I met Tamar I felt pretty bad, so she was a catalyzer, she was home, a place I belong to, it was a drastic change. But I can't separate it from processes I went through. I presume that therapy is also part of it, it all came for me together, therapy, Tamar, but I think the real push is Tamar. Because I have Tamar, so I don't feel alone." In this respect Michael feels that throughout his whole life he has been preoccupied with searching for connection and belonging, which he views as related to his parent's divorce. But now he views things from an adult's point of view and he understands them; they could have done things differently, but this is what they knew to do.

The Story of the Preoccupied

Karen was 20½ when she began university. In some ways she was different from the other three. She had not left home, so that in her case the transition to university did not involve adjusting to living away from home. In the group design study, state loneliness was lower at the beginning of the year for those living with parents than for those living away from parents. Further, her pattern of loneliness scores was such that she scored low on state loneliness, but just as high as Lili and Michael on trait loneliness.

Early Memory. "My very first memory is from the Yom Kippur War, I was then 2½ years old, almost 3, we lived in an apartment house where the shelter was in the basement, I remember it was night, my father was of course not with us, and we went down to the shelter with my brothers, and we sat in the shelter and it was very organized . . . and I had a lot of friends in the building, and two really close girlfriends of mine. . . . It was very scary, a feeling of helplessness, I remember it."

Her second memory: "We were supposed to go on a family trip on a Saturday, and I scribbled on the wall, just before, and I remember my mother asked who did it, and I didn't tell, and it was clear I had done it, and we didn't go on the trip until I would tell the truth, because I lied, I remember me sitting and her sitting across from me with a very serious look on her face." I asked Karen about her feelings, and she responded: "embarrassment, helplessness, an unpleasant feeling." This memory of conflict with her mother is perhaps consistent with her current struggle for separation-individuation in late adolescence.

Karen's Loneliness

Three months before starting university, Karen and Bill, her boyfriend of 3 years, separated. Loneliness for her goes with the pain of that separation: "During the period that Bill and I separated I felt loneliness about 24 hours a day. My best girlfriend and my parents all said it is a good thing we separated, so I felt lonely with how I felt, and was very lonely during the separation, because I felt that no one understands me. While I was in the relationship I was less lonely, but still at times when I had difficulties with Bill I felt I had no one to share these problems with, as I didn't want to share these with my mother."

In trying to talk about loneliness, it is clear that for Karen, unlike Michael, loneliness is not a feeling she has thought much about. She thinks she feels loneliness when she is in a bad mood, but she doesn't know if it is the hen or the egg. A situation that arouses feelings of loneliness for Karen is at the folk dancing nights, on the occasions when everybody around her is dancing in couples and she doesn't have anyone to dance with; either she is not invited, or the men who invite her are not to her liking, but she wants so much to dance and then she feels terribly lonely.

The Transition to University. Karen adapted socially very quickly, and after only 2 weeks of classes she had already made friends. She says, "Lonely, I am not," as reflected in her low state loneliness score. She seems enthusiastic and hopeful about her new social environment: "It is lots of fun to meet new people, so I came to university with the sense that this is a good opportunity to meet more people and widen my circle of friends, which was quite narrow. Today it is great, I don't feel in the center, but I feel part of it. I am satisfied, I study a lot and enjoy it, and people are wonderful, and the class seems very nice, and there are lots of boys."

I asked Karen if it was typical of her to form relationships quickly when she is in a new situation. Unlike Lili and David, she sees herself as a very open person. On the outside she thinks she is seen as a self-confident person, and this is not always how she feels inside, yet she forms relationships with ease. This mixed picture of self-confidence is also evident in her reassuring self-statements at the transition to university: "I decided that enough with the lack of self-confidence, now I am in my own right and I will meet people!" Finally, she qualifies this picture of being outgoing and sociable by indicating that at least with girls she has no problem connecting quickly; however, "with men it is different, I am withdrawn."

Loneliness Toward the End of First-Year University

At our second interview, Karen still seems very happy at the university, she likes her studies, doesn't feel lonely, and feels surrounded by people. Despite this sense of being surrounded with people, Karen has the fear that people don't really want her company, and particularly with men she is afraid of being exploited. She painfully tells me of a guy in her course who came to her home a number of times and studied with her for hours for an exam. She taught him the material, and they watched movies until late at night. He told her about himself and she liked his sensitivity. She really liked him and thought perhaps this relation had the potential to develop into something, but after the exam she didn't hear from him anymore. She is very angry and hurt and it makes her feel *lonely* to think that for the exam he was interested in her, but that he was not interested in her *for who she really is.*

Karen's wish to be understood and loved is reflected in her self-description: "I am very sensitive, I take things to heart. I am afraid of confrontation, most of the time I keep things pushed inside myself, eating myself from within. Sometimes I am very depressed, but it doesn't last long, I find many reasons to laugh and smile, and I also cry and it passes. Often I do the listening to other people, but I don't always find who to tell, and people don't like to listen, and I look for someone to take things off my chest, and my mother isn't always capable of understanding. I like to pamper and I want to be pampered, I like to love, to show I love, to choke out of love, and I want it to happen to me."

This description of the kind of love Karen wishes for sounds much like what Main, Kaplan, and Cassidy (1985) referred to as a "preoccupied-enmeshed" style of attachment.

Karen Toward the End of Her Third Year

Karen Goes on a Diet. Of all the interviewees, Karen changed the most in her appearance. I accidentally bumped into her at the university about a half a year before I interviewed her for the third time, and for a minute I didn't recognize her. She lost a lot of weight (30 kg.), changed her haircut, wore a short dress. Karen no longer looked like a girl, but really looked like a woman. This change in her physical appearance was very meaningful for her, and she referred to it a number of times during the interview and in her self-description: "I went through a big change with the diet, and I looked inside myself, and I gave myself the opportunity to be with myself, to get to know myself, because before I tried to escape, if by surrounding myself with many people or with the food, but I decided to give up being overweight, and I dared to take off my biggest shield. . . . There was a period I really detached myself, and I was alone, and I tried to get to know myself alone. So today if I describe myself I can say that I am a person that likes a lot of company, but I can also be by myself and like it. I remember when I was in first-year university I really felt like a little girl, I would see married girlfriends, and it looked to me like a far thing, and today I'm even willing to think of it. I feel more mature and more ripe, I went through a lot in these 3 years."

The Quest for a Love With Mutuality and Validation

Karen's story of the process she went through during the last 2 years is a story with two major themes that are partly related: The first is about separation-individuation from her parents, whereas the second is about the search for a mutual relationship with a man.

The first man is a friend from her studies with whom she falls in love and has long discussions into the night. She feels attracted to him, and although they reach a great deal of closeness in the relationship, he is not interested in a romantic involvement with her. Then she gets romantically involved with Gary. This relationship goes hand-in-hand with a rebellion against her parents, in that they don't approve of him. She experiments with rebelling and does things she didn't used to do—smokes, drinks, goes to discotheques, and leads more of a wild life. She loves Gary deeply and for a while it seems like he is really in love with her; he opens up to her and she puts everything into the relationship. Yet at some point Gary is also interested in seeing other girls and Karen is extremely hurt and frustrated, feeling like she is doing all the giving. After Gary she meets Ron and falls into his open arms, only to get disappointed once more. Ron likes her a lot, but after a relatively short period of intense involvement, he admits to her that he is not truly in love with her. For Karen, this is not good enough; she is searching for true reciprocal love.

After she and Ron separate, she stays in bed for a whole week, and really cuts herself off from everybody. But then she decides to take things into her own hands: "So I decided to take responsibility, and to do what I want. Up to now I was for everybody else and I invested in relationships, and I never got anything in return, so, no more, now it is me for myself." Two weeks later, friends of hers introduce her to Jonathan. At the beginning she doesn't give of herself; she thinks he will be only a way of forgetting Ron. She is happily surprised when the relationship continues to develop. At the third interview, after 4 months of the relationship with Jonathan, she feels that perhaps for the first time she is in a mutual relationship in which Jonathan is investing in the relationship and doing a lot of the giving. For the first time, she feels that he really accepts her as she is.

Looking at the maps she drew at the earlier interviews, she comments, "Before I used to surround myself with people, now I have fewer connections, and at the university people ask, 'Where did you disappear?' I find myself more alone, but not lonely, I know that when I need I have someone to turn to, because today I really have relationships with people who truly love me and I love them."

The Quest for Connectedness

What can we learn from David, Lili, Michael, and Karen about loneliness as process? All four rated high on trait loneliness during first-year university; however, despite some common themes, their narratives seem to point to the multifaceted nature of the loneliness experience. In terms of the relational deficit dimension, their stories were ones about emotional loneliness, whereby they all seemed to be operating from the quest for connectedness.[7] The lack of a social network (i.e., social loneliness) appeared to be a manifestation of state loneliness, and in a matter of weeks the students made some connections at the university (even David the "loner" did not seem to complain of social estrangement). The core of their loneliness seemed to stem from the lack of close emotional ties. However, this lack was multifaceted in that it had different shades and colors.

To understand the kind of relational dimension that is lacking in different types of loneliness, it is useful to refer to the other side of the coin, namely, the multidimensionality of relatedness. Josselson (1992) postulated a multidimensional relational space that consists of the following eight dimensions: holding, attachment, passions, eye-to-eye validation, idealization, mutuality, embeddedness, and tending. The basic assumption underlying her model is that "although each of the dimensions is probably present to at least some extent in everyone's life, people often develop along particular relational pathways that highlight one or two relational themes in favour of others" (Josselson, 1992, p. 9). Within this model Josselson outlines the pathological poles of these dimensions, of which the ones relevant to the present work are: "aloneness" as the absence of attachment, "loneliness" as the absence of mutuality, and "rejection" as the absence of eye-to-eye validation.

Looking at the four stories through this prism offers some insight into the variability of the trait loneliness of these students, despite their similar trait loneliness scores. Karen's story seems to be one of struggling for a connection with validation and mutuality. Michael's story is a quest for an attachment that can be trusted to be permanent and thus will provide belonging (cf. Josselson, 1992). Both Lili and David desire an intimate attachment, but their loneliness seems to stem from a fearful avoidance of intimacy (Bartholomew, 1990). Unlike the "dismissing" style of avoidance, which is characterized by a defensive denial of the desire for attachment bonds, the "fearful" is characterized by a conscious desire for social contact counteracted by fears of the consequences of attachment.

In intersecting the relational dimension that is lacking with the time dimension (i.e., chronicity of loneliness), it appears that the four cases tell us a different story about loneliness as process. Tracing these trait-lonely students from the transition to university to the completion of their undergraduate degrees, their loneliness narratives seem to show different degrees of continuity and change. Placing these four cases on a continuum from continuity to change, David, who at first seemed to change the most from the fall to the spring of his first year in that he started to get involved with the opposite sex, turned out to be the one most disappointed with his lack of change. In the third interview, he repeatedly referred to his difficulty in forming relationships, as if he became aware that there are faces out there. In answer to my question whether there has been a change in his desire for relationships, he replies, "I have actually always had the desire, and always have it, the loneliness doesn't feel good, perhaps it is more of a companion than it is for other people, because in many periods in my life I was lonely, so this feeling is not a stranger to me and I can live with it, but the will is always there, not to be lonely, yet the inhibitions are apparently even stronger."

Lili, whose narrative has certain similarities to David's, appears next on the continuum. She has gone through some changes, such as forming a strong attachment to her roommate and becoming somewhat more sociable. Due to a family crisis, and perhaps her counseling experience, her perception of her relationship with her parents has shifted and has become more ambivalent. Nevertheless, in relationships with the opposite sex she seems to continue to be a fearful avoidant, caught in an approach-avoidance conflict (Bartholomew, 1990).

In some ways, Michael has gone through the most change as he shifted from a feeling of painful loneliness to escaping emotional loneliness by his attachment to Tamar. Like Lili, his process of change was perhaps facilitated by therapy. However, Michael is also aware of his difficulty in freeing himself from his fear of abandonment, which draws on his earlier experiences.

Finally, Karen's struggle with separation-individuation is coupled with her preoccupation with attachment. She seems to be motivated by the "fear of loneliness" (Fromm-Reichmann, 1959) in her search for validation and mutuality. Her story, like that of other young women, is a story of "self-in-relation," in which the self is developed in the context of important relationships (Surrey, 1991).

Looking at this continuum, it appears that loneliness that stems from fearful avoidance of intimacy like that of David and Lili is more difficult to escape than the loneliness that stems from the fear of abandonment and a preoccupied stance like that of Michael and

Karen. In the former cases, the inhibitions and the passive and introverted stance seem to interfere more with taking off on the journey of the quest for connectedness. This may be even more true for men, because difficulties in risk-taking in the initiation of social relationships have been found to contribute to loneliness for males more than for females (Schultz & Moore, 1986). In contrast, in the latter cases, once an attachment is formed, either with the help of therapy and/or life events, these individuals thrive on the fulfillment of their connectedness needs, even if they do not feel completely secure in these relationships.

It appears that although these cases scored similarly on an objective measure of trait loneliness, in referring to loneliness one cannot speak of a trait in the regular sense. Instead, trait loneliness is not only multifaceted, it is also a process that is continually evolving, with some types being perhaps more changeable than others. The fact that this selected group of trait-lonely students did not complain of loneliness in its "state" sense, in that after some time even they felt at ease in the university environment, underscores the importance of the distinction between state and trait loneliness. However, it appears that although the story of state loneliness seems to sound similar across first-year university students, when it comes to trait loneliness, we are faced with different stories. Hence, rather than talking about the "chronically lonely" as one group, one needs to differentiate between types, and this differentiation may relate to the changeability of this "chronicity."

An analysis of the students' early family relations and experiences is beyond the scope of this research. Some hypotheses on these issues could be derived from the early memories and the students' spontaneous reports (such as the effect of parental divorce in Michael's case). However, the question of the antecedents of the patterns of loneliness revealed in the interviews needs to be addressed in future research, including prospective studies of young children.

Loneliness as process may be particularly evident in the case of young adults, as they are faced with the developmental tasks of identity and intimacy (Erikson, 1968). Park and Waters (1988) have argued that both relationships and traits will be better understood "when both are treated as developmental rather than static entities" (p. 176).

Similarly, transactional models of development emphasize the possibilities of change across the life course in individuals and their environments, and it has been demonstrated that many individuals may dramatically change their social patterns over their life (Skolnick, 1986). Thus, instead of considering trait loneliness as an enduring aspect of personality, we need to understand further under what conditions it changes and how it changes in different types of loneliness.

Epilogue

Studying loneliness as process requires a longer lag of time than that which is most often found in loneliness research. Indeed, in meeting with each of these four interviewees recently to show them their story, I found out that both David and Lili have each been romantically involved for the last 5 months; that Michael and Tamar continue to live together, although Michael feels somewhat less sure that his loneliness is a thing of the past; and that Karen will be getting married to Jonathan in the summer.[8]

Finally, in weighing the contribution of the narrative approach to the study of loneliness, I am reminded of Rubenstein and Shaver's (1982) caution against the study of loneliness suffering the fate of social psychology, which they view as "unfortunately remarkable for its ability to reduce profound and fascinating human issues to rather superficial and uninteresting generalizations. . . . One safeguard would be to return to the complexities of phenomenology" (p. 221). I found the attempt to understand what David, Lili, Michael, and Karen had to tell us about loneliness most rewarding.

Notes

1. One exception is DeJong-Gierveld and Raadschelders (1982), who refer to whether the individual perceives his or her loneliness as unchangeable.

2. Their trait loneliness scores were 1.5 to 2.4 standard deviations above the norms reported by Russell et al. (1980). In addition, they were characterized by an insecure attachment style on the Hazan and Shaver (1990) adult attachment measure (for the association between insecure attachment and loneliness, see Shaver & Hazan,

1987). These students also obtained extreme scores on the Depressive Experiences Questionnaire (DEQ) (Blatt, D'Afflitti, & Quinlan, 1976) in Self-Criticism and/or Dependency (for a review of the DEQ, see Blatt & Zuroff, 1992; and for a study of the DEQ and loneliness, see Wiseman, 1993).

3. For details on the instructions and an example, see Josselson (1992, pp. 251-260). The instructions for the time points of the relational space maps in the present study were as follows. In the first interview (at the beginning of the year), we asked the student to draw maps for two relatively recent times: One year into their first year of army service (about age 19), and the second for the present, namely, at the third week of their first year at university (the ages varied from 20½ to 25). In the second interview (in which we also focused on early memories), the student was asked to begin with a relational map for age 5 and then to draw a map for the present, namely, toward the end of first-year university (about 6 months after the last relational map). Finally, the fifth relational map was drawn at the third interview for the present, namely, toward the end of third-year university (with the ages varying from 23 to 27½). In the second and third interviews I also asked for a self-description.

4. The purpose of these interviews was presented as part of a study regarding the interpersonal relations and experiences of university students. That is, it was not introduced as a study on loneliness.

5. A recent study that examined the association between attachment style and the way people reacted to the Iraqi missile attack on Israel during the Gulf War found that avoidant people used more distancing strategies (Mikulincer, Florian, & Weller, 1993). See also Ayalon (in press), for a discussion of the experience of the sealed room during the Gulf War.

6. Research has shown a positive relationship between loneliness and depression, and at the same time has demonstrated that loneliness and depression are distinct phenomena, that neither is the cause of the other, and that they seem to share some common causal origins (Russell et al., 1980; Weeks, Michela, Peplau, & Bragg, 1980). This overlap underscores the importance of understanding loneliness to deal effectively with many depressed clients (Young, 1982).

7. DeJong-Gierveld and Raadschelders (1982) also found that the loneliness types in their typology referred only to forms of emotional loneliness.

8. In response to reading their stories, the participants seemed to validate my "reading" of their stories of loneliness.

References

Acklin, M. W., Bibb, J. L., Boyer, P., & Jain, V. (1991). Early memories as expressions of relationship paradigms: A preliminary investigation. *Journal of Personality Assessment, 57,* 177-192.

Ayalon, O. (in press). Images of destruction. In F. Cruz (Ed.), *Stress, anxiety and emotional disorder.* Portugal: University de-Minho.

Bartholomew, K. (1990). Avoidance of intimacy: An attachment perspective. *Journal of Social and Personal Relationships, 7,* 147-178.

Blatt, S. J., & Blass, R. B. (1992). Relatedness and self definition: Two primary dimensions in personality development, psychology and psychopathology. In

J. Barron, M. Eagle, & D. Wolitsky (Eds.), *Psychoanalysis and psychology: An APA centennial volume.* Washington, DC: American Psychological Association.

Blatt, S. J., D'Afflitti, J. P., & Quinlan, D. M. (1976). Experiences of depression in normal young adults. *Journal of Abnormal Psychology, 85,* 383-389.

Blatt, S. D., & Zuroff, D. C. (1992). Interpersonal relatedness and self-definition: Two prototypes for depression. *Clinical Psychology Review, 12,* 527-562.

Block, J. (1993). Studying personality the long way. In D. C. Funder, R. D. Parke, C. Tomlinson-Keasey, & K. Widaman (Eds.), *Studying lives through time: Personality and development* (pp. 9-41). Washington, DC: American Psychological Association.

Cutrona, C. E. (1982). Transition to college: Loneliness and the process of social adjustment. In L. A. Peplau & D. Perlman (Eds.), *Loneliness: A sourcebook of current theory, research and therapy* (pp. 291-309). New York: Wiley-Interscience.

DeJong-Gierveld, J., & Raadschelders, J. (1982). Types of loneliness. In L. A. Peplau & D. Perlman (Eds.), *Loneliness: A sourcebook of current theory, research and therapy* (pp. 105-119). New York: Wiley-Interscience.

Elliot, R. (1983). Fittting process research to the practicing psychotherapist. *Psychotherapy: Theory, research and practice, 20,* 47-55.

Erikson, E. H. (1968). *Identity, youth and crisis.* New York: Norton.

Fromm-Reichmann, F. (1959). Loneliness. *Psychiatry, 22,* 1-15.

Hazan, C., & Hutt, M. (1994). *Patterns of adaptation: Attachment differences in psychosocial functioning during the first year of college.* Manuscript under review.

Hazan, C., & Shaver, P. R. (1990). Love and work: An attachment-theoretical perspective. *Journal of Personality & Social Psychology, 59,* 270-280.

Hojat, M., & Crandall, R. (Eds.) (1987). Loneliness: Theory, research and applications. *Journal of Social Behavior and Personality, 2* (Pt. 2).

Horowitz, L. M., & French, R. S., Anderson, C. (1982). The prototype of a lonely person. In L. A. Peplau & D. Perlman (Eds.), *Loneliness: A sourcebook of current theory, research and therapy* (pp. 183-205). New York: Wiley-Interscience.

Jones, D. C. (1992). Parental divorce, family conflict and friendship networks. *Journal of Social and Personal Relationships, 9,* 219-235.

Jones, W. H. (1987). Research and theory on loneliness: A response to Weiss's reflections. *Journal of Social Behavior and Personality, 2,* 27-30.

Josselson, R. (1992). *The space between us: Exploring the dimensions of human relationships.* San Francisco: Jossey-Bass.

Kazdin, A. E. (1981). Drawing valid inferences from case studies. *Journal of Consulting and Clinical Psychology, 49,* 183-192.

Main, M., Kaplan, N., & Cassidy, J. (1985). Security in infancy, childhood, and adulthood: A move to the level of representation. In I. Bretherton & E. Waters (Eds.), *Growing points in attachment theory and research: Monographs of the Society for Research in Child Development, 50,* 66-106.

Marangoni, C., & William, L. (1989). Loneliness: A theoretical review with implications for measurement. *Journal of Social and Personal Relationships, 6,* 93-128.

Mijuskovic, B. Z. (1979). *Loneliness in philosophy, psychology and literature.* Assen, The Netherlands: Van Gorcum.

Mikulincer, M., Florian, V., & Weller, A. (1993). Attachment styles, coping strategies, and posttraumatic psychological distress: The impact of the Gulf War in Israel. *Journal of Personality and Social Psychology, 64,* 817-826.

Mikulincer, M., & Segal, J. (1990). A multidimensional analysis of the experience of loneliness. *Journal of Social and Personal Relationships, 7,* 209-230.

Park, K. A., & Waters, E. (1988). Traits and relationships in developmental perspective. In S. W. Duck (Ed.), *Handbook of personal relationships* (pp. 161-176). New York: John Wiley.

Peplau, L. A., & Perlman, D. (1982). Perspectives on loneliness. In L. A. Peplau & D. Perlman (Eds.), *Loneliness: A sourcebook of current theory, research and therapy* (pp. 1-18). New York: Wiley-Interscience.

Perlman, D. (1987). Further reflections on the present state of loneliness research. *Journal of Social Behavior and Personality, 2,* 17-26.

Perlman, D., & Peplau, L. A. (1982). Theoretical approaches to loneliness. In L. A. Peplau & D. Perlman (Eds.), *Loneliness: A sourcebook of current theory, research and therapy* (pp. 123-134). New York: Wiley-Interscience.

Rook, K. S. (1988). Toward a more differentiated view of loneliness. In S. W. Duck (Ed.), *Handbook of personal relationships* (pp. 571-589). New York: John Wiley.

Rubenstein, C. M., & Shaver, P. (1982). *In search of intimacy.* New York: Delacorte.

Russell, D. (1982). The measurement of loneliness. In L. A. Peplau & D. Perlman (Eds.), *Loneliness: A sourcebook of current theory, research and therapy* (pp. 81-104). New York: Wiley-Interscience.

Russell, D., Peplau, L. A., & Cutrona, C. E. (1980). The revised UCLA Loneliness Scale: Concurrent and discriminant validity evidence. *Journal of Personality & Social Psychology, 39,* 472-480.

Schultz, N. R., & Moore, D. (1986). The loneliness experience of college students: Sex differences. *Personality & Social Psychology Bulletin, 12,* 111-119.

Shaver, P., Furman, W., & Buhrmester, D. (1985). Transition to college: Network changes, social skills, and loneliness. In S. Duck & D. Perlman (Eds.), *Understanding personal relationships: An interdisciplinary approach* (pp. 193-219). London: Sage.

Shaver, P., & Hazan, C. (1987). Being lonely, falling in love: Perspectives from attachment theory. *Journal of Social Behavior and Personality, 2,* 105-124.

Shaver, P., & Rubenstein, C. (1980). Childhood attachment experience and adult loneliness. In L. Wheeler (Ed.), *Review of personality and social psychology* (Vol. 1, pp. 42-73). Beverly Hills, CA: Sage.

Skolnick, A. (1986). Early attachment and personal relationships across the life course. In P. Baltes, D. Featherman, & R. Lerner (Eds.), *Life-span development and behavior* (pp. 173-206). Hillsdale, NJ: Lawrence Erlbaum.

Stokes, J. P. (1987). On the usefulness of phenomenological methods. In M. Hojat & R. Crandall (Eds.), *Loneliness: Theory, research and applications* (special issue). *Journal of Social Behavior and Personality, 2,* 57-62.

Sullivan, H. S. (1953). *The interpersonal theory of psychiatry.* New York: Norton.

Surrey, J. L. (1991). The "self-in-relation": A theory of women's development. In J. V. Jordan, A. G. Kaplan, J. B. Miller, I. P. Stiver, & J. L. Surrey (Eds.), *Women's growth in connection* (pp. 51-66). New York: Guilford.

Thorne, A., & Klohnen, E. (1993). Interpersonal memories as maps for personality consistency. In D. C. Funder, R. D. Parke, C. Tomlinson-Keasey, & K. Widaman

(Eds.), *Studying lives through time: Personality and development* (pp. 223-253). Washington, DC: American Psychological Association.

Weeks, D. G., Michela, J. L., Peplau, L. A., & Bragg, M. E. (1980). The relation between loneliness and depression: A structural equation analysis. *Journal of Personality & Social Psychology, 39,* 1238-1244.

Weiss, R. S. (1973). *Loneliness: The experience of emotional and social isolation.* Cambridge: MIT Press.

Weiss, R. S. (1987). Reflections on the present state of loneliness research. *Journal of Social Behavior and Personality, 2,* 1-16.

Wiseman, H. (1993). *Interpersonal relatedness and self-definition in the experience of loneliness* (Scientific research report AG 90/5). Tel Aviv: Israel Foundations Trustees.

Wiseman, H., & Lieblich, A. (1992). Individuation in a collective community. *Adolescent Psychiatry, 18,* 156-179.

Young, J. E. (1982). Loneliness, depression and cognitive therapy: Theory and application. In L. A. Peplau & D. Perlman (Eds.), *Loneliness: A sourcebook of current theory, research and therapy.* New York: Wiley-Interscience.

It's the Telling That
Makes the Difference

Adital Tirosh Ben-Ari

$\mathcal{M}$ark was 27 when we met at one of the small cafes in Berkeley, California. His intense blue eyes stared at an invisible spot as he began to put together the pieces that made up his story:

> It was during the holiday season. We had taken a friend of ours to the doctor and were waiting for her in the car. My mother raised the subject of the dance planned for the following night. She asked me why I had decided not to go. She waited a few seconds, sighed, and said, "Well, I keep hoping that sometime you are going to have a girlfriend that you will bring along," and I said, "That's never going to happen." She asked, "What?" and I said, "I am gay." She was silent for a few minutes, then whispered, "You must be kidding," and I quietly shook my head, "No, I am not." That is how I told my mother.

Mary, a soft woman in her late 50s, began her story:

> It was around Thanksgiving weekend. We were all staying at our friend's house. There was a big dance coming up the following night. I had bought tickets for everyone. The whole family planned on going, including my 87-year-old mother.

153

A week before the party, Mark asked me to take his ticket
back. . . .

We had taken our hostess to her doctor's appointment and
were waiting in the car. We were very quiet and didn't even
look at each other. I have a very clear memory of that moment. I remember asking myself what was going through his
mind and if this silence was significant. Then, breaking
the silence, he asked, "Did you take back that ticket?"
"Yes," I said, disappointed, "I'd really like you to go but there
will be other times." But he shook his head and said, "Oh
no, there won't." And I asked, "Why not?" and it was then
he told me that he was gay. This is how I learned that I have
a gay son.

Two personal and distinctly different accounts of the very same
incident: a son's and a mother's attempts to arrange their lives within
a meaningful context. At present, both Mark and Mary think of that
weekend as a turning point in their lives.

The aim of this chapter is two-fold: It documents the attempts of
two individuals to personally organize their life experiences around
a particular turning point, using the narratives of Mary and Mark to
illustrate what gay men, lesbians, and their parents may go through prior
to, during, and following the discovery of a child's homosexuality.
Researchers have argued that predictive and longitudinal research
focuses mainly on demonstrating stability over time, which may result
in neglect of a more interesting question, that of conditions accounting for change (Anthony & Cohler, 1987; Cohler, 1987; Rutter, 1987).
Recently, Boxer and Cohler (1989) have called for studies that interpret or "make sense" of changes in the lives of gay men and lesbians.
This chapter addresses this call: It examines a change in people's lives—a
turning point—employing a narrative or interpretive approach.

I will also introduce a new framework that may facilitate our understanding of the dynamics involved in the process of "coming out"
as perceived by both gay and lesbian young adults and their parents.
The existing literature on coming out includes mostly anecdotal
writing (Borhek, 1983; Fairchild & Hayward, 1979; Rafkin, 1987;
Silverstein, 1977). Little research has been devoted to understanding

the reactions in the family to the discovery of a child's sexual orientation (Ben-Ari, 1995; Muller, 1987), and generally, the impact of gay men and lesbians on their parents' well-being has been overlooked (Boxer, Cook, & Herdt, 1991). I will confront these issues and look at coming out from a new perspective by applying the concepts of privacy and intimacy and the dynamics between them to the process in which parents learn about their children's homosexuality. In so doing, I will also examine the coming out process and its implications for the well-being of the parents.

A dictionary definition describes "a turning point" as a point at which a decisive change takes place; a critical point; a crisis; a point at which something changes direction (*Webster's Encyclopedic Unabridged Dictionary*, 1983). In the context of life experiences, a turning point marks a change in people's lives. What precedes the so-called event is perceived as qualitatively different from what follows. Perceiving an event as a turning point is in and of itself an attempt to organize life experiences according to one or a few underlying themes. It employs an orientation that promotes a sense of coherence and continuity. In many cases, it also assumes a retrospective outlook.

Bruner (1986, 1990) suggests that narrative form reflects an effort to restore a sense of order and meaning to experience. That is, stories are ways of organizing experience, interpreting events, and creating meaning while maintaining a sense of continuity. Recently, the concept of "narrative" has been employed frequently in accounting for human experience (Gergen & Gergen, 1986; Mishler, 1986). Sarbin (1986), for example, argues that thinking, perception, imagination, and moral decision making are based on narrative structure. White and Epston (1989) propose a view of therapy as a process of "storying" and/or "re-storying" the lives and experiences of persons. The therapeutic context, they claim, provides opportunities to reauthor and create new and possibly liberating narratives.

One of the main arguments of the narrative approach is that constructing a "subjective truth" is at least as important as revealing "objective truth" (Borden, 1992; Spence, 1982). Eliciting the significance of the experience and its meaning to the individuals involved in it is the principal concern. To elicit first impressions and minimize the potential influence of a theoretical framework, open-ended and almost identical questions were presented to Mary and her son. When interviewing Mary, I asked her to describe her experiences as well as her perceptions of her son's experience throughout the process of coming out. In a similar fashion, Mark was asked to describe his as well as his mother's experiences throughout the very same process. Thus two first-person accounts and two descriptions of the other person's perceived experiences were available on completion of the interviews. The following is a presentation of these four perspectives of a single incident: a son revealing his sexual orientation to his mother. Obviously there are differences between the versions. Nonetheless, the purpose of discussing these differences is not to detect discrepancies among the stories, but to interpret and understand in terms of their respective contexts.

The relationship between privacy and intimacy is usually characterized as being either complementary or contradictory (Derlega & Margulis, 1982; Sullivan, 1953). This chapter, on the other hand, views the relationship between them as essentially dialectical and integrates both the contradictory and complementary aspects of the relationship into a developmental sequence.

There is general consensus about the affinity between privacy and intimacy. In fact, in *Webster's Encyclopedic Unabridged Dictionary of the English Language* (1989) they are used interchangeably. As a social concept, privacy includes both descriptive and normative aspects. The former are reflected in connotations of solitude, secrecy, and autonomy, whereas normative features include the right to exclusive control of access to private realms (Sills, 1986). Various definitions of the concept of intimacy and interdependence of partners, extent of self-disclosure, and warmth and affection (Perlman & Fehr, 1987) tend to emphasize themes of closeness—sharing, exchanging, and knowing the innermost.

The dialectic between privacy and intimacy demonstrates itself in as much as the development and maintenance of privacy and largely precludes closeness and intimacy, for secrecy precludes sharing. However, autonomy, the sense of independence that is an adjunct to privacy, may evolve over the history of the relationship and eventually allows intimacy to develop. Thus what seems to be contradictory at an early stage is absorbed when intimacy is achieved and maintained.

There is extensive research on intimacy in interpersonal relationships (Chelune, 1987; Fisher, 1984; Perlman & Duck, 1987; Perlman & Fehr, 1987). Generally it is seen as characterizing friendship, marital, and courtship relationships (Burgess, 1981; Chown, 1981; Cunningham & Antill, 1981; Reisman, 1981). Although there have been studies of infant-mother relationships (Pawlby, 1981) and parent-child relationships in the middle years of childhood (Shield, 1981), very little work has been done on the quality of the relationships between parents and their young adult children (Nydegger, 1991), in particular, on intimacy as a quality of those relationships. This chapter tries to confront this lack. It examines the development and maintenance of intimacy between parents and their young adult gay and lesbian children as they go through the process of coming out.

In their stories, Mary and Mark differentiate between predisclosure, disclosure, and postdisclosure thoughts, feelings, and experiences. A similar sequence underlies the organization of this chapter. It is important to point out, however, that the distinction between predisclosure, disclosure, and postdisclosure is predicated on adapting a retrospective outlook.

Predisclosure

All that can be said with any certainty about predisclosure is that it ends at disclosure. Yet significantly, both Mary and Mark felt the need to somehow define this period and seemed to want to consider how long this stage lasted, when it started, what it referred to, and what characterized it.

Mark talked about wanting to come out as well as his reservations about it.

> I feel close to my mother. Her not knowing was an incredible barrier. I was hiding probably the most major facet of my life from her. I felt that I was living a lie by not telling her that I am gay.

Reflecting on his fears, he added,

> I did not have any real ones, my mother is pretty liberal, I knew that there wouldn't be any major problems. And yet I knew that once I said it, I would never be able to take it back. The words would be out there and there would be no way to return. . . .

Mark characterizes predisclosure as a period of tension and conflict. He describes constant struggle: wanting to share and wanting to hide, on the one hand, longing to be open and honest about his homosexuality with his mother, and on the other hand wishing to remain secretive about the very same issue.

During predisclosure, these two opposites gradually evolve into either serious consideration of the possibility of coming out or a tendency to avoid it. Although the former leads to closeness, the latter pulls individuals further apart. In that respect, one could look at predisclosure as reflecting a dynamic between privacy and intimacy. Prior to disclosure, gay men and lesbians experience tension between the need to exercise control over the access to particular information (privacy) and the need to share that very same information (intimacy). According to this line of thinking, disclosure occurs when the need to keep information private subsides and the wish to be open and share this information becomes more important.

I asked Mary what she had thought were Mark's motives in coming out to her. She replied,

> I used to constantly ask myself the same question. At different times I came up with different answers. At first, still in the grip of pain, I asked myself why he did it, whether he was trying to hurt me, or to get back at me. I found myself constantly thinking about what it was that *I* had done. Later, I learned that he had been tired of hiding and pretending to be someone he was not. It took me several years to realize that Mark came out to me primarily because he valued our relationship. He felt that hiding that aspect of his life from me would cause our relationship to stagnate or even deteriorate. I really think he wanted to be honest and to share with me what he was going through back then.

In trying to account for Mark's motives to come out to her, Mary gives us a clear example of the developmental nature of interpretation. Her attempt to "make sense" of her son's behavior evolved through three major stages. Initially she focused mainly on herself, as if she or her behavior could possibly explain his behavior. She then moved to concentrating on him as the main locus of interpretation: He didn't want to live a lie, or he was tired of pretending to be someone he was not. Finally, she began to talk in terms of their relationship. It has been my observation that when parents make this transition, that is, when they move away from seeking understanding in either themselves or their children, to thinking about the relationship between them, then they start adjusting to the discovery of their child's homosexuality.

Reflecting on Mark's then-anticipated fears, she said,

> Now, I can hardly think of Mark being afraid of telling me anything about his life. I don't think he was afraid that I would do something. But knowing that he did keep this information from me for a significant period of time is in and of itself indicative. Even now it is hard for me to admit that he did not tell me because he was afraid to and yet, between the time he himself discovered his sexual orientation and until he told me, well it has been a fair number of years. . . .

Self-disclosure literature has proposed various explanations for the tendency either to disclose or to avoid disclosure. Motives for disclosure include the development of joint views, goals, and decisions that facilitate the "we-feeling" (Levinger & Shoek, 1972); enhancement of the ability to meet one another's needs (Jourard, 1971); validation of one's self-concept (Kelvin, 1977); the attempt to develop and maintain close relationships (Derlega & Grzelak, 1979); development of the ability to exercise self-expression and social control (Derlega & Grzelak, 1979); avoidance of loneliness; and the prevention of conflict escalation (Derlega & Margulis, 1982).

Studies on homosexual identity formation have also suggested specific explanations for homosexuals' disclosure of sexual orientation to parents (Cramer, 1985; Kus, 1980; Ponse, 1978; Troiden,

1989; Wirth, 1978). Hopes that disclosure will reduce the price exacted for "passing" (i.e., as heterosexual), permit greater honesty, open up channels of communication, strengthen family bonds, deepen love, and provide opportunities for mutual support and caring feature as reasons for disclosures.

However, self-disclosure is not always perceived as a positive experience. Self-disclosure is avoided because of incurred risks of criticism, ridicule, loss of power (Komarovsky, 1976); increased vulnerability to exploitation (Kelvin, 1977); the experience of hurt and betrayal and the fear of what the recipient of information will do with it (Phillips & Metzger, 1976); and possible danger to the relationship if the disclosure alienates, upsets, or hurts the recipient (Rosenfeld, 1979). Gay and lesbian children, according to the research, avoid disclosures to their parents in particular because of fear of rejection, worry about parents' sense of guilt, guilt about parents' physical and mental pain, apprehension about being forced to seek treatment, desire to protect the family from crises, and uncertainty about their sexual identity (Cramer, 1985; Kus, 1980; Wirth, 1978). Underlying all these specific fears is the realization that disclosure is irreversible. Mary describes being suspicious during the predisclosure stage. Suspecting that Mark was gay long before he told her, she recalls asking herself if it was normal that he didn't do the same things as his older brother. Was it normal that he never had a girlfriend, never expressed any interest in going out with girls? She also remembers, however, that as a teenager, he went through a period when he didn't want to be around anyone; days in which he stayed at home without leaving his room. She recalls that she often asked herself what the meaning of all this was and where it would all lead. Now she believes that it was during this period that he came to terms with his homosexuality. It is important to note, however, that Mark did not discuss this period of time in his story. This is a fact that will be discussed later.

Recognizing that gay men and lesbians are not alone in being secretive prior to disclosure introduces yet another component to the predisclosure dynamics. In many cases, they, like their parents, become both concealers and people from whom information has been concealed. Research shows, for example, that the majority of gay people believe that at least one of their parents knew of their sexual orientation before it was disclosed. Indeed, there is evidence to confirm that most parents somehow know about their child's sexual preference before they are told (Bell & Wienberg, 1978; Ben-Ari, in press; Robinson, Skeen, & Walters, 1987; Saghir & Robins, 1973). Many parents who suspect their child might be gay choose not to share this suspicion with other family members or with their gay son or lesbian daughter.

Mark admitted that he knew his mother suspected he might be gay before he actually came out. Both the mother and her son, in fact, were withholding information. Mark was secretive about his sexual orientation; Mary kept her suspicions to herself. Yet Mark knew about his mother's secret, much as Mary knew about her son's. Thus a complex of secrets and concealed awareness of the other party's secrets evolved throughout the predisclosure stage.

As early as the turn of the century, Simmel (1903/1953) was recognizing the tension between secrecy and disclosure. He argued that disclosure is always just beneath the surface of secrecy, constantly threatening to break the veil. Secrecy amplifies differences and establishes barriers between people. Yet at the same time, secrecy tempts one to violate those barriers. Ponse (1978) studied the ramifications of secrets for interpersonal relations and concluded that people feel isolated and alienated when they feel compelled not to admit knowing that which has never been revealed and acknowledged. Recently, Nydegger (1991) suggested that secrets between young adult children and their parents are likely to inhibit mutual understanding.

A secret creates particular family dynamics. It divides the family into two subgroups: those who know and those who do not. The subgroups are not mutual, nor are they equal in status, which adds an element of tension to the network of family relations. Generally, those in the know have a sense of inclusion, while the others feel excluded. The former are in a position to exercise control over access to the secret. They decide who is a concealer and from whom information is to be concealed. Control over access to particular information adds a new power component to the relationship. Thus it is not unreasonable to assume that a secret may change the distribution of power within the family.

Foucault (1979, 1980, 1984) has suggested that "knowledge and information is power" and that they are inseparable in shaping people's lives. It is his conviction that one's individuality is a vehicle for power in much the same way that power/knowledge is a vehicle for individuality. These notions are instrumental to our understanding of the disclosures in interpersonal contexts in general and of the coming out process within families in particular. Because information is power and power is a vehicle for individuality, it stands to reason that gay men and lesbians who keep their homosexuality private are still in the process of defining themselves as gay and lesbian individuals. Mark, like many others in the gay community, probably needed to keep this fact secret while confronting questions pertaining to his own identity. Indeed, research suggests that usually gay and lesbian individuals first come to terms with their sexual orientation and only later disclose it to others: first, to identified members of the gay community, and later to nongay people, including family members (Cass, 1984; Troiden, 1988, 1989).

The first family member with whom Mark shared his secret was his sister. Mark knew that she had many friends in the gay community and that she would not have a problem accepting him as a gay brother. Our data (Ben-Ari, 1995) suggest that the majority of gay men and lesbians would first disclose their homosexuality to a family member other than a parent: a sibling or a member of the extended family. They think of the first disclosure to a family member as a trial, a "rehearsal" before the real performance. During a certain period of time Mark and his sister were the concealers; Mary, her husband, and the older brother were the ones from whom information was concealed. At the same time, Mary became a concealer. She developed her own suspicions about Mark's homosexuality. Three people in the family were both concealers and people from whom the information was concealed: Mark, his sister, and Mary. The father and the older brother were the ones from whom information was concealed, and as far as both Mark and Mary, know had no idea about Mark's and Mary's secrets. These dynamics changed immediately on disclosure: Mary became a concealer of the very same information that was kept from her. At the same time, her own secretive suspicions naturally disappeared.

Mary and Mark think of predisclosure as a period of time during which they felt distant from one another, and their relationship deteriorated. "Not telling" enabled both of them to keep their secrets and protect their privacy. By the same token, withdrawing to the safety of their secrets left little space for exchange, sharing, and closeness.

Disclosure

Mary and Mark have different perceptions of what transpired during actual disclosure. Within a narrative framework, the significance of an experience and its meaning for the individual involved takes precedence over objective fact. This is the basis for the distinction between subjective and objective truth (Borden, 1992; Spence, 1982). This notion seems most relevant as we look for differences in how Mary and Mark develop their stories. For instance, Mary is sure that Mark carefully planned the disclosure down to the very last detail. On the other hand, Mark casually implies that he had intended to come out "sometime" during that weekend. Mary thought that Mark deliberately chose a time when she would be unable to make much fuss.

> Not only were we not at home; we were house guests. He made his disclosure when our friend was in the doctor's office, allowing only a very brief exchange between us. When the friend returned, we both tried to act as if it had never happened, hadn't been said. But I think he was very stiff at that point, and felt a little self-conscious. Later that day, I asked him when he first knew, and he told me that was too private and personal a question.

Mark's narrative focuses on a different aspect of the exchange:

> I was watching her through the rear mirror. She was in the back seat. I could see her. She could watch my eyes. We were both looking at each other through the mirror. . . . At some point I think we both avoided looking at the mirror. Later that evening, I was sitting in front of these people's house and my mother came to talk to me. She asked me if I

was sure that I was gay, if I wasn't just going through a
phase. She also said that if it was true, she wouldn't know
what to do about it. That was about all we talked about.

Mark and Mary's perceptions of the disclosure reflect the differences in the meanings they attribute to it. What is being added to
Mary's story when she attributes planning on Mark's part? What is
being added to Mark's story when "planning" is omitted? What does
it mean for Mary if disclosure had been planned? What does it mean
for Mark if disclosure had not been carefully planned? Generally,
when people share similar views about the importance of an event,
they also have similar notions as to the amount of planning required.
Generally, the initiating person is more likely to recognize the planning involved. It is interesting to note, however, that in our case Mary
is sensitive to the planning aspect of disclosure.

Neither Mary nor Mark includes details that might imply doubts
pertaining to issues about which they currently feel certain. Yet the
other person does. For example, although Mary talks about Mark
coming to terms with his sexual orientation, Mark does not refer to
his own coming out process in his story. By the same token, Mark
emphasizes his mother's questioning of his homosexuality, and Mary
doesn't mention it in her account. These differences can be explained
in light of how they currently perceive themselves. Mary views herself
as a very accepting person. She actively participates in support groups
for parents of gay and lesbian children. In fact, she now believes that
her son's disclosure was meant to teach her and others how to uncon-
ditionally accept people. One could argue that this can be thought of
as the fourth stage in Mary's gradual interpretation of Mark's motives
for coming out. It is within this new spiritual and universal outlook
that she perceives his disclosure.

Mark, on the other hand, presents himself as never having doubted
his homosexuality. It is important for him to come across this way,
and emphasizing his mother's doubt in contrast to his own self-
confidence serves this function. Although he sees his sexual orientation as an integral part of his identity, his basic attitude toward his
homosexuality is offhanded. He believes that being casual about homosexuality is the best way to educate people and to overcome negative

social or parental attitudes. Like many other gay men and lesbians, he assumes that acceptance as a gay person is identical to acceptance as a human being. "If they can't know about who I am, then I don't want them to know anything about me."

On the basis of interviews with 27 parents and 32 gay men and lesbians, Ben-Ari (1995) has developed the view that in most cases, gay and lesbian young adults disclose their homosexuality to their parents because they want to get closer to them. Indeed, telling parents about their homosexuality generally does improve the relationships between these children and their parents. Most of the interviews reflect a consensus during the time of the interviews, and in retrospect, the main motive for disclosure is "to be honest with parents; not to hide; not to live a lie."

That increased sharing and closeness motivate such disclosures is also reflected in attempts to create settings that promote intimacy. Usually parents are told individually; the parent to whom the child feels closest is generally told first. The preference is also for disclosure to be done in person, where there is opportunity for eye contact, intimacy, and nonverbal exchanges.

Like their gay and lesbian children, an overwhelming majority of parents also prefer that their gay children disclose their sexual orientation to them (Ben-Ari, 1995). They also prefer to receive "private" disclosure and that it be done in person. During the interviews, many parents expressed their regrets at not being told sooner. They feel that they missed an important part of their children's lives. Mary says,

> I really feel bad that I missed those years of his life, that I could not share with him when he was in high school, whatever he was going through. I think all mothers who have learned to accept this, feel this way. We miss. In my case, I missed 10 years of his life which he couldn't share with me, the questions and fears he had. Now, I wish I could replay those moments, hug him, and tell him how much I love him anyway.

Nonetheless, many parents differ from their gay and lesbian children with respect to how they first view the reason for disclosure. When trying to account for their behavior following the discovery, parents are likely to admit that at the beginning the initial pain and other intense feelings prevent them from viewing disclosure as their children's attempt to get closer.

Postdisclosure

I met Mark and Mary more than 5 years after the initial disclosure. Mark remembers his mother right after disclosure:

> A little bit of surprise, quite a bit of disbelief, and unwilling-ness to deal with it. The hours and the days that fol-lowed, I think she kind of put it in the back of her mind and did not think about it because she had this social en-gagement she was going through, and she couldn't stop to process this knowledge. After that she talked a lot to my sister who has a lot of gay friends.

Mary remembers,

> I was pretty shocked, I think that when you are shocked like that you kind of have a dead feeling, you don't really know what to say next. I didn't cry, I was just shocked and thought what am I going to do now. I don't think I even reassured him that that's OK with me. . . . [Very quietly she added,] I don't think I even did that.

Parental reactions to learning about their child's homosexuality are often seen in terms of typical grief responses, including shock, denial, guilt, anger, and acceptance. These parents grieve the loss of an image of their child with which they mistakenly interacted over the years (Muller, 1987; Robinson, Skeen, & Walters, 1987; Silverstein, 1977; Switzer & Switzer, 1980; Wirth, 1978).

Mary's experience, however, does not reflect a typical process of grief following disclosure. Although describing herself as being shocked initially, she could not recall going through denial, anger, self-blame, or guilt. This is understandable given that Mary had suspected for some time that Mark was gay. It is possible that parents who suspect their child might be gay may experience some of the typical grief reactions before the actual discovery. One of the interviewed mothers said she mourned the loss of her son's image long before he came out to her. Indeed, our data did not confirm the traditional view and did not reveal significant differences between specified grief reactions (e.g., shock, denial, shame, guilt, anger, and rejection), which may imply that parents do not necessarily go through a grief sequence after learning about their child's homosexuality (Ben-Ari, 1995). Although several explanations can account for this finding, it is not unreasonable to assume that because the majority of parents suspect their child might be gay before they formally learn about it, they, like the previously mentioned mother, grieve prior to disclosure. This explanation can also account for the fact that for most parents, prediscolosure is the most difficult period. The same mother said that her experiences prior to disclosure were most difficult because she suspected and mourned at the same time, without having her son or anyone else to confirm or refute her suspicions.

Like many other parents, Mary thinks about her postdiscovery stage in terms of a chronological sequence. She differentiates, for example, between her thoughts and feelings right after she was disclosed to, during the first year, and at the time of the interview:

> Later on, maybe 6 months later, I think that I came to gradually accept more and more that this was really true. I felt very protective toward him and extremely concerned. I was more worried about him than I was about how I was feeling. After realizing that he could not change, I didn't even think about it anymore, I started to accept reality.

The search for an underlying theme that would characterize a period of time or a certain experience is indicative of the effort to organize and create meaning out of a particular experience. Thus the process of ordering past experiences in a chronological sequence assumes an interpretive approach.

When I think about it now, the emotion I found that I had within the first 6 months, or the first year, and still have to some extent is loneliness. I tend not to share this with anybody who I think will think less of him. Everybody in our family thinks very highly of him. I guess, I don't want anybody to think: Ha, he is not what we thought he was. Among my closest friends, there is no one with whom I could share the experience of having a gay son.

Mark's recollection of his mother's postdisclosure experience is somewhat different. He remembers, for instance, that during the first 6 months, or even the first year, his mother didn't want to ask him about his personal life.

She was embarrassed to talk about it, or she thought it wasn't any of her business. I think she really didn't want to know what could be going on. She didn't want to know if I had a lover. She didn't know how to communicate about gayness with a gay child.

It has been suggested that parents of gay people need to come out, too. In fact, one argument is that an indicator of parental acceptance is their own disclosure and openness about it (Wirth, 1978). Often, gay men and lesbians also perceive parents' openness about their children's homosexuality as an indication of their acceptance (Rafkin, 1987).

On completion of the interviews, I asked Mark and Mary, "What could the other person have done so it would be easier for you?"

Mark thought that if his mother had been able to communicate with him about his homosexuality earlier, it would have made the whole experience easier. He felt that his initiative to get closer to her was not reciprocated. Mary said that it would have helped if Mark were closer, physically and emotionally, so she would not have to be so alone.

At present, the son and the mother value their close relationship and appreciate the sharing aspect of it. They see Mark's disclosure as the event that gave a different quality to their relationship. Mary and Mark both wish they could have told each other about their need for closeness back then. They both emphasize that it is sharing with the other person that could have eased their experience.

This chapter suggests a new perspective for looking at the process by which parents learn about their child's sexual orientation. It introduces the concepts of privacy and intimacy, as well as the dynamics between them as underlying themes in such a process. One of this chapter's main concepts is that gay men and lesbians come out to their parents mainly because they want to get closer and be able to share their lives with them. Parents can ease their experiences following the discovery of their children's homosexuality by perceiving it as a quest for intimacy. By the same token, gay and lesbian individuals are not the only ones who keep information about their homosexuality private before disclosure. In most cases, the parents of these individuals also keep related thoughts and suspicions secret.

Blenkner (1965) suggests that filial maturity occurs when individuals realize they can no longer look at their parents as a rock of support in times of trouble and begin to understand that their parents need their comfort and support. A recent study by Nydegger (1991) also considers the parental dimension of filial maturity, which parallels that of the child. Two essential aspects of this parallel process are distancing and comprehending. As the first pulls parent and child apart, the second tends to draw them together, and the former is generally a precondition for the latter. A key factor in the development of comprehension between parents and young adults is the willingness of children and parents to be open with each other. The process by which parents learn about the homosexuality of their gay son or lesbian daughter clearly demonstrates this dynamic.

It is the telling that makes the difference. It is also the telling about the telling that can make the difference. . . .

References

Anthony, E. J., & Cohler, B. J. (Eds.). (1987). *The invulnerable child.* New York: Guilford.

Bell, A., & Wienberg, M. (1978). *Homosexualities: A study of diversity among men and women.* New York: Simon & Schuster.

Ben-Ari, A. (1995). The discovery that an offspring is gay: Parents' gay men and lesbians' perspectives. *Journal of Homosexuality, 30.*

Ben-Ari, A. (in press). The process of coming out: A dialectic of intimacy and privacy. *Families in Society.*

Blenkner, M. (1965). Social work and family relationships in later life with some thoughts on filial maturity. In E. Shanas & G. Strieb (Eds.), *Social structure and the family: Generational relations.* Englewood Cliffs, NJ: Prentice Hall.

Borden, W. (1992). Narrative perspectives in psychosocial intervention following adverse life events. *Social Work, 37*(2), 135-141.

Borhek, M. V. (1983). *Coming-out to parents: A two-way survival guide for lesbians and gay men and their parents.* New York: Pilgrim Press.

Boxer, A. M., & Cohler, B. J. (1989). The life course of gay and lesbian youth: An immodest proposal for the study of lives. *Journal of Homosexuality, 17,* 315-355.

Boxer, A. M., Cook, J. A., & Herdt, G. (1991). Double jeopardy: Identity transitions and parent-child relations among gay and lesbian youth. In K. Pillemer & K. McCartney (Eds.), *Parent-child relations throughout life.* Hillsdale, NJ: Lawrence Erlbaum.

Bruner, J. (1986). *Actual minds, possible worlds.* Cambridge, MA: Harvard University Press.

Bruner, J. (1990). *Acts of meaning.* Cambridge, MA: Harvard University Press.

Burgess, R. L. (1981). Relationships in marriage and in the family. In S. Duck & R. Gilmour (Eds.), *Personal relationships* (Vol. 1, pp. 179-196). New York: Academic Press.

Cass, V. C. (1984). Homosexual identity formation. *Journal of Homosexuality, 20,* 143-167.

Chelune, G. J. (1987). A neuropsychological perspective of interpersonal communication. In V. J. Derlega & J. H. Berg (Eds.), *Self-disclosure, theory, research, and therapy* (pp. 9-34). New York: Plenum.

Chown, S. M. (1981). Friendship in old age. In S. Duck & R. Gilmour (Eds.), *Personal relationships* (Vol. 2, pp. 231-276). New York: Academic Press.

Cohler, B. J. (1987). Vulnerability, resilience and the study of lives. In E. J. Anthony & B. J. Cohler (Eds.), *The invulnerable child.* New York: Guilford.

Cramer, D. W. (1985). *Coming out to the family: An exploration of the role of selected aspects of family functioning in the disclosure decision and outcome.* Unpublished doctoral dissertation, Texas A&M University.

Cunningham, J. D., & Antill, J. K. (1981). Love in developing romantic relationships. In S. Duck & R. Gilmour (Eds.), *Personal relationships* (Vol. 2, pp. 27-51). New York: Academic Press.

Derlega, V. J., & Grzelak, J. (1979). Appropriateness of self-disclosure. In G. J. Chelune (Ed.), *Self-disclosure origins, patterns, and implications of openness in interpersonal relationships.* San Francisco: Jossey-Bass.

Derlega, V. J., & Margulis, S. T. (1982). Why loneliness occurs. The interrelationship of social psychological and privacy concepts. In L. A. Peplau & D. Perlman (Eds.), *Loneliness: A sourcebook of current theory, research and therapy* (pp. 152-165). New York: Wiley-Interscience.

Fairchild, B., & Hayward, N. (1979). *Now that you know.* New York: Harcourt Brace.

Fisher, D. V. (1984). A conceptual analysis of self-disclosure. *Journal of the Theory of Social Behavior, 14*(3), 277-296.

Foucault, M. (1979). *Discipline and punish: The birth of the prison.* Middlesex, UK: Peregrine.

Foucault, M. (1980). *Power/knowledge: Selected interviews and other writings.* New York: Pantheon.

Foucault, M. (1984a). *The history of sexuality.* Middlesex, UK: Peregrine.

Gergen, K., & Gergen, M. (1986). Narrative form and the construction of psychological theory. In T. Sarbin (Ed.), *Narrative psychology: The storied nature of human conduct.* New York: Praeger.

Jourard, S. M. (1971). *The transparent self.* New York: Van Nostrand Reinhold.

Kelvin, P. (1977). Predictability, power and vulnerability in interpersonal attraction. In S. Duck (Ed.), *Theory and practice in interpersonal attraction.* New York: Academic Press.

Komarovsky, M. (1976). *Dilemmas of masculinity: A study of college youth.* New York: Norton.

Kus, R. J. (1980). *Gay freedom: An ethnography of coming out.* Unpublished doctoral dissertation, University of Montana.

Levinger, G. K., & Shoek, J. D. (1972). *Attraction in relationship: A new look at interpersonal attraction.* Morristown, NJ: General Learning Press.

Mishler, E. (1986). *Research interviewing: Context and narrative.* Cambridge, MA: Harvard University Press.

Muller, A. (1987). *Parents matter.* New York: Naiad.

Nydegger, C. N. (1991). The development of parental and filial maturity. In K. Pillemer & K. McCartney (Eds.), *Parent-child relations throughout life.* Hillsdale, NJ: Lawrence Erlbaum.

Pawlby, S. J. (1981). Infant mother relationships. In S. Duck & R. Gilmour (Eds.), *Personal relationships* (Vol. 2, pp. 123-139). New York: Academic Press.

Perlman, D., & Duck, S. (Eds.). (1987). *Intimate Relationships: Development, dynamics, and deterioration.* Beverly Hills, CA: Sage.

Perlman, D., & Fehr, B. (1987). The development of intimate relationships. In D. Perlman & S. Duck (Eds.), *Intimate relationships: Development, dynamics, and deterioration* (pp. 13-42). Beverly Hills, CA: Sage.

Phillips, G. M., & Metzger, N. J. (1976). *Intimate communication.* Boston: Allyn & Bacon.

Ponse, B. (1978). *Identities in the lesbian world.* London: Greenwood Press.

Rafkin, L. (1987). *Different daughters.* San Francisco: Cleis Press.

Reisman, J. M. (1981). Adult friendships. In S. Duck & R. Gilmour (Eds.), *Personal relationships* (Vol. 2, pp. 205-230). New York: Academic Press.

Rivenbark, W. H. (1971). Self-disclosure patterns among adolescents. *Psychological Reports, 28*(1), 35-42.

Robinson, B., Skeen, P., & Walters, L. (1987). The AIDS epidemic hits home. *Psychology Today, 21*(4), 48-52.

Rosenfeld, L. B. (1979). Self-disclosure avoidance: Why I am afraid to tell you who I am? *Communication Monographs, 46*(10), 63-74.

Rutter, M. (1987). Continuities and discontinuities in socio-emotional development from infancy to adulthood. In J. Osofsky (Ed.), *Handbook of infant development.* New York: John Wiley.

Saghir, M. T., & Robins, E. (1973). *Male and female homosexuality: A comprehensive investigation.* Baltimore: Williams & Wilkins.

Sarbin, T. R. (1986). *Narrative psychology: The storied nature of human conduct.* New York: Praeger.

Shield, M. M. (1981). Parent child relationship in the middle years of childhood. In S. Duck & R. Gilmour (Eds.), *Personal relationships* (Vol. 2, pp. 141-159). New York: Academic Press.

Sills, D. L. (Ed.). (1986). *International encyclopedia of the social sciences.* New York: Macmillan & Free Press.

Silverstein, C. (1977). *A family matter: A parents' guide to homosexuality.* New York: McGraw-Hill.

Simmel, G. (1953). *The sociology of Georg Simmel* (K. H. Wolff, Ed. and Trans). Glencoe, IL: Free Press.

Spence, D. (1982). *Narrative truth and historical truth: Meaning and interpretation in psychoanalysis.* New York: Norton.

Sullivan, H. S. (1953). *The interpersonal theory of psychiatry.* New York: Norton.

Switzer, D. K., & Switzer, S. (1980). *Parents of the homosexual.* Philadelphia: Westminster.

Troiden, R. R. (1988). *Gay and lesbian identity: A sociological analysis.* New York: General Hall.

Troiden, R. R. (1989). The formation of homosexual identities. *Journal of Homosexuality, 17*, 43-73.

Webster's encyclopedic unabridged dictionary of the English language. (1983). New York: Portland House.

Webster's encyclopedic unabridged dictionary of the English language. (1989). New York: Portland House.

White, M., & Epston, D. (1989). *Literate means to therapeutic ends.* Adelaide, Australia: Dulwich Center.

Wirth, S. (1978). Coming out close to home: Principles for psychotherapy with families of lesbians and gay men. *Catalyst, 3*, 6-22.

❦ 8 ❦

Life Histories as Social Texts of Personal Experiences in Sociolinguistic Studies

A Look at the Lives of Domestic Workers in Swaziland

Sarah Mkhonza

Introduction

A number of studies address the issue of analyzing linguistic practices of people through ethnographic methods such as the narrative. Brown (1987) points out that it is important to examine linguistic capabilities of people in a sociopolitical context, especially low-income groups, because they do not make their own choices in the languages that they speak.

This study is about the lives of domestic workers who lived during the colonial period in Swaziland, a small country in southern Africa. It is an attempt to look at what the linguistic practices in social control during the colonial period were and also to assess the perceptions of

AUTHOR'S NOTE: This study is part of a Ph.D. dissertation that is to be submitted at Michigan State University. It was funded by AFGRAD/USAID.

Swazi people on language policy. Swaziland is a country that was under British rule up to 1968. One can argue that the social stratification that was created by dualism (the division of Swaziland into a Western and a traditional economy) was also maintained through language in that when most people entered wage employment, the inability to speak English created serious problems for them. Even today, it is those who can speak English who are able to advance themselves within the socioeconomic ladders of that society.

A Personal Social Text

I am a Swazi woman, black, and educated in Swaziland and in American universities. I am employed by the University of Swaziland as a lecturer in sociolinguistics. As a member of the Swazi elite I can speak English, the language of our colonizers. I am aware that my job is based on this privilege. Due to involvement in language planning, I started to have questions of my own about people's lives and how language affects them, especially women in low-income groups.

I have employed a number of domestic workers. I also have relatives who have worked as domestic workers. I had wondered what the experiences of these workers were at work and how these could be incorporated into language policies. I also had questions about how domestic workers dealt with the issues of language, race, and class during the colonial period and after. I did a sociohistorical construction, reading books on domestic work during the colonial period and came up with information on male domestic workers in Zambia, Zimbabwe, and South Africa, but very little information on Swaziland, especially information about women. Investigating language and experiences of women through the life history offered me a way to try to answer these questions.

Theories of Language Planning

A number of studies have demonstrated that language is power in society (Fairclough, 1986; Tollefson, 1991). Although language does not create inequality in society, it is one of the main means that is used to maintain it. The issues of language and power can be viewed at the macro (national) and micro (person-to-person) levels.

Fairclough (1989) analyzes the relationship between language and power by pointing out that language is a vehicle through which power is imposed on people through the creation of ideologies that make people accept what is said as true. It is by looking at social situations and the relations of power dictated by language that we can understand how relations of power are constituted in people's everyday lives. Fishman's concept of situational domains of language behavior provides a way of studying role relations in a specified culture. In his study of Puerto Ricans, he outlined six domains: home, school, church, work sphere, neighborhood, and public places (Fishman, 1968).

This study focuses on the domain of work. Tollefson addresses the importance of language in the work place and how it dictates who gets jobs and who does not. Learning a language is not "an ideologically neutral act" (Tollefson, 1991, p. 206). The requirement that people learn a language like English in order to get a job results from unequal relationships (Tollefson, 1991, p. 209).

This study was done to investigate the effects of language on women as they go about their everyday duties at work. By deconstructing the social narratives of women who worked in domestic work, we can see how social forms of consciousness are created and also how such forms represent social relations of domination that are created through language.

Subjects of Study

The subjects were chosen through purposeful sampling. I interviewed 20 domestic workers who had worked in domestic work for at least 5 years. Ten of these were over the age of 45 and they had worked during the colonial period. These women were interviewed so as to establish a sociohistorical construction of domestic work. The other 10 were below the age of 45. They were interviewed so as to establish a postcolonial understanding of the work they do.

The domestic workers were interviewed and their life histories with language at the work place were recorded in siSwati and later transcribed and translated into English. The interviews were detailed and structured into 1-hour interviews with each person, which would establish (a) biographical data and a focused life history, (b) experiences at the work place and specific questions on experiences with language at work, (c) perceptions of experiences at the work place with specific questions on language policy, and (d) prospects for the future. The data were collected in 1993.

I have used data taken from five life histories, which are sociohistorical constructions in this partial report in an attempt to answer some of my questions about language research. I chose these life histories on the basis of how representative they are of spatiotemporal issues about the colonial period. I tried to choose at least one life history that represents life on Boer farms, British farms, Swazi Nation Land, and others that build a mosaic of experience on the linguistic issues that are pertinent to this discussion.[1] I have used pseudonyms in order to maintain anonymity.

1. Linah Maseko is a woman who entered domestic work as a young girl. She did not earn money because she was to play with the white man's children in exchange for a bag of maize that would be sent to her parents once in a while. She was bitten by a snake and her leg was amputated when she was about 15 years old. She worked in Swaziland and eventually went to South Africa with her employers. She is now married and stays in a suburban house.

2. Lobutimba Xaba started off as a young domestic working for the Swazi royal family. When she entered domestic work, she worked for the Andersons, and now she is employed by a governmental institution, making tea for the staff members.

3. Mary Gama worked for Mhhwabadla, Mrs. Lock, and a man she remembers as a Scottish man. She cleans floors in a doctor's surgery now.

4. Losimilo Nhleko worked for Malabhu, Mr. Morgan, and the owner of Dups Bazaar, and now stays at home, making her living as a farmer.

5. Tryphina Dlamini worked for a Boer farmer called Mahlakaniphane and eventually went to work at her uncle's home as a domestic
worker. This is where she learned how to sew. She bought herself a
sewing machine and decided to earn a living by sewing and has now
retired in her clean home.

Creating the social mosaic or experience by taking from each
woman's life can help us see the women in the political context, but
in this short chapter it is not possible to give attention to all the details
about the workers' lives.

A Sociohistorical Intertext of
the Social Institution of Domestic Work:
Its Life Histories as Factual Texts of Experience

> I was born in 1930. When I was born, the school in my area
> had just started. I went to school for a short time. I started
> when I was 12 years old. After I passed Standard III, because
> our home was built on a Boer's farm, we had to go and
> work for the "plaas" [farm in Afrikaans] for 6 months and
> we would come back after 6 months. So this Boer took me,
> I went to work and he did not allow me to come back
> home. I stayed there for 4 years because when I left I was
> 15 years old and came back when I was 19.

This extract is taken from the life history of Losimilo Nhleko, a
Swazi woman who worked as a domestic worker in the 1940s. The
forced labor system that farm dwellers had to live under had a great
effect on her life. These were regulations that were created under a
law called the Masters and Servants Act, which dates back to 1856.
Under this law, Africans who had their homesteads on farms had to
provide labor for the farmer without expecting any pay. Keegan (1986)
points out that the contract was a verbal agreement that the farmer
made with the male household member, binding all his children to
provide labor on the farm (p. 131). This is why Losimilo Nhleko and
her sisters and brothers had to take turns working "for the plaas" so

that the family could live on the farm. The children of farm dwellers had to go and work in farms instead of going to school. Losimilo had to leave school and go to work in the kitchen as a domestic worker. Working for the Boers meant trekking from Swaziland to South Africa with the sheep when it was grazing time.

> Our land was the land of the Boers. This Boer would take us to go and work in Breyten. He used to have land both in Swaziland and South Africa. In April the sheep would come down to Swaziland to graze on the farm. They would be here grazing in May, June, July, August, September, and then in October they would leave and others would have to drive the sheep back to Breyten. We girls used to work for them when they came in April. April was called "Mabasa." In April everybody knew that the sheep were coming down. They would give birth and then the Boers would come down and stay for the whole winter so that they could see if their sheep were well looked after. They would come down with us from Breyten and when they go up they would go up with you so that you can go and work that side.

> I used to work in the kitchen, doing the washing and looking after children.

The telling of the self that is done by Losimilo Nhleko places her life in the historical context that shaped it. The concessionaires arrived in Swaziland during the time of King Mswati. However, it was in the time of Mbandzeni, at the end of the last century, that most of the land was signed off to the white settlers, mainly Boers and the British. Swazis ended up living on one third of the land and the concessionaires owned two thirds. When Losimilo grew up, her family lived on the farm and had to work for the farmer and got no pay. Kuper (1947) points out that people who lived better lives were those who lived on Swazi Nation Land, because they could still do what they wanted on the land. The everyday life of Losimilo consisted of the routine of domestic work. She did the washing and cooked and looked after children.

Although race was a determinant of difference, class also played an important role in Swaziland at that time. Swazis who lived on

Swazi Nation Land had to show allegiance to chiefs and the royal family. Lobutimba Xaba tells how she grew up looking after children at the royal kraal.

> I was born in Hhohho, at Vusweni. . . . I grew up at the royal kraal in Lobamba. . . . My grandmother went to Lobamba. My grandmother had to go and work for the king. In siSwati, the king needs someone to sleep near the door, the female king. She had to sleep near the door. A long time ago whatever came in through the door had to start with the commoner. That is why they needed someone, an elderly person, to come and stay at the royal kraal, so that the queen mother can send her. That is why I ended up staying with my grandmother there. . . . I stayed with my grand-mother until it was time to go to school. I went to school and then there was a problem with the children of the big people and then we had to leave school and go and look after the children. . . . We were eager to go and work for our king, so we left school. . . .

Lobutimba Xaba worked for the royal family until she reached puberty. She moved from one royal household to another after she left school. As a commoner, she reports with pride the service she offered to the royal family. She was not paid, but lived with the members of the royal family as a child of the family, raising child after child. Later in her life she went into domestic work after the royal households could no longer make use of her because she had come of age and wanted to have boyfriends.

Roles and Routines

The social roles of the domestic workers were learned when the domestic workers got into domestic work. They were taught how to cook, clean, and look after children. Lobutimba says her employer liked her because she worked hard. She taught her how to cook different kinds of food.

> I was taught by the wife. The woman, the "Mesisi," said
> when she hired me, "OK, Nellie, I like you. I will teach you
> how to work. I'm going to teach you. Do you know cooking?"
> "No, Nkosikazi, just little bit." I didn't know. She said,
> "OK, I'll teach you well." And she taught me saying, "When
> you cook this, you cook it so." Until I learnt, because when
> you want to learn, you do understand. This was when I
> first arrived. After 4 days I knew what to do. I said, "OK,
> Nkosikazi, take your newspaper and sit and read and just tell
> me what kind of food we are cooking. I will cook it for you
> and you will see if it is not nice."

The designation of roles and the interpretation of the roles by the
women portray them as actors who came to understand their situation as defined by the employer. They interacted in domestic work
by learning their routines, which meant doing almost the same thing
daily according to the designation of the roles as defined in domestic
work. Social interactionists point out that the process of designation
and interpretation is the main means of maintaining interactions in
society. The workers had to do their repetitive roles, which included
waking up and fixing breakfast. This meant the acceptance of time
constraints as allocated by the employer. Personal time became the
time of the employer in domestic work. Lobutimba worked for Mr.
and Mrs. Anderson, an English couple, and learned her routines very
early because she was willing to learn. Her experience shows stratification and the designation of roles and acceptance of her role as an
employee. Life at the Andersons was regulated by the clock. She
describes a day in her life as follows:

> Six o'clock, I knock on the door and "umnumzane" opens. I
> put the kettle on the stove. I have already washed my hands
> because I am going to touch food. I put the kettle on the elec-
> tric stove. The kettle boils. I make the coffee for the Mesisi.
> I go to the bedroom with the tray and I knock. "Mesisi,
> Mesisi," I whisper. "Coffee time," I say it to the Mesisi. I
> leave the coffee and I go and start shining the floors. I dust
> the dining room. When they wake up they will find the
> place looking nice and the food smelling nice. When the

> white people are about to eat breakfast, I will make some
> more coffee, fry eggs and bacon, cut bread, and bring marga-
> rine and cover up everything with a net. I continue with the
> work. They will just come and eat. They would leave for
> work and leave me with the baby. The baby gave me prob-
> lems. He was crying and I would stop working and also cry
> and worry about the work because if I do not finish the
> white man will sack me. I would wash clothes when they
> had gone. At lunch time they would come back and have
> coffee and tea and then leave for work. At 3 o'clock I had
> to make fire in the coal stove and put the meat for supper
> on the stove.

Learning how to cook meant learning the new vocabulary of different
kinds of meat and also how to prepare it.

Routine in Afrikaaner households was slightly different as the
workers did not have to cook all the meals. Mary Gama says she woke
up and cooked breakfast, and after her employer and her children
were gone she had to clean the house.

> I used to wake up and make fire on the stove and then I
> would cook breakfast, thin porridge. I would cook it and dish
> it and put it on the table. They would eat and they would
> go, the woman and her children. I would remain and
> clean the house everywhere and dust and then I would get
> R1.50 for all the work.

Learning of roles for the workers was a necessity because they had
come to work. They needed the money.

Creation of Social Identity in Domestic Work

Although life in domestic work was marked by the learning of
roles and routines in the process of socialization, it is clear from the
experiences of most of the workers that these were not learned in
amiable situations. Fear was pervasive in most of the interactions and
encounters with the employers. There was fear of expulsion and also

fear arising from ignorance of the other, especially in first encounters. The psychosocial maintenance of power of the whites in colonial Swaziland relied on creating fear of the whites. Fear was a common theme for most workers who worked in Afrikaaner households. Social identity was created in fearful situations.

Tryphina Dlamini told how life with the whites was marked by fear. Their fear of whites dated back to their childhood. They feared whites because they had not seen them before. She says when they saw the white man on his horse coming from the distance, they would go into hiding when they were young.

> Ha! Had we seen the white man before? When we were young we did not know white people. . . . When his horse appeared over there . . . we would hide. He will not see where we went. He would shout and no one would answer. We had closed every little hole. We would run away from the white man. We grew up eventually and then we got used to them. When we were clever we did not fear the white man anymore.

The workers also created the social identity of their employers through naming. The way they used naming when it came to their employers was different from what they were told to say in direct address. On a daily basis they often used the titles that were common at the time. The direct translation of the titles shows that the whites elevated themselves to the category of kings. The title Nkosi (king) was used when addressing men, Nkosana (prince) was used when addressing the sons of the employer, and Nkosazana (princess) was used when addressing young women. There were Afrikaaner and English versions of these. The wives of the employers in the life histories of the women were referred to as Nkosikazi (queen) or Mesisi (Mrs.).

The workers gave the employers Swazi names, particularly the men apart from the general title of umnumzane (master). Although the employers had their own names, the Swazis called them by nicknames that they had coined from their features or manners. There was Mahlakaniphane (clever one), who owned the farm near Sigombeni where Tryphina Dlamini worked. Linah Maseko worked for Ndlumhlophe (white house). Some of the workers knew their employers' real names, whereas others did not.

The rigidity of who shows respect to whom was dictated by the the rules of the social institution. The worker had to obey the employer. Tryphina Dlamini said:

> You had to do what you were told. There was no way you could not. What place was this? You did not see mother and father. How could you not do as you were told? Where were you?

Although the social relations between the worker and the employee were interpreted racially, they were also determined economically through what one was paid. Remuneration is an indication of personal worth. The workers who worked on Boer farms were not paid anything but given rations of brown sugar, mealiemeal, and soap. The women who were paid were those who did not work under the forced labor system, but they constantly pointed out that they were paid very little.

The making of meaning through designations that are based on race is one of the prevalent themes in the life histories of domestic workers. The workers had different types of meat from the employers, different dishes, and slept in their own place. Brown (1987) believes that physical objects acquire meaning as nonverbal forms of communication in rigid institutions because they communicate the social realities that prevail in the institution.

Most of the use of physical objects as a social code was done in relation to food. The worker had her own dishes, her own food, her own type of meat, and did not eat with the family. This also applied to sugar and margarine. Lobutimba Xaba explained that she had her own meat and utensils. Although she cooked for her employers, she did not eat their food but had to also cook her own.

> I had my own food and my own pot. My meat was called dog's meat. It was bought especially for me. I cooked it on another stove. There was a coal stove and an electric stove. Your food is not cooked like that of the white people. Yours

is plain food. You would also not eat margarine. You did not eat white sugar, you ate brown sugar. I am surprised these days when we all eat brown sugar because it was for black people. You got a ration of food when it was finished. You ate your food after they had finished. You ate it in your house.

The time when you ate was also controlled by the employer as was the place where you ate. Linah Maseko pointed out that she had to sit on the floor when she ate. Sitting on a chair was not allowed because the chairs were for white people. She also pointed out that even when it came to dishes, she had to use her own·dishes. Hers were enamel dishes.

> They did not want you to eat out of the same dishes as they did because you were black. Even when you washed the dishes you had to wash theirs first and then wash yours last. You always knew your dishes. They were not the same. You see, they were the green and blue ones which do not break.

Space was also used in a binary manner that pointed out social status. It became a social code that was used to communicate who was who in the symbolic interactions that took place. The worker had her own space, just as the employer had his or her own. The restrictions were determined by the owner of the space.

Mary Gama told how she slept in the kitchen and had to wake up early and take her blankets to the garage, where the dogs slept.

> I slept in the kitchen. I would wake up early when it is still dark, I wake up. I would take my blankets to the garage. You see, in the garage where his car was kept together with his dogs. I put my blankets there. I would then come and take his pots, the black pots, the three-legged pots, their legs were removed. I would go and cook porridge and put it on the table. Then "oubaas" [old boss] would leave after eating.

Being a domestic worker also meant that the workers always avoided things that would get them expelled from work. The Boer employers also made regulations that affected the women's bodies. Being a worker meant that you had to make sure that you did not become pregnant because the Boers did not want the domestic workers to get pregnant while working for them. This way the employer had control over the worker's body. Mary Gama pointed out that if one became pregnant, one had to leave and come back after the child was born. She stayed at work and had her baby after she had left her job.

> The only thing the Boers did not want was for you to get pregnant. He would say you must not become pregnant at his home. Once you became pregnant you had to leave. I don't know what they did not like about becoming pregnant.

The raising of the women's consciousness about their rights at work was achieved, in most cases, by their change of job. Lobutimba Xaba pointed out that when she was working for the whites in the colonial period, it did not matter whether it was her day off or not. If her employers said she should work she would work. Even if her boyfriend came, she had to do what her boss said. It is nowadays that she knows how to show discontent when her rights are violated, because she is working for an institution and she can join others when they put their grievances across to employers.

> Even when your boyfriend came at the time when you knock off, if the white person comes and says, "You know what Lobutimba, this afternoon I supposed to go to the ca- sino." You just had to accept the fact that there was no day off for you. You would not cry or say anything because you were begging them for the job. Jobs were scarce, unlike to- day, when they say do this job and I join them and get angry because I see others get angry. Why shouldn't I?

To Lobutimba Xaba, getting angry in the colonial period was some- thing she could not do. She said that even Swazi culture does not allow people to get angry or show that they are angry. She said when she got annoyed she would retire to some private place and cry and then come back to the employer looking happy and smiling.

The Linguistic Elements in the Life Histories

Denzin (1989) points out that people's lives are linguistic as well as economic and political. The political context shaped the linguistic lives of the workers in that they found that they had to learn the languages of their employers even though at home they spoke siSwati with their parents.

Most of the domestic workers went to mission schools. Tryphina Dlamini told how the mission school she attended was organized. Her experiences highlight the lack of good teachers. She was only able to get to Standard II and then had to go and work on the farm.

> There was a school there at Sigombeni, which was a Methodist school. Classes were run inside the Methodist church. The elders went to Manzini, to the main mission and asked girls who could read who were older than us to come and teach us. We went as far as Standard II. We did not care about education. We did not know how useful it was. Our teachers were paid very little money, they were also not qualified. They were just helping us with the little education they had.

The policy of the British toward African languages was that they should be learned in school. In the case of siSwati, because it had not been standardized at the time, Zulu was the language that was taught in school. Because Zulu and siSwati both belong to the Bantu/Nguni family, this did not cause any problems for the students.

Language and Education on Farms

Although most of the domestic workers spoke siSwati and learned Zulu at school, their language education was different. Each person's experience was shaped by his or her individual experience. Those women who worked on farms left school when the time to work on the farms had come. They took the 6-month contracts, which they called "inkwenteleka" in siSwati, and joined the seasonal movement of the sheep. Losimilo Nhleko tells of her school life and brings out the sadness that having to join the working team on the "plaas" brought into her life.

> I left school because we lived on a farm. I was still attending school when one man came and said the white man had sent them to come and fetch me so that I can go and work on the farm. I cried tears. That is when I left school and went to work on the farm. With us girls, we used to take one whole year working in the kitchen. If you look after them well they would not allow you to go home. I worked for 4 years and nobody from my family came to take over from me!

Losimilo compared her life to that of her brother, who could afford to attend school because he went to school when the sheep came back from Breyten.

> There is one of my brothers who was able to attend school. When he came back with the sheep in April he would attend school. When he went up with the sheep he would take his books with him and read them when looking after the sheep. When the sheep came back he would pass on to the next grade. I could not do that because I started working on my 15th year and spent the 16th, 17th, 18th, and 19th year. All these years! How could I go to school with my chest fully developed?

Language and Education
on Swazi Nation Land

Women who lived on Swazi Nation Land were not forced to work on the farm. However, the forces of patriarchy were against their going to school. Mary Gama recalls how they had to run to school when they had taken milk to the dairy because their parents did not want girls to go to school. She says they expected girls to grow up and get married.

We did not go to school because we were sent there, we had
to steal away to go there. . . . We used to take milk to the
dairy. After we dropped the milk at the dairy, we would run
away to go and learn at Nyakeni wearing our string skirts
[luvadla]. Our parents thought that we had taken milk to
the dairy. They did not want us to go to school because we
were female. . . . When we got there the teacher would
teach us how to write. He would just teach you how to
write your name. It was not like today when there are universities and all these things. We would learn [a] and [ma]
and [ba] and then we would go to the dairy and take the
milk and run home. We would hide our skins on the way
when it is raining because we were going to school. They
said schools are civilized places.

But their ruse was eventually discovered. Mary Gama continues,

We would go to school without our parents knowing that
we went to school, but they eventually got to know because
when we came back the milk was sour. The clerk would
take out our containers and put them outside. When we
came back we would rush and take our containers and go
home at the end of the day. The milk is all whey. Then they
would ask us, "How come you always come back with the
milk spoilt?". . . . We told them that we go to school and
they beat us. And they said why are we going to school because we are going to get married? It is only the males that
are sent to school. . . . They would beat us and we would go
into our grandmother's hut and hide there. . . . We stopped
going to school.

Different women had varying experiences of language education.
Although Linah Maseko's family lived on Swazi Nation Land, her
parents were not against education. However, the relationship her
father had with a farmer resulted in her having to leave school and
learn language at the farm house. Although farm schools were common in South Africa, they were not common in Swaziland. When Linah
Maseko's father died, a white farmer came to ask Linah's mother if
he could relieve her by taking one of her children to go and play with

his children. Because Linah's mother wanted her kids to have an education, the farmer was asked to educate Linah and also give Linah's mother mealiemeal instead of paying her because she was too young. She left school and continued her education on the farm.

> I was born at Phonjwane. Let me say that it was a poor home. We were many in my family. We used to take turns to go to school. Some of us would go one day and look after cattle the next. Then there was a white man who asked for me when my father had died. He asked if he could take one of us children. My mother agreed and I went and stayed with the children of the white man. . . . We used to wake up in the morning and clean the dining room of the white people and the kitchen. When they woke up they found everything ready. After that I would prepare the water for the children. I would make fire in a little stove which made the water warm. When the children wake up I would wash both of them. We would then leave with the children and go to the fields where I would pick cotton. I would pick the cotton and watch the children when they are playing. . . . When the children were at school I would be taught by the Nkosikazi from 10 to 11. She taught me English. She would write all the things and then I would also write them. She also taught me how to pronounce the words. I then picked up and my English improved.

Linah pointed out that the wife of the farmer did not continue to teach her when Linah was bitten by a cobra. This incident was a turning point because it affected her for the rest of her life. Linah says she was bitten by a cobra when she went to the chicken house to pick up the container that they fed the dogs in. This incident affected her because she spent years in hospital, and eventually her leg was amputated. The farmer eventually moved to South Africa, taking her along with another Swazi man who was employed as a tractor driver.

When they were in South Africa, they bought her an artificial leg. She worked for the artificial leg and never got paid for all the years she spent on the farm. Because the farmer had left Swaziland, he was no longer giving her mother mealiemeal, which was one of the conditions on which they had agreed. When Linah inquired about going home, they told her that she could not leave unless the rest of the money that had been used to buy the artificial leg was paid up. She worked for this farmer into her old age and never got paid any money. Linah's experience was very unique from that of the other workers because she continued to learn on the farm. Her life history had many turning points in that even though she also expressed fear of whites she eventually got married to a white man.

Language at the Work Place

Language at the work place for most workers meant the language of the employer. The women's experiences differed according to the employer's knowledge of languages. Some employers could speak siSwati, whereas others could not.

> At the farm where I worked they used to speak Afrikaans. The man also used to speak some Zulu, not siSwati. We used to understand Afrikaans because when you stayed with them you would learn. It is easy to learn when you stay with the people all the time because you will hear something and wonder what the person said. You will bother yourself because you have to know what was said.

The question of creating understanding between the domestic worker and the employer seemed to be determined by the person who appropriated power. A domestic worker felt obliged to understand what the employer said. Losimilo thought that it was imperative to hear what was said if you were a worker. This is why they took it on themselves to learn the language of their employers.

> You have to hear and like to hear what was said so you would ask others what she said, what this means or you call someone who knows and ask them and she will tell you "when she says this, she means this." Even when you are alone you teach each other, especially Afrikaans, it was easy

to learn it especially when you stay with children. Like me,
I stayed with children, looking after them. You will learn
and eventually learn and eventually start to understand a little.

When the employers spoke Afrikaans to workers who had not
started to understand what was being said to them, there was a lot of
misunderstanding. The workers who had just come seemed to have
serious problems. The South African domestic workers seemed to
cope better because they already understood Afrikaans. The Swazis
had a tough time. Losimilo tells how she helped a woman who had
a problem because she did not understand when the Mesisi told her
to wash the clothes and rinse them. Instead of rinsing them she covered
them. Losimilo retold their dialogue:

Madam: Jy man kyk hier so.
  (Hey man, look here.)
  Wat hierdie meid gemaak hierso?
  (What this maid did here?)
  Wat, wat ek het jou gese?
  (What, what did I tell you?)
  Se vir haar sy moet was hom en spoel hom.
  (Tell her she must wash him and rinse him.)
Losimilo: Ek het hom gese.
  (I told him.)
Madam: En nou?
  (And now?)
Losimilo: Ek weet nie.
  (I don't know.)
  Sy het nie mooi geweet nie.
  (She did not understand well.)

Even though Losimilo told the narrative very well, it is obvious
that she did not know Afrikaans very well because she uses "hom"
the male pronoun instead of "haar" the female pronoun. My informant told me that this was not good Afrikaans. It showed evidence of
mother-tongue interference. The narrative also shows that the employer had tremendous power over the employees. It is mainly made

up of commands and questions. The power of a domestic worker who could speak Afrikaans is shown in that although Losimilo could interpret and answer the questions the madam asked, the domestic worker who had made the mistake was totally silenced because she did not understand what was being said.

The communication breakdown that used to occur in domestic work and other work places where the people were not educated resulted in the creation of a language called Kitchen Kaffir. Kuper says that the whites in Swaziland did not bother to speak the languages of the Swazis. She says they were content to speak to them in Kitchen Kaffir. This language became a social code that the workers had to speak when they were at work. Losimilo Nhleko said,

> At work we spoke what was a mixture of Zulu and English. The white people did not speak siSwati. They spoke something like Zulu, let me say that it was Zulu.

Although the domestic workers said they spoke Zulu, when they were asked to demonstrate what the language that the employers spoke was, one realizes that it was not Zulu, but Fanakalo, a language that was spoken in the mines in South Africa. The version of Fanakalo that was spoken by the domestic workers when they imitated their employers seems to have a lot of Zulu in it. Losimilo tells how her employer used to speak:

> She would say to me, "Wena hamba lapha . . . hamba lapha noma lapha kamelweni. Wena vula lapha shelufini. Wena thatha lo, noma vula lapha wardrobini. Wena that lorogo kamina yena fana kaso kaso." Yes, that is what he would say. He would speak Fanakalo.

Translated into English the instruction says,

> You go there . . . go there . . . in the bedroom. You open there in the shelf. You take this, or open there in the wardrobe. You take that dress of mine that is like this and like this.

The basic matrix of Fanakalo is the Zulu language, to which is added mostly English and Afrikaans nouns. The sentences are simple in structure, most of them being subject-verb-object (SVO) sentences. Although the thinking of most people is that Fanakalo is the language of slavery, the domestic workers did not think that. They thought that it was a way of trying to get them to understand. Losimilo said that this was a language that was spoken so that the workers could understand what the employer was saying.

> There were many languages, let me say that. There were many languages that they had heard. It was not spoken by someone who wanted to speak with you in siSwati. In order to give you an example of someone who does not understand siSwati, the employer would speak to you in this language because you also do not understand English. Because you are speaking with someone who does not understand English, you do not speak proper English. But since the one speaking does not understand siSwati, the result is a mixture. This was because you wanted to work with each other.

Lobutimba Xaba pointed out that learning English was a way of trying to understand the employer so that communication could be easier. She says that she learned all the names for different types of meat from her employer. She learned what "frying steak" was. She also learned how to cook the different types of meat from observing the wife of the employer. She says she learned phrases such as "What is for supper tonight, Nkosikazi?" She observed that white people are tolerant of people who do not know English, unlike Swazis, who make fun of people who do not speak English well. She brought this up, directing her response to me in a way that showed that we did not belong to the same class and age group.

> Before the Mesisi goes at 1 o'clock you ask her, "What is for supper tonight?" She tells you and then she takes out the meat. I had started to understand English. Even in siSwati you say, "Sizodlani ntambama Nkosikazi?" [What will we eat in the evening?] "noma, Yini supper ntambama"

[or, What is for supper this evening?] A white person will understand. They do not say you break English as you educated people say. A white person is happy to understand you and answer you. You educated people are silly, let me say that. You think your education did not come from us, your parents. You just became educated. You are like this because of your mother. She was doing this so that you cannot be like her. Yet when your eyes are opened you will look down upon us and cartoon us and say, "Did you hear this woman? She was saying broad instead of bread?" You are supposed to correct us.

Lobutimba also said that she learned her first English expressions by listening to the wife of her employer when she was speaking to her son.

I did not know their language. In other cases there was a boy they had: They would say to him, "Ronnie, please will you go to the bathroom. Go and fetch a soap in the bathroom." And then I would note that the bathroom is where they wash. Then I would catch what it is. Then I would learn the names of things like that because I am the one who works in the house. When I dust I would know what the thing is and see it closely and then learn what it is. They would send their son and he would get things for them quickly. They knew I was from the royal kraal.

Lobutimba Xaba also said that she learned most of the basic expressions such as "listen here" when the employers were talking to their children. Most of the expressions she gave were imperatives.

They would say, "Angela! Don't do this," then I learnt that it means you must not do this; you must not do this. And then I picked up and it helped me because even now where I work people speak different languages. . . . I don't know English very well but I try to speak it.

Some of the domestic workers who could understand the languages spoken by the employers were also helpful in explaining what was said by the masters. Linah Maseko pointed out that the master spoke siSwati very well, but when he was away she used to interpret.

> I used to help the others when Nkosikazi spoke to them when her husband was not there. I would interpret what she was saying, like when she is calling them and telling them to go and milk the cows.

Most of the domestic workers I interviewed could write Zulu. They could read the Bible, having left school in the early grades. However, when they were at work, they did not use writing much. Most of them could not read and write English. They often carried notes from their employers not knowing what was in the notes. Mary Gama tells how her employers wrote the shopping list that she often carried to the different stores and butchers. She pointed out that this was done so the employers would get the type of meat they wanted.

> The whites used to write a letter and say go and buy there and fetch meat from the butcheries. They would write and you would keep running with this thing and give it to these shop owners. You will then see them giving you if they get them. You don't know what the white person has written. Again when you go to the butcheries he has written, and you will come back with those things. They wrote so that you can get the thing you want because speaking English. . . . A long time ago the storekeepers were white people, Boers in the butcheries. The white man would want the type of meat he wants. Then he would write, and I will just lay bhaca [the letter]. He then reads it, he reads it. He [the shopkeeper] takes out what the white man wants and he reads again, and he reads, he takes the things out and they become a pile and I put them in a basket. . . . You were not given money. I am sure they paid at the end of the month.

The differences in language may have been a problem for some farmers, but the farmer that Linah Maseko worked for spoke very good siSwati. He used to interpret for the domestic workers when they had problems understanding his wife. The workers were happy when they heard him speaking their language. Linah Maseko said,

> We would be happy when we heard him speaking because you would be surprised that this white man speaks siSwati and you can understand. We were pleased because he spoke our language.

The speaking of the language of the workers made the workers feel that their culture had been embraced by the employer. Linah Maseko said they were encouraged in their work when their employer spoke to them in siSwati. This was a form of acceptance of them.

Language and Power at Work

A look at the interactions of the workers and their employers shows that the grammar of everyday life consisted of language that gave power to the employer. The grammar of the self that the worker acquired was determined by the employer. This included naming, the expressions that are used on a daily basis, and the general use of language in cases where there were no communication problems.

Naming and the Self

The repertoire of the self that Africans came to acquire in domestic work was created by the employer. The names used were sometimes determined by the employer. The employers had their own cultural attitudes toward the naming of domestic workers. They sometimes struggled with the African names of their employees or used names that came to their minds. Tryphina pointed out that even though the Boers asked for your name in Fanakalo when you got to the farm, saying, "Ngubani logama kawena?" (What is your name?), they would not call it properly. She used the name Lobutimba to give an example of how they mispronounced names. She said Lobutimba could be pronounced as "Buzimba," which leaves out the prefix that is used on girls' names in siSwati. She said to get around the problem of pronouncing the African names, the Boers used one name for most African domestic workers. She said the typical name for a domestic worker was Annie. They would use this name for almost every domestic worker.

> The name that a Boer uses for an African is Annie. Once you are a worker your name is Annie. Annie! She would call all of you Annie and when you all looked at her when she called you, the Annie she was looking at was the one she was calling. She would say, "Annie 'kom!' " The one she was looking at had to run.

Brown (1987) points out that naming is a powerful linguistic device. Appropriating the power to name objects is appropriating the right to predicate. Grouping the name of the African domestic workers into one name can be seen as a way of "emptying their personal identity" (Brown, 1987, p. 127). This is because it made the women's identities indiscernible. The workers had a life at work that was not distinguished from that of the next worker. This is appropriation of the power to give identity on the part of the employer.

Tryphina pointed out that Boers used the name "kaffir" for blacks when they were angry. The Africans would be angry when referred to as kaffirs because they considered this name an insult. However, when Annie was used, they were not hurt because the name does not have racist connotations.

The children of the employers also called the workers kaffirs. Mary Gama said that the children of the employers were rude to them and called them kaffirs, a word that is equivalent to "nigger." From the way Mary Gama told this story, it was obvious that she felt that the dogs were treated like the workers, if not better.

The Everyday Grammar of Interactions and the Worker

In this metaphor of society as text, the women had to learn new vocabularies such as the "kaffirpot." This example was given by Tryphina Dlamini. She said that the three-legged pot was given this

name. When I asked her why, she said, "It is because it was our pot."
Although she did not like the adjective attached to the pot, it was
obvious that she had come to accept the meaning and saw the three-
legged pot as an extension of her self-identity. This is because the
whites had defined the pot as a pot for blacks. Acceptance of the self
meant accepting the definition of the self that was made by the
employers through the physical objects one found in domestic work.

Another issue of language and power was revealed by the repertoire of the everyday expressions that the workers came to acquire.
These were partly influenced by the fact that the workers did not
learn the whole language. Life was restricted to everyday expressions
that were used in domestic work. The grammar of everyday life
consisted of structures that were repeated in the performance of
different chores around the house.

Losimilo Nhleko told how she was spoken to in Afrikaans most
of the time. From the expressions she uses, one learns that all she
learned was the phrases for questions and commands. She used the
following Afrikaans expressions:

Waar kom jy?
  (Where do you come from?)
Waar was jy gistermiddag?
  (Where were you yesterday afternoon?)

Tryphina used imperatives to show how instructions were given
to them in Afrikaans. The expression "maak gou," which means "do
it quickly," was constantly used. She gave the following examples:

Maak gou koffie, toe.
  (Make quickly coffee.)
Maak tee.
  (Make tea.)
Annie kom.
  (Annie come.)

These expressions show how questions and imperatives that a
worker could never use to the employer were used by the employer

to the worker. Social talk was controlled by the social position the person occupied.

Language and Power in Interpersonal Relationships

Linah Maseko pointed out that the whites had power because they were white. They could say what they wanted at any time. The black people had no say. They had to listen to what they were told. They could not show anger. To show anger was a sign of disobedience.

> A long time ago even if you had a problem, you could not call a white person and talk to him. If you called a white person they would show you the way home and tell you to leave. . . . There was nothing you could talk to a white person about. What could you talk to a white person about? There was nothing you could say because if you say anything you would be sacked. . . . It was the law. Whites were above blacks.

Linah Maseko worked for a farmer who could speak siSwati very well. She said that he used to insult them in siSwati. There was one worker who would jest with him in the same manner as he did with them. Although this domestic worker was portrayed by Linah as assertive and nonchalant, she almost got shot because she kept joking when the farmer was angry.

One narrative that showed that the master had the power to say anything to the worker had to do with remuneration. Although the women often said they were paid little when the king intervened and sent someone to check the wages of the workers, the employer told the worker not to say the correct amount that she was paid. Lobu-timba Xaba told how the employer told her to lie to the person who was checking and say she is paid more than what he paid because they would chase him away from the country. The employer spoke to her in Fanakalo and said,

Lobuzimba wena yazi manje skhathi wena fika lomuntu
lapha Swazini lobuya lapha kaSobhuza, Khuluma kawena
mangakhi mali wena khuluma mine nika R25.00 goba uma
ungakhulumi loko hhayi khona lunga. Azikho lungile kimi.
Bazangixosha lapha kaNgwane.

Translated into English, this means,

Lobuzimba, you know when the Swazi person from King
Sobhuza comes and asks you how much I am paying you,
you must tell him I pay you R25.00 because if you do not
say that it will not be all right. They will chase me away
from Swaziland.

Lobutimba said she agreed to tell lies and say she was paid more even
though she earned very little.

Pleasant Memories

Work as a domestic worker was not portrayed as all torture with
no good experiences. There were enjoyable times. They enjoyed the
food and interactions with other workers. Mary Gama says she used
to eat a lot at her employer's place.

Food! They used to give us food. They used to cook! I became very fat.

She remembered with nostalgia the trip to the old post office where
she took the tea of the "oubaas." She says they would come from
different directions with trays in their hands. This was also a meeting
place for them. One got a chance to see one's friends.

Some of the workers felt that even though it was a hard life, they
learned a lot. They learned how to look after their own houses and
also to appreciate cleanliness. Tryphina said she learned to work hard
and also how to cook food differently. She took some time to teach

me how to bake bread using potatoes as a raising agent. She also said she learned how to make soap from pig fat and soda.

Opinions on Language Policy in Swaziland

On issues of language policy in Swaziland, the women emphasized the practical value of English in that it helps people get jobs. They felt that both siSwati and English should be used in Swaziland. Lobutimba felt that siSwati was the language of Swaziland and should be spoken. She expressed concern about the way the youth speak it badly.

> Our siSwati is OK. We want siSwati to be spoken, and it must be spoken correctly. . . . English is also OK. It is the language that we speak when we want jobs. If I speak English a Zambian can employ me so that I can wash clothes for him and earn money. Even in the schools we want both English and siSwati.

Some women answered the question in relation to their children. Mary Gama said that she thought that her children should learn both languages in school because English helps them to get jobs.

> My children must speak my language. They can speak the one they learn in school, but they must learn my language. English helps them to get jobs, my child. My children grew up learning English. I sent them to school.

Future Aspirations of Workers

Workers were asked to imagine how they could change their lives if they could live again. Most of them emphasized getting an education. They said they would make sure they stayed in school and learned everything. Mary Gama said she would be educated and learn

English. She said she went to Sebenta and they kept teaching her siSwati and she did not like that because she could write Zulu.

> If I could be young again, I can go to school, and learn so that I can know how to read English. I like to go to school. By the way I went to Sebenta and they said we should learn siSwati. They wrote things and said we should fill up and I said I would like to learn English. . . . There was no one who could teach us English. Since I had learnt Zulu, I did not want to learn siSwati.

One woman associated the question with the behavior of young girls who decide to have boyfriends instead of living lives more fruitfully and said that she would not have a boyfriend if she had a chance to change her life.

Implications for Further Research
and Reflections on Narrative Research

The use of life histories as a research method in sociolinguistics still needs to be investigated. It relies mostly on the teller. Even though the data one gets are from the perspective of the teller, the researcher does shape the text in that the answers are a response to the questions that are asked. I noticed that in telling their life histories in the first section, in which they were telling the general life history, the domestic workers tended to leave out the linguistic information. Although the difficulties in using the language of the work place were there, they seemed to be part of the situation that they took for granted. I had to ask more specific questions before the respondents would focus on the issues of language.

There were several times when the women addressed me personally, bringing out their frustrations about using languages they do not know well when talking to those who know them. This helped me get what the feelings about language between classes are. I also had to adopt a more relaxed, conversational form of interviewing. The women were more at ease than if they were being interrogated. Because it was time for elections, some women suspected me as someone who was collecting data on politics. I had to explain what the interviews would be used for before they would agree to participate.

Relying on the workers for information on language afforded me just one view of the story. This is evident in the samples on Fanakalo. Because the workers speak African languages, their Fanakalo shows the evidence of coming from someone who knows the prefix and suffix systems of Bantu/Nguni languages. This becomes a close imitation of Fanakalo and not the real Fanakalo that is spoken by the nonspeakers of Bantu/Nguni languages. This does not mean that the Fanakalo is wrong, but it shows that it is the version of Fanakalo that the workers used in their interactions with their employers.

It is very important to ascertain what the worker means because the use of euphemisms is very common among Swazis, especially Swazi Christians. The influence of religion on expressions was evident as the workers would use a word that was not specific, because to use the other word would be unacceptable to the domestic worker for religious reasons. One worker was telling me that the farmer and his wife used to defecate on themselves and said "bebatonela," which might mean they used to wet themselves. I had to be specific in asking my questions.

Conclusion

Though the information about the women varies according to each woman's experience, it does provide useful linguistic data from which generalizations about social codes, reasons for low language skills, and problems that arise in interactions and attitudes toward languages can be made. The women's life histories also show that the acquisition of social reality through language in an institution means the subjective internalization of taxonomies and designated schemes of social categories of space, time, hierarchies—all of which are experienced through language.

People learn linguistic repertoires in institutionalized social roles. As people play their everyday roles, they make meaning in interaction with others. Language is used to direct actions, and when this is done at the work place, in a language the worker cannot understand, it gives a lot of power to the employer and those who understand the language. The frustration of those who do not understand it should not be ignored by language planners.

The lives of the workers show that language is used to control people by depriving them of language skills, thus keeping them from going up the defined social ladders of society. The processes of enforcement that are used to do this vary with each social situation. In order to understand how these processes function, the domains of language use have to be studied through research methods that can give people in lower classes a voice so that they can express their life experiences. This way, language planning can become less of an academic exercise and more of a way of validating the experiences of those whose lives are mostly affected by language problems. What happened in domestic work during the colonial period is re-created in different ways in postcolonial Swaziland.

Note

1. Life histories of Mary Gama (September 12, 1993), Tryphina Dlamini (September 2, 1993), Linah Maseko (September 11, 1993), Losimilo Nhleko (August 31, 1993), and Lobutimba Xaba (September 12, 1993).

References

Brown, R. H. (1987). *Society as text.* Chicago: University of Chicago Press.
Denzin, K. N. (1989). *Interpretive biography.* Newbury Park, CA: Sage.
Fairclough, N. (1989). *Language and power.* London: Longman.
Fishman, J. A. (1968). *Advances in language planning.* The Hague, Netherlands: Mouton.
Keegan, T. (1986). *Rural transformations in industrial South Africa.* Braamfontein, South Africa: Ravan.
Kuper, H. (1947). *The uniform of color.* Johannesburg, South Africa: Witwatersrand University Press.
Tollefson, J. (1991). *Planning language, planning inequality.*New York: Longman.

❧ 9 ❧

Extending Boundaries

Narratives on Exchange

Ardra L. Cole

J. Gary Knowles

Grace

I have traveled a lot. I took courses in Copenhagen and England. I have also traveled all across Canada, including the two territories, just to gain more knowledge about each area of Canada. The geography and meeting and talking to people I have found fascinating. I have traveled in England, Wales, and Scotland and then, for a month, I traveled in all of the Scandinavian countries. One year I took a tour of eight countries in 14 days but I always have said that I would love to go to New Zealand or Australia and, when this chance for an exchange came, I

Sue

This exchange program was, I guess, part of my career plan. Exchanges in New Zealand seem to [occur] in little pockets of teachers and [you find out about them] mostly by word of mouth. I knew about going on an exchange from teachers who had done it and had a wonderful time.

We don't like the idea of traveling a day here and a day there. We had come to a stage where Joanna [our older daughter] is 11 years old and if we didn't do something now she would be too old to travel around with us—it would affect

AUTHORS' NOTE: An earlier version of this chapter was presented as a paper at the annual meeting of the American Educational Research Association, San Francisco, April 1992.

thought I would put New Zealand
first. That was my first choice.

her educationally to take her out of
high school. So it was either this year
or not at all.

Developing Our Study

Grace and Sue are experienced classroom teachers who, through participation in an international Educator Exchange Program, traded classrooms,[1] schools, homes, and countries for the Canadian academic year 1991-1992.[2] Grace is a single, Anglo-Canadian woman. Sue is married to Peter and has two daughters, Helen and Joanna, and is also of Anglo heritage. She is *Pakeha,* a Maori word describing white New Zealanders of non-Maori heritage, usually European (see, King, 1985). Both women are in their mid-30s and have about the same amount of elementary (or primary, as it is called in Aotearoa, New Zealand) school teaching experience behind them. When we learned about their arrangement, our interest was piqued because our own national and cultural backgrounds mirrored theirs: One of us, Ardra, is long familiar with the cultural and school contexts of the Canadian education system; the other, Gary, with the contexts and culture of New Zealand schools. Both of us have also taught in schools—Ardra in Canada, and Gary in New Zealand. When we approached Grace and Sue before the school year, asking if we could "observe" their experiences, they eagerly agreed to join us in a study of their experience of teacher exchange.

We outlined three primary objectives of the study. First, we wanted to gain insights into the different contexts and cultures of the school systems of Canada and New Zealand from the perspectives of the two teachers. We were especially interested in this topic because we sensed that exposure to new and sometimes contrasting settings would provide ongoing opportunities for professional development.[3] Second, we wished to explore, in general, the concept of international teacher exchange programs as a professional development experience. And third, we wanted to understand, in particular, the experiences of the two exchange teachers and how the exchange program and the related activities influenced their professional development.

In this chapter, we represent elements of the two teachers' experiences of one another's classrooms, schools, and cultural contexts, and illustrate how experience in unfamiliar, even dramatically different contexts influenced their personal and professional development. We frame our interpretation with Dewey's (1938) notions about the role of experience in education and development. In particular, we view exchange experiences as educative opportunities that "have the promise and potentiality of presenting new problems which by stimulating new ways of observation and judgment will expand the area of further experience" (Dewey, 1938, p. 75).

Obtaining and Developing Narratives

Because our research project involved participants separated by great distances and international boundaries, we had to rely on telephone and mail for some of our communications and data gathering. We conducted extensive face-to-face and telephone interviews (all of which were audiotaped and transcribed) with each teacher over the duration of her exchange: In-person interviews with Grace, the Canadian teacher, took place prior to her leaving Canada and also occurred in New Zealand; in-person interviews with Sue, the New Zealand teacher, all took place in Canada. The telephone interviews were shorter, limited by budgetary concerns. The interviews took the form of informal conversations between each of the teachers and the two of us.[4]

Both teachers agreed to keep a journal of their experiences, which they delivered to us by mail at regular intervals. Although both women were experienced journal keepers (and had already planned to keep a journal for the duration of their exchange), we initially gave some suggestions as to how they might organize their journal writing and make regular entries for the purposes of the study. We also provided an excerpt from Holly's (1989) publication on the form and purposes of journal writing. The journals provided a forum for the teachers to chronicle events as they happened; record impressions, thoughts, and reactions to events and experiences; and to "work through" and make sense of their experiences both within their classrooms and the broader cultural contexts. The journals were the narrative thread that gave continuity to the patchwork of experiences represented in the intermittent interviews and mail correspondence.

The two teachers wrote their journal entries in very different formats and styles. Sue initially elected not to use the wide-margined, loose-leaf paper that we supplied. She wrote in a predated, lined, commercially printed diary that had 3 days to each page. Thus, right from the start, her writing was defined by the preprinted page and tended to be abbreviated and direct, even sometimes staccato-like because of the restricted space. The form and her writing style did not allow for extensive reflection on any topic. She wrote for her own record of the exchange experience, recording family activities as well as school experiences. Only after the pages of her preprinted diary were filled at the end of the calendar year did she begin to use the less restrictive format of the loose-leaf paper. She told us, then, that she had changed the focus of her writing somewhat and that she was no longer placing as much emphasis on issues outside of the "business of teaching and working." She also told us that, from this time, she also kept another, more extensive "family" journal, complete with memorabilia from travels within Canada and the United States.

Grace, on the other hand, wrote more flowing, extensive, and reflective accounts. Like Sue, she also wrote for herself, recording her many and varied exploits out of the classroom. More than Sue's record, her journal recorded intricate details of life in her newfound temporary homeland. These she photocopied and mailed to us.

Presenting the Narratives

In our presentations, we attempt to respect the integrity of the teachers' accounts. The narratives we present are theirs, not ours. Our role in narrative construction was mainly organizational. From an analysis of the interview transcripts, we were able to pick up thematic strands and patches of conversation that we then interwove with the narrative threads from the journals. The narratives we present are merely a re-presentation of the original accounts organized in a manner that, we believe, captures the richness and detail of the year's experience, respects each teacher's individuality, and highlights some of the themes that emerged through our reading of the narrative texts. Narrative, both as a process and a phenomenon, has a central role in personal and professional development. It provides a process and a structure for teachers to make sense of their own experiences, and for others to better understand and support such opportunities for teachers:

> Through telling, writing, reading, and listening to life stories—one's own and other's—those engaged in [the work of teaching, consulting, and professional development] can penetrate cultural barriers, discover the power of the self and the integrity of the other, and deepen their understanding of their perspective histories and possibilities.
>
> Understanding the narrative and contextual dimensions of human actors can lead to new insights, compassionate judgment, and the creation of shared knowledge and meanings that can inform professional practice. (Witherell & Noddings, 1991, pp. 3-4, 8)

Thus we proceed with the presentation of elements of the two teachers' experiences—an interactive narrative dialogue. We begin with the teachers providing some background information about their career and professional development histories and about their respective learning contexts.

Teaching in Canada

I grew up in a family of teachers and my father was a principal of a high school. I have always been kind of interested in education. My mother was also a teacher before she had children. I have always enjoyed children and it has always been a fascination with me how they learn. [I have enjoyed] going to different countries and just watching the children, even if it did not involve schooling.

Teaching in New Zealand

I have been teaching for about 12 years. I did a year in Auckland and a year and a half in a country area. When we got married I could not get a [regular teaching] job in Auckland so I just applied for any [teaching] job. The one I got turned out to be special education in a handicapped school and it was really wonderful. Then, I took special education [courses] for 4 years, had the girls,

Just talking with people and observing people on the street, and just kind of being involved in their lives—all of those things have really helped me grow as an educator. It makes you stop and think about the way you do things. You don't go to a place to decide who is doing "it" right and who is doing "it" wrong. You go to get new ideas, to question what we are doing here [at home]. You may not be able to do anything about it because one person is not going to change the whole [system], but travel does change you, in a way, because you get to think in different ways.

I have taught for 10½ years. I started teaching at a little country school with three teachers. Then I moved to [my present school] where I have been for about 10 years. I have always taught Grade 1 or Grades 1 and 2.

and went back [to teaching] part-time.

When I was teaching part-time, I had 6- and 7-year-olds for 2 years. Then, I applied for the job I have now with 10- and 11-year-olds.

I have been involved in professional development programs, [for example,] doing Advanced Studies for Teachers (AST) after school and at night. [We take the courses at Auckland] Teachers' College. There are eight 60-hour papers [courses] and an exam at the end. You can do just [about] any subject. I have taken Teaching Art, Communication, Conducting "Buzz" Groups, Social Development, Social Studies, all of the curriculum areas. [I do this] not for a career move [out of teaching] but because I feel I want to move more within the teaching profession—I don't want to stay in the same job forever. I do it for the new ideas and the practical things that you bring back to the classroom.

[In our school] we have moved toward an individualized program, especially in Language Arts. We got rid of the basal readers, and the phonetic approach, and developed a more "whole language" approach. I think it's wonderful. The kids are doing great things. My kids in Grade 1 are able to express themselves and write pieces of work that I don't think we wrote when [I was] in Grade 4. It's so exciting to see what they are doing. It depends when you come in what the room is like. We have a session every day where we have everybody working together; other times, the kids have free choice of what they want to do.

I have a new reading loft which is very exciting. It's square, made out of wood, and the kids can climb up on a top platform. It has railings and indoor-outdoor carpeting—so they can go up there and sit and read quietly or they can go underneath. It's got two big windows that they can use as a puppet theater or, when we are "doing money," they can use them for a store and people can go and buy things at the store. [It was built by] our Parent-Teacher Association, which is very strong. I tried for 3 years to get this thing made so I was really pleased when I got it. I saw something like it in Denmark (on a much smaller scale). When I came back I said [to the principal], "I have to have a loft." So I drew it up and he helped me with dimensions of things because it had to be made so that it would come apart to go through the door.

Reading is a very, very important highlight of my classroom. I would almost say that all of the kids love to read no matter what level they are at. They love to read and they love the loft because they can just get up there with a book. They have "buddy work," too, [in which] they read with children from another grade.

The kids do a lot of writing [on their own] also. In environmental studies, we usually do units and the children become involved in different things, like sandboxes or water or research. This year when we did a unit on dinosaurs, the kids were divided into groups and they were able to get books and use the table of contents and index, find the names of the dinosaurs, and write down [information] about them. I thought, for 6-year-olds, it was pretty good.

I'm really excited about the way language [teaching] in the classroom has developed since I started [teaching]. Right from the beginning I did not like the traditional program in the school. It was very phonics-based. The kids learned to read but they really didn't understand what they were doing. They spent a lot of time just sounding out words. [With] this [new] way, even the poorest, most immature student is able to get a book and read it. He or she is not held back by the fact that she cannot remember what this letter says. They "read" by context instead of letter by letter and word by word.

The children are also involved in discovering concepts of math. They used to learn only by rote (e.g., 3 + 4 = 7). Now they work with manipulatives so that they understand what 3 + 4 is. Instead of giving them a ditto sheet of number facts to complete, you might give them a blank ditto and say, "Your number is 8. See how many number facts you can give me for 8." And, the kids will give you different number facts than you ever thought of. It's exciting what they are doing.

My kids are probably freer [than students in other classrooms]. As long as the children are moving in the direction they are supposed to be moving—if you can put a lot of fun into learning and maybe take away a lot of the structure that we used to have, where they had to sit there and be very quiet—why not if the kids are enjoying it? I have kids who don't want to go on summer holidays and don't want to go home on weekends because they like [school] so much!

Usually when the [children] start [in my class] they are anywhere from a mid-kindergarten to maybe about Grade 2 in ability [range]. Maybe I have two or three children who can read simple books and the rest [do] not [have] even a general knowledge of language and how it is made up. Home background varies also. [In the community] there are a lot of single parents and parents where the father is not home a lot. There are all different income ranges and a lot of [marriage separations]. It is not a multicultural community in any way.

I have done a number of [extracurricular] things in the school: helped coach basketball and volleyball, [organized] the Jump Rope for

My school [in New Zealand] is from [the equivalent of Grades] 1 to 6 [with] nine [classroom] teachers, a teacher of special needs, and an itinerant teacher of special needs on a program we call the "Edmonton Scheme." We are one of about four schools in the area that takes very slow children and puts them with a teacher and a teacher's aide.

My school is quite low socioeconomically so we pick up an equity grant that makes up for financial differences that might otherwise occur. Many of the children's parents are either unemployed or have low incomes. We have a high Polynesian [student] intake and a high non-English-speaking language group of

Heart Program and the milk program. This year I helped direct the musical *Alice in Wonderland*. [In New Zealand] I would like to be involved in sports—I have never done it by myself.

children so that we need this assistance, the extra money. [There is a] very big multicultural group—[children from] Maori, [Pacific] Island [Polynesian], Fiji Indian, Korean, and Chinese families.

My children in New Zealand were a Standard 2, 3, 4 [about Grades 2 and 3] vertically grouped class. We have two parallel classrooms [i.e., two classes of Grades 2 and 3 split], which means that no classroom gets overloaded with children. Having two classrooms also means that personality conflicts between students and teacher can be avoided because we can split the children up.

The primary wing of our school is very cohesive. We work together. Sometimes we will have five teachers involved [in a unit] and all of those students will rotate [among the teachers]. We do a lot of things together so that the kids not only know me but they know the other teachers too and they feel very comfortable with them.

The principal makes the decision [about placement] but invariably teachers are involved. At the end of the year, we sit together to collate the rolls and [strive for] a balanced group of children on each roll—some smart ones, some below average, and some average. Then we total up the roll and say, "I will swap you for so and so" because you just know the kids you are going to clash with. We end up with what we each consider to be a fair group [or distribution].

In [my New Zealand] school we exchange ideas and plan units together. We sit down as a junior school or as a middle school (which is where I teach) and look at all the topics and units we need to cover for the term, and pull out the ones that are timely or interesting, or whatever. Someone will go to the library and get all the resource materials we need. I might get the *School Journals* [a New Zealand Department of

Education publication] and plan the art. And we bring all that together for one unit. Then, from that unit, we each take out what we want to teach. It ends up with the whole school teaching the same thing at the same time. It is a 3-year plan and the children never repeat [the same content material].

The preceding narratives reflect elements of the perspectives on and experiences of teaching that Grace and Sue took to their respective exchange classrooms and contexts. In the following section, we provide a sense of how these preconceptions acted as lenses through which they initially interpreted their experiences in their new settings.

Social and Economic Contexts

Settling In in New Zealand

New school, new staff, new students, new adventure. I was surprised at how "at home" I felt amongst my new surroundings. I don't think I could have gotten a better exchange. The staff here is very helpful, warm, and friendly. During my first week they called me up, dropped in for tea, and asked what I needed. They are a very supportive group and I'm sure I will enjoy working with them.

Even though I'm halfway around the world, I feel quite at home here. Many of the routines and expectations are the same. From the second I stepped off the plane, I've never had any feeling of being alone. I

Settling In in Canada

First day of school. Children [have] very limited skills. Things are very different!

[I knew] nothing about the school at all [before I came]. I believe the school is quite strange. The county people tell me that it's different. I asked one of the teachers, "Do you ever go out socially?" (In New

always knew I had someone I could call if I wanted to talk. I knew if I wanted to do something, there were five or six people I could go to and say, "Do you want to do this?" As everyone told me, in New Zealand when they say, "Drop in," they mean it. Very often I go over to Sue's parents—I drop in and end up staying for dinner. They have become my New Zealand parents and I feel very comfortable with them. I also feel very comfortable with the staff, especially a couple of them. You don't ever really feel alone—everyone is interested in what you are doing.

———————————

[People] have gone out of their way to make me feel at home. Everybody is always making sure that I have something to do. They are interested in what you are doing and they want to hear about it afterward. They want to include you in a lot of things. They want to make sure you have something to do and that you are okay.

———————————

Zealand, for example, all the teachers would maybe go to a movie.) She said, "Why would I want to go out with some of them?" So, actually the staff don't mix well together. There are divisions, in other words.

I had been at the school a couple of times before [school began for the year]. I was really surprised because the first day, after we had our children for about an hour, there was a school assembly. At home [in New Zealand] we would put on a show and do some great things and have some singing. Then someone would talk, and there would be a few more songs—it would be a fun time. [Here it] was very formal. The children sat on the floor and the new teachers were introduced and they stood up, said "Hello," and then sat down. And that was my introduction to the school.

———————————

[In New Zealand] if we had a new member on staff (like it would be done for Grace) there would be songs of welcome and a morning tea. [Here] I walked into the staff room at recess to find no lights on and nobody else there. The morning tea is our social time [in New Zealand]. Everybody goes for morning tea time and there is a little jar out and you pay 24 cents if you want a cup of coffee.

It has been my experience in every school that I have been in that the staff room is the hub of activity, especially at lunch time. Part of the ritual is to bring special treats and someone makes coffee and tea. It is usually a welcoming, inviting environment. It's homey. That's where things take place and where all of the socials are planned. This has not been my experience [here]. That's why I am finding all of this surprising.

[I relied on] the children to tell me who was who because I hadn't had any social [contact with faculty], whereas in New Zealand for the two new staffers and the assistant principal, they actually had a barbecue party on Saturday night before school started so that staff could get to know other people.

Relatives of my exchange family have certainly gone out of their way for me. I feel as if I have known them all my life. I felt very good about coming to New Zealand but I never expected it to be THIS wonderful.

I am so busy, every day just seems to fly by because something new happens. The school is exciting because it is new, and the kids are very eager, in some ways, to do a lot of things. There is always something [social] planned. Usually by Monday I know what I am going to be doing next Saturday. It got to the point that, at school, they thought they should have a social calendar up [on the wall] just for me so I could write down everything I was doing [that] everyone would know.

It has taken us a long time to make friends with the people here. I don't think it takes so long [to make friends] in New Zealand. I guess it depends on the sort of people you are. I'm quite an outgoing person, and I like to have people around. I enjoy other people's company. I got a real shock coming here. I'd been warned that it would happen but we [still] got a real shock that nobody bothered to include us in things until we made our own friends. I don't think that would happen in New Zealand.

It poured rain again today and the children were unable to go out for fresh air. The rooms are so damp and cold it makes me think of the warmth of home. I've never felt so cold inside except in Scotland.

Today the heat is terrible. The classrooms seem too full of gear— no central storeroom; own personal equipment; no pooling of resources.

Many of the children spend their day in bare feet. Even though it's cold and rainy they don't seem to feel it. Since it's third term [and spring here], they've turned off the little heat the school has. If the schools were this cold at home, the furnace would be running. It's something I'm beginning to get used to though.

The things you hear on the news are kind of scary. You know things are happening out there and maybe you are more cautious. I feel very different about the way this house is locked up and [how] you would never put Christmas decorations outside because they would just [disappear]. They say, "Always make sure the car is in the garage and the garage is locked and the gate is locked." There seems to be a real uneasiness about what is happening in New Zealand and that, I must admit, surprised me when I first got here. You always hear only all the good parts.

The social and economic contexts of New Zealand and Canada, though vastly different in some respects, are remarkably similar in others. In the broader social context, New Zealand is presently grappling with serious societal issues that are directly reflected in the schools and the curriculum, some of which are high levels of unemployment, which have spiralled over the last decade, and the tenuous economic status of the country; a depressed economy; a serious erosion of the general standard of living over the last 3 decades; questions about the role of the welfare state, the underpinning of New Zealand's infrastructure; the place of the indigenous Maori culture and language within society; accommodation of immigrants, especially those from South Pacific Islands and Southeast Asia; deteriorating race relations; and serious crime/law and order issues. It was to this complex national context that Grace was introduced.

Ontario, where Sue spent her exchange year, is described by the rest of Canada as a "have" province, home of the majority of the country's population, commerce, and industry. Because of the province's large size and significance, the sociopolitical issues prevalent in the greater Canadian cultural context are magnified there. The issues are similar to those with which New Zealand is struggling. The economic climate is, also like that of New Zealand, fraught with rising unemployment (a dramatic turnaround from the latter years of the 1980s), rising costs, and lowered productivity, and questions about political foundations and universal welfare services are currently in the forefront of the provincial news. Both New Zealand and Ontario also have recently seen changes in governments and have been heavily affected by the widespread, global recession. And in the year following the teaching exchange, the Ontario government began modeling many of its economic strategies after those of New Zealand.

Narratives in Context

As we read and reread the narratives of Grace and Sue, we were struck by the similarity of the topics they raised in their writing and conversations, even though they were speaking of and from each other's home environments. Of course, they also had similar issues and tasks to face as they landed, met new people, adjusted to climatic differences, prepared for school, taught daily, and so on. Not only did they address concerns and view similar processes or procedures from quite different perspectives, it was clear that they each brought to the new contexts particular frames of professional and cultural references, benchmarks, expectations, and personal conceptions. These they used as a basis to observe their experiences and assess or judge the worth or usefulness of particular lines of action or events they encountered in their newfound settings. The cultural milieus in which their prior experiences were bounded seem to offer some explanation of their behaviors and practices.

At face value, Grace appeared to be welcomed into the school community in a vastly more personal manner than Sue. Are we to assume and generalize, therefore, that New Zealanders are friendlier and more welcoming of visitors than Ontario Canadians? (Of course, one could quickly generalize that because New Zealand is small, isolated, and the people friendly, entry would obviously be greatly facilitated.) We cannot generalize from singular experiences. We caution ourselves on this point. Nevertheless, the fact that both teachers had preconceptions of their entry into their newfound home environments may well have had a profound effect on their materialized expectations and the recordings of those experiences. And, as will be evident later in the narratives, Sue's early experiences of school and community in Canada were influenced by other events.

Next, we present some of Grace's and Sue's reflections on their experiences in each other's classrooms and schools. Stark contrasts between the ways in which the two schools operate—structure, atmosphere, organization of the school day, curriculum, rules, and norms and patterns of interaction—provided opportunities for them to reconsider their own teaching situations at home.

At School in New Zealand: Reflections on Classrooms, Curriculum, and Teaching

I have 26 Standard 1-2 students—7- and 8-year-olds. Because [the class is based on] vertical grouping, I end up with extra children—like, [children from the] lower 3 and 4 [Standards] come into my class for mathematics—so that makes it really interesting. I have students from China, Fiji, Samoa, Tonga, as well as New Zealand Maori children. It's a real mixture. The multicultural aspect is probably the basic thing that really sticks out. Each one of those cultures brings very interesting twists to the classroom. Some of the [stu-

At School in Canada: Reflections on Classrooms, Curriculum, and Teaching

In New Zealand we have big windows and the classrooms [are arranged so that] to get to my room I have to come in through [other teachers' rooms]. There are outside doors but once you get in [the building], the only way a teacher [in an inside classroom] can get to her room is to walk through [other teachers' classrooms]. So she trots through [the other rooms] where the teachers are working [conducting conversation such as], "Hi! How are you? Oh, I like what you are doing. Can I borrow that?". . . .

dents] are very quiet. A lot of the girls from the Pacific Islands tend to be quiet, and education is maybe not their main aim in life. And the boys are *very* domineering. A lot of the Maori boys are very loud. I have some ESL (English as a Second Language) children, and they struggle to grasp the [English] language itself, as well as the content we are teaching.

The classes are large, and rules and regulations seem much more relaxed than in Canada. The atmosphere overall seems far more relaxed. The kids are able to come in and go out at their own free will. The classrooms don't seem to be as rigid. They don't line up to come in or they don't walk quietly down the hall like they do at home. They are supposed to walk in the halls but it takes a lot to get them to walk in a line. I guess little things like that make me feel more relaxed than at home. The students and staff tend to dress very casually here in New Zealand. No one is afraid to participate [in sports activities] because they're not dressed in frills. Girls very, very rarely wear a skirt to school. Boys come dressed in various ways, but always very casual—no real dress up. Bare feet is something that you see a lot of, even though it is cold out. [At first] it made me shiver but you get used to it. There are some days when I wanted to be in my bare feet too. It doesn't bother anyone to see a teacher in bare feet whereas, at home, a teacher

Here, [there is a] concrete wall [between the main building and] my classroom. I don't know what it's like outside because I have opaque glass on the windows and then wire on the other side of the wall. My room looks over the blacktop area so that it is all protected with a wall and wire window so I don't know what the weather is like if I haven't been outside. I can't see. At home I have big windows on either side [of the room] and I would have wandered through others' rooms quite a lot.

The way I teach, the type of classroom I run, and the type of teaching I do is very, very different than the image teachers [here] have of [good teaching]. Lots of people have told me that, and I can just see it. [In other teachers' classrooms] the children all sit in rows. They are totally quiet. I cannot believe how quiet they are. In the Grade 2 class next door, at lunch time they all sit in seats to eat their lunch. In my class, they sit wherever they like to eat their lunches—that's private time. They chat and if they make a mess, they clean it up. If they spill a drink, they clean it up.

It is all very formal and very rigid [in the school], and the people are like that too. They portray different images. The image they [present] at school is totally different from the image they [present] at home. [For example], one [woman teacher] drove [to a neighboring town] 15 minutes by car to buy alcohol [for a dinner party she was having]. She did not buy it in town because that is not the image of a teacher [that she wishes to present].

would not take off her sandals and be in her bare feet. Here, I would.

_____

We start every morning with Fitness. When the bell rings, the [senior] kids (that is, Standards 1-6, about Grades 2 through 6) know to get into their fitness groups. We do [Fitness] for about 10 or 15 minutes and then they come inside. They always do some kind of physical activity. It may be jogging, which we do every Monday and Friday—we go for about a mile run. On other days, we do aerobics to music, and on other days we do something called Circuits, which are 12 different physical activities involving push-ups, stretches, skipping, bench-stepping—just various activities like that. Children circulate every 2 minutes. The whistle blows, and they move to the next activity.

[Then] we all go into our own classrooms. Basically, we set up so all the seniors do vocabulary development and writing, and story writing and spelling. Then they have "play" from 10:20 a.m. until 10:45 a.m., and then we have math. All the seniors have math at the same time be-

I am different. [The other teachers] all wear very formal clothing. I don't wear my jeans to school but I usually wear my corduroy pants and a sweatshirt. And I sit on the floor.

I think [the teachers] are really frightened of what the children are going to be like when they get them next year. I really think they are frightened of how loud and boisterous and noisy [the children] are going to be. They [think children] should be quiet, sitting and working at a desk.

_____

The bell rings at ten to nine and [the children] come in, sing "O Canada," we take the roll, and then I do a news time with the children. They have a time to share their news every morning. If they don't want to share, they just pass. We do a bulletin— "Today is Wednesday and the weather is. . . .," and then I write somebody's "news." It's actually story writing. I also have two helpers who come in and [work with] groups of children. The other children have a choice of activity in the room. They can choose activity centers, sand, blocks, or a related activity, which might be [something like] lists of other children's names. They like to make lists—people's names, things they study, colors. In another corner I have a color center with yellow, blue, and green food coloring and eye droppers. They mix [the colors] to see what they get.

During that time, I don't want to know what the others are doing. They are all busy but it's a choosing time for them. I just hang my head

cause they change classes with some of the [other] children. Then, in the afternoon, we do reading. They have a 5-minute "small play" and then we do "themes."

On Wednesdays we have a sports afternoon from 1:00 p.m. until 3:00 p.m. The children divide into groups for games. There might be four or five different activities going on, like paddle tennis, baseball, netball, or softball. The Acquapath we are doing now is definitely different from anything you would do at home. Acquapath is a swimming program that is geared to make the kids more confident in water. It is an interesting program because the [classroom] teachers are [also] teachers of the Acquapath [program]. Whether you have any swimming experience or not, you are the one in charge of the 20 kids, and you are marking them on different things. It is a big responsibility to have that many children in a pool at a time. At home you would have the lifeguards teaching [a program such as this] because they have the qualifications to do it. Having that many [students] in the water at the same time is really hard. They need a lot of parent involvement.

down and work with one group at a time—I rotate them. As the children finish their story, they go over to a table where there are colored markers, and [they] start doing a picture to go with their story. I call up another child and then they do a story with me. That takes us up to the first recess in the morning. We stop about 10 minutes before recess for sharing time.

We sit in a circle and [the children] show all of the things they had done that morning, or their story if they had written one. Some days we don't get through everybody's story. If someone had written a story and didn't have time to share it, then [that person] would be first to give a story tomorrow. All the kids listen as they read and "finger-point" to the words. I have a kiwi stamp, which I put on the page and hand, which tells me immediately who has read and written a story.

When they come in from recess [the children] automatically get a book. I have "shared reading" out of Big Books that I make in the classroom. It's so much fun—they come and read with a pointer and they love it. We [work with the Big Books] for about 20 minutes and they have a choice of reading activity [such as] poems or word games. My room has lots of activities situated around so they can read with a pointer. [In another activity] they walk around with big, long pointers and read. We have about six Big Books in the room now. We also do lots of [word games]. That takes us to lunch time.

[After lunch] we have a story and a song, about 10 minutes of printing, more singing, and then [after recess] we do environmental studies. It's quite a social time [in which] we make and do things [such as] Halloween activities [in October].

I have physical education [scheduled] every day but I only teach it three times a week so that I can work on reading [instead]. [The principal] came in one morning to watch me teach. He said that he really liked what I was doing, and so he has given me a free hand to do what I want. He is quite happy with my work.

[The principal] keeps inviting people to come and see this "strange new way of teaching." I asked not to have more than three visitors at a time but today he tried to push for five people in one day. I explained that two extra people was really too much, and that I certainly didn't want five people. I also asked him not to book people on a Friday, but he asked if a special friend of his could come on this Friday.

Last week I had 11 people through my room—11 people! [The children respond], "We've got some more customers." [I have the visitors] sit on a chair to watch and, after that, they are given a pencil and paper and asked to help the children with their programs. I need the help in my room.

This is my children's first year of writing. My [whole language] program works. It comes from New Zealand—it is not mine personally. I think [teachers here] have had the theory [of whole language] thrown at them and they just didn't know how to put it into practice; then, all of a sudden, there is somebody who is putting it into practice and having a lot of success (people tell me that they would be happy if their Grade 2 students wrote like that, and this is only half way into year one).

I have decided to write out my story writing program with all my ideas and work cards and [put them in a] kit to sell. [The principal] has found out that there is no reason why not. I have so many visitors, and they all want my ideas, so I shall try this idea. I have the "OK" from the Board office. [The principal] wondered if the Board may want to buy it.

It is interesting to see all the volunteer helpers in the school. In Canada, we're lucky to get one or two for the school. It's wonderful that so many are willing to give up free time to help the children. Basically, I have been involved with the parents through my ESL children. [The parents] take the [students] out and work with them on reading, vocabulary, and writing—anything I am involved in that I would like them to work on a little more. I have also been working on a parent reading program. They are the ones who take the poor readers, or the ones who are having a little bit more trouble with the reading, and read with them every day. These children are getting an extra dose of reading to help them bring up their reading levels and skills. Some of these parents have actually taken a course—a 3-hour

My school in New Zealand does badly [as far as parental support is concerned] because we have a high proportion of working parents but we do get very good support when there is something on in the school. Here, there is hardly any support. When we went down to [my daughter's] Science Exhibition at [her] school [there was no one there]. In New Zealand, it would be standing room only. You really can hardly get in the door of the intermediate school to see the Science Fair. Here, there was only one other family looking.

[In New Zealand], from the time the children start school, the parents are encouraged to be part of it. They're in and out of school, on [field] trips, etc. Here, the children go to kindergarten in the morning and the parents say "Farewell" at the door. Even when picking up their

course—on how to help children in their reading, or how to be a parent volunteer. They really seem to enjoy working with kids and it is wonderful to have the extra help.

I was surprised to find the children sitting in groups according to abilities. I changed that because I don't like them sitting like that (although we still do a lot of our reading in those groups). I've always tried to mix up ability levels—I think the students learn a lot from each other. That way the slower ones learn from the quicker ones. [I was also surprised that] some of the kids left my room for math. At home, we usually keep the same kids all of the time. The other thing is that these kids are all different ages because they start school on their fifth birthday, or they have up until last year. At home, everybody starts in September of the year they are 5; therefore, most of the kids are within a certain [age] range. With these kids, there can be almost a 3-year spread between them when you have a Standard 1-2 class, even a 4-year spread with some.

There seems to be far less emphasis on manipulatives and far more on memorizing. Children, even at my level, are encouraged to do formal homework every week. They seem to stress academics more although the children do not seem to be more advanced. You tend to give the children more questions to do in a book instead of having them work with [concrete] things. Because you don't have the resources to work with, maybe some of [the children]

children, they wait in the car park; they're not allowed to come into the corridor.

At home I would be outside much more because of the space, the land, and the area in the playground. I do a lot of math and science outside. Teachers think about education differently.

The difference between the Canadian and New Zealand curriculum is that [in New Zealand] it is all taught together. It is not taught as Grade 2, for example. All the juniors [K-2] would be having the same experience at the same time. [For example, once they completed a unit on the zoo or the beach] they would never repeat that unit again. I don't use my unit [plans] again. I use my resources but I always write a new unit [plan].

[In my school in New Zealand] we had a powerful [challenging] group of children. They were naughty, but really neat, and they did some great things. They wrote letters to me the other day and [when] I got them I felt strange and distant. A month ago, it would have meant a lot more but the kids here are "my kids" now. When I was in New Zealand they were my class, but they're not my kids anymore; they are [the other teacher's] kids.

move into the abstract level before they are ready.

When we are doing math in Canada, we always have manipulatives right there ready to use. Here, there are basically no manipulatives. There are a few blocks that have to be shared among the seniors. These are senior classes so it is a little bit different from [my own class] but, [for example], there are very few measuring tapes. For geometry they had two sets of tiny geometric figures from which we were supposed to teach "shapes." You can get things from around the classroom or you can get things from the environment, which is good, but you need something to start with. I think a lot more of their work is done abstractly because they don't have the things to work with. I think that is a disadvantage to a lot of lower-ability children who need to have the concrete materials with which to work.

———

[We] Canadian teachers have far more supplies [available in Canadian schools]. We also have many extras—corrugated paper, bulletin board edging, lots of construction paper, bristol board, glue, paper bags, plates, and envelopes. New Zealand teachers have to be far more creative. They have white and black paper, crayons, pastels, powder, glue, and small packages of colored paper that you handle like gold. New Zealand teachers and students are not as likely to waste paper because it's not so easy to get. Students also pay for pencils, notebooks, rubbers [erasers], and rulers. They pay a small school fee too. This money plus a

[One of the other teachers] said that she had written to Grace. The teacher said, "There is a lot of play in [Sue's] room."

———

We really thought that [schools in] Canada would be like we hear [schools in] America to be—so far ahead technologically. [There is] a lot of money, much more money in Canadian schools than we have [in New Zealand] and I expected better equipment. But, [for example,] the story books are boring and dull in comparison to what I am used to having. There is an amazing amount of funding to spend on the schools and you wonder where [the money] goes. When I asked for something at school—like a math book—I got it. It just arrived. Now, in New Zealand that would be "$60 out of a $200 budget" and I would feel really

small grant from the Ministry pays for the running of the school.

In New Zealand, or in our school, they have three computers for the whole school. In Canada we have at least one computer in every classroom. There are a lot of programs you can get through the resource center. If you want a special program, they have a whole selection. They will send you a program to use for a month or however long you want it. Here, there are so few [programs]. We have had one [computer] in our classroom since the [computer] course [I'm taking] started—probably only by taking the course were we able to get one into the classroom through a lot of wheeling and dealing. It has been in the classroom now for 6 weeks and the children have had a chance to use it for their writing but, because it is there for only such a short time, they don't get as many chances and their time has to be limited on it. At home [in Canada] very often, I will let them work on the computer until they say that they are finished.

---

naughty asking for it. I would probably borrow somebody else's and try to copy it. [In New Zealand] my art budget [for] the whole school was $2,000—for the *whole* school. [Here] I will probably use that [much] in my classroom this year. [In New Zealand] our budget to replace physical education equipment was $800 for the whole year. Here, there is just so much stuff. Wonderful!

The resource room is like Aladdin's cave—so much equipment and no accounting for its use! Children don't provide their own stationery. Everything is provided!

The difference in the amount of equipment in the two settings makes [New Zealand teachers], I think, more resourceful. We make far more things; whereas Canadian teachers will go out and buy [teaching aids] and then put them up or use them once. [For example], pretty bulletin boards that are up all year have fancy edging all the way around, and they are up as a teacher-made display. [My bulletin board] is a child-like display and it probably looks gaudy to [the other teachers]—it has kids' paintings on it. But it's like, "If you can buy it, then get it." [The teachers] asked [the principal] to buy all of these manuals—the same for all the classrooms!

New Zealand teachers get no preparation time unless teachers agree to combine classes for subjects such as physical education or music. Canadian teachers don't know how lucky they are. It's not that conditions are bad, it's just that [in New

I get 120 minutes of preparation time for every 6-day cycle, which I never get in New Zealand.

Zealand] they lack some of the things we take for granted.

In both places, I have always spent a lot of time at work. Here I spend a lot more time planning because you have to be so careful that you have the equipment that you are planning to use; whereas at home I know what is available. I also know where I can get my hands on it or where to go [to access it]. Here, you don't have a learning resource center. You have to look and see what you have and plan around that—or you go to the library and find books on [the topic]. But you don't have a lot of those resources right at your fingertips. At home, I spend most evenings doing work, which leaves me free on the weekends to do other things. [Here], if something [else] comes up on a weeknight, then I can manage to do it because I feel that is part of the growth and education of being here.

Both in Canada and in New Zealand you have to [keep student] records. You have to keep track of the children's daily work as well as any formal testing you give. Here, in New Zealand, you have a folder that follows the children from the time that they are new entrants right up until at least Standard 4. [It] is very useful because you can look through and see a child's [development]. If they are having trouble in Standard 3 you can look through and kind of see that, "Ah, yes, they were having trouble in Standard 2 in this area and they are still weak here, so maybe this is the area we should be focusing

In New Zealand I would be in school at 8:00 [a.m.] and I would leave about 5:00 p.m. And, I would probably go in for an hour on the weekend, usually to frame our pictures [with] colored paper. (I do Art on Friday and I like to have [children's work] on the wall for the kids when they come [in on Monday].) Here, I leave [home] at ten to eight [in the morning] and I am home at 4:30 p.m.—and I have a 15-minute drive. So I am not spending as much time at school here as I did in New Zealand. Here I work during my lunch time [because] there is nothing else to do. I eat my lunch [in the staff room] and then I go back to the classroom. There is nobody else there—[the other teachers] eat their lunch and then they just leave. A couple of them go home for lunch.

[One of the other teachers] came in to see my running records today. She is very interested in [finding] a tracking/monitoring system for juniors. I have shown her how to evaluate the running record and [how to] teach from it.

I heard something quite strange today. [The teachers who attended a session on a new student evaluation system] told me that New Zealand bought the program from Ontario to initiate in New Zealand schools.

---

on instead of going on and on." In
[Ontario] Canada, we also have to do
record keeping. We have the report
cards that are very thorough. A copy
of the report card goes into the OSR
(the Ontario Student Record). That
OSR follows the child through from
the time they are in kindergarten
until they complete high school. The
[administration] doesn't want little
bits of the children's work in [the
OSR]. They just want official documents. I believe we did talk, at one
time, about having something that
would follow [a student] through but
it has never actually been set up.
Here it has. They also have [a different system of] reporting here. For
the junior reporting, a written report
only goes out once a year; for the
seniors, it goes out twice a year.

Comparisons

In the preceding portions of their narratives, Grace and Sue
focused on various aspects of their teaching experiences. Although
we did not request their attention to specific topics by defining the
subject matter of their journals, we are again forced to acknowledge the
similarity of their comments. Much of their descriptions or explanations of their new environments and circumstances rests on comparisons between "home" and "here." At first glance, this comparison
appears focused on judgments about the new contexts. Yet we sense
these comparisons represented efforts to make sense of their new
contexts. The tendency toward such comparisons is not unexpected.
Other teachers reporting on their international exchange experiences
(e.g., James, 1983; Nesdoly, 1988; "Teaching on Exchange," 1978)
acknowledge making extensive comparisons of educational and cultural differences between home and host countries.

In some cases, as in Nesdoly (1988), such a comparative perspective is likely to result in both a dissatisfying and a miseducative experience. A particular teacher embarked on her exchange from Canada to Greece with romantic and highly idealized expectations. Those illusions were shattered, however, by the reality of day-to-day life. Hence she was unable to look beyond either her prior expectations or her own cultural norms, a phenomenon not unlike the experience of some new teachers in formal preparation programs (see, e.g., Cole & Knowles, 1993). "Teacher on Exchange" (1978) and James (1983), reporting on their experiences teaching in England, on the other hand, made home/host comparisons about all aspects of their exchange. Unlike Nesdoly, however, their own standards were not used as a basis for judging other practices but merely served as a reference point.

For Grace and Sue, contrasting experiences in each other's classrooms and schools presented a challenge to their conceptions of their own situations. For example, in their initial descriptions of their home schools and classrooms, it seemed that Grace and Sue had similar classroom programs and approaches to teaching, and yet Sue was seen by the teachers in Grace's school as having a "strange way of teaching." And, whereas Grace described her classroom as activity- or play-centered, a colleague in her Canadian school reported in a letter the apparent anomaly of Sue encouraging "a lot of play" in Grace's room. Similarly, what Sue described as an equitable way of working with children of different abilities Grace found to be just the opposite. Also, Grace's description of the New Zealand curriculum as one placing more emphasis on memorizing and "academics" than on concept development through manipulation of materials was in direct contrast to Sue's description of teaching in her New Zealand school. We see these as examples of how experiences in unfamiliar settings provide opportunities for the ongoing reconstruction of knowledge. In the next section, Grace and Sue continue to make sense of their new settings (and, we expect in the process, gain insights into their home situations) by comparing and contrasting professional relationships in their respective contexts.

Professional Relationships in New Zealand

Because of vertical grouping, teachers must work together more closely than at home, where each room is an isolated, independent unit. This seems to create a better understanding in the school—creating fluency and familiarity from one level to the next. The teachers here are warm and friendly. [At home], we do some group teaching, but not enough. I think the teachers in New Zealand (this school anyway) communicate better with each other, which gives the school a sense of "oneness." The lack of communication back home is something we have noted and discussed several times throughout my teaching career.

I think the "working together" is wonderful. It is a great advantage that teachers do work together more. We tend to work together in the primary wing at home but most of the time one teacher will instigate it. For example, I will go and say, "Let's all do a unit on something." But it would be once or twice a year that all the primary teachers would work together.

Professional Relationships in Canada

People tell me that they don't mix school with personal life. On New Zealand Day, a Saturday night, we had a potluck dinner. It was the first function we had as a staff. I thought that was really interesting—the first social function, and it was here at our house. Nobody else would have one [not even] at Christmas.

Nobody infringes on your personal self. [The principal] doesn't ask me [anything that] is not "his business." Unless I volunteer the information, he will not ask me. He has been really good when I have asked for things. He is really helpful but very, very formal. He does not intrude on you at all. And that is how it is. It's very formal.

"Personal rights" are really strong here. If somebody asked you something in New Zealand and you did not want to answer you could quite politely tell them to "mind their own business." But here, nobody would ask you anything personal. I had to sign a form [before] my phone number could go on a [public list].

Somebody explained to me that nobody would confront me if they thought I had done something wrong in the school. They would have to put it in writing. At home, if somebody thought I had done something wrong they would tell me that what I did was stupid; we would talk about it, and that would be it. Here, it is all written down, and it goes to the Board office, and then comes back—the process is related to the human rights legislation.

At home, [the teachers] are quite different—they are much more relaxed, much friendlier, much easier to speak to. [Here the teachers portray] a professional image and a home image. [At home in New Zealand] I know most of the staff, I know all their children and their children's names, and I am interested in what they do. The teenagers come into the school when there is a day off and we chat. There are no boundaries [between home and school]. [Here], there are boundaries. [Here, the attitude is], "That's my private life and nobody knows about it." [At home] you know what is going on in other people's homes so much more. [Here], you don't know anything.

The reason people don't bring their spouses [to any social functions] is because [the spouses] get sick of the teachers "talking shop." [At home] we don't "talk shop" even at lunch time—unless it is something urgent.

Here, people [seem to] travel quite long distances to go to work: [Two of the teachers] drive about an hour; two live in [a city close by]; one lives in [another town]. In New Zealand, we all live quite close to school.

I have become very friendly with the other Grade 1 teacher who teaches part-time, and with [another one of the other teachers]. We do lots of things together. We actually plan our units together all the time now. [One of us] brings a whole lot of books, I will bring something else, and we write the objectives and evaluate together. That is something that is not typically done here.

> I discussed with [two other teach-
> ers] the possibility of them joining
> [the Grade 1 teacher] and me for a
> junior school assembly once a week—
> to sing, celebrate birthdays, present
> certificates, show work, etc. They
> said they would try it once to see if
> they like it.
>
> [One of the teachers] is coming
> regularly to my room [to observe].
> She is trying lots of language-cen-
> tered activities that I am using and is
> delighted with the results. She has
> taken a copy of my day book [too].
> She is surprised at how much we
> share in New Zealand. I showed [an-
> other teacher] who was having prob-
> lems with a low-ability writing group
> how I would set up a remedial pro-
> gram.

Bridging Boundaries, Forging Links

Grace clearly values working together with other teachers and, in
the period immediately before she left for New Zealand, highly com-
mended the way in which the teachers in the primary wing of her
school worked together. From her vantage point at the time, the
Canadian teachers worked closely with one another. On reaching
New Zealand she realized that although at home they did "some
group teaching," it was "not enough." The New Zealand context
markedly colored her thinking about this topic. In the section we
titled "Settling In" and in the immediately preceding section, we
presented portions of Grace's narratives in which she praised the
professional work environment, wanting to adopt similar practices
on her return to Canada. Once again, the contrasting experiences
contributed to the reconstruction of meaning. Whereas Grace initially described teachers in her Ontario school as "cohesive" and
indicated that they worked together, her experience in the New
Zealand school challenged her to think differently about her earlier

characterization. She had an opportunity in New Zealand to broaden her perspective on professional relationships and experience new possibilities.

Meanwhile, Sue, on exchange at the Ontario school, was initially almost overwhelmed by the isolation and apparent rigid boundaries between teachers' classroom territories, evidence she thought represented teachers' unwillingness to collaborate or work together. Little by little the situation changed. First, teachers tentatively dropped by the door of her room, then more frequently came in as they became more accustomed to Sue's openness and nonconcern at their entry into her space. Over the course of the exchange, it appears, Sue became a catalyst for changing notions in the minds of some teachers in the Ontario school. The teachers in the primary wing began working together quite closely, at least around the tasks that Sue and they defined together. And, no doubt, this way of operating reflected Sue's approach in her home school in Auckland, New Zealand.

This change in interaction patterns is an example of the kind of indirect influence teacher exchanges can potentially have. On returning to Ontario, and should she choose to reenter her previous teaching position, we wonder to what extent Grace will act as a continuing and further catalyst. Although we can only speculate at this point, it is likely that Grace, returning home with renewed conceptions and experiences of collegial interactions, will be able to make greater strides toward establishing more collaborative working relationships in her school, in part because she will step into the imprints left by Sue.

Educational Contexts

In their narrative accounts, Grace and Sue also reflected on issues related to school governance and administration, once again comparing and contrasting the two contexts. They wrote about such things as career advancement and the hierarchies of each school system; budget cutbacks as a result of decreased funding by the respective governments and the implications for resources, staffing, and class size; and the role of the teachers' unions in educational decision making.

Although Canada and New Zealand have similar colonial settlement and cultural roots, they have, structurally, quite different education systems. And both countries at various times have overlooked the educational needs of their indigenous peoples. New Zealand has had a centralized national education system (with strong regional nodes) that only recently has been fractured as efforts to decentralize and initiate strong local control have been put into effect. New Zealand is also experiencing the effects of changing organizational structures and administrative control and a serious erosion of the financial base for education. A state of flux and uncertainty within the national curriculum partly evidence this. There is a national curriculum that often has been recognized for its innovative practices; however, performance in national examinations continues to direct students away from university education. Strong vocational and community education programs also exert powerful influences on the preparation of New Zealanders for the work force.

Education in Canada is under the jurisdiction of the individual provinces. In the province of Ontario, as in New Zealand, schools are in a state of transition as government agencies and educational institutions attempt to keep up with the changing social, political, and economic climate. Reform and restructuring in public education and the education of teachers are under way. In New Zealand, major organizational and structural changes also are being made as the colleges of education and universities join in the preparation of teachers.

The collective voice of classroom teachers is heard in different intensities in the two countries. In New Zealand, the teachers' voice has been recently somewhat muffled. Although teachers traditionally have been of strong voice, primarily through their direct participation in decision making associated with the administration of schools and curriculum, their status shows signs of change. Reliance on teacher secondment as a means of filling national, regional, and local administrative and field service positions within the system, and broad and direct participation by classroom teachers in other aspects of school governance and professional development are long-standing. Classroom teachers have played significant roles within the system as evidenced, for example, by the design and implementation of inservice or professional development programs, curricular design and implementation, the administration of the education system, the preparation of new teachers, and the standing and recognition in their community. But flux within New Zealand society and the education system is changing the status of teachers and the conditions under which they work and develop.

Certainly the pay scales of teachers in the two settings are vastly different, with the Ontario teachers receiving much greater remuneration, a point difficult for Sue to accept given that her funds did not go far in Canada. Furthermore, recent changes have diminished the functions of regional boards of education within New Zealand (e.g., the Auckland Education Board), and individual schools have become more autonomous, accountable, and directly responsible for major elements of their funding and operation.

Teachers in Canada are professionally organized in a national federated body that has provincial associations and regional affiliates. As Grace indicated, the teachers' federation and affiliates in Canada are strong and vocal, their influence on government and school board policy and practice clearly apparent. The teachers' voice in Ontario is heard loud and clear as new roles and responsibilities for teachers are being defined. In a difficult economic and political climate, with increased pressures for teachers to do more for less, the teachers' federation is asserting its influence to defend its members. At the same time, it is attempting to promote an image of the teacher that reflects concepts of professionalism, empowerment, and leadership. Conditions such as planning time, class size, and respectable salaries—considered to facilitate professional growth—are among those receiving renewed attention. Inservice education and professional development activities are being designed with an emphasis on long-term professional growth and ongoing renewal.

Travel

As they had hoped, both Grace and Sue had the opportunity to travel and they reveled in the opportunities. It was also an expressed expectation of the experience. The following narratives give some evidence of the extent to which Grace and Sue (and her family) moved around. We present only brief excerpts from their travel accounts. Grace, in her journal, provided more extensive narratives than Sue; yet even so, we are reminded of how partial such narratives are when compared with the daily complexities of moving around in a foreign country.

Experiencing New Zealand	Experiencing Canada and the United States

Absolutely wonderful! The people are really friendly. I have not been doing a lot of tourist things. I have just been doing a lot of New Zealand things, like going to karaoke parties (the "in" thing at the moment) and just going for walks on the beach with one of the teachers and eating out with different people at their homes and kind of getting to know everybody. The staff at the school is very friendly and very accommodating and I am really enjoying that. I am finding it very difficult to write because so many things are the same. I am just kind of living a New Zealand life.

During the weekends I have been doing a lot of things like sailing, going to the beach, swimming. I went to the ballet and am going again on Saturday [to see] *The Nutcracker Suite*. I went down to Muriwhi on the Labour Day weekend—it's a beautiful beach—and had a marvelous time eating fresh mussels cooked in wine, garlic, and herbs. Cooking over an open fire is my favorite thing to do. Sue's relatives have kind of adopted me as part of their New Zealand family now. It feels rather nice. We had a good time tramping through

The first 6 weeks, I didn't really get to know anybody here at all, and we [the family] depended on each other. Maybe we didn't give it a chance because we were away most weekends—we traveled [a lot] but I think that to come here as a single person I'd have been really lonely.

I had not traveled a lot before. I have been to Australia and on cruises, and Peter and I have been to the [South Pacific] Islands.

It didn't really come home to us until we started to travel around—as we drove to Florida—what a "tired old country" New Zealand is. I made a mistake of going right through the middle of Cincinnati because I missed the bypass. It's a pretty big place to go right through the middle of. The towns, the enormous towns that we went through, and how scary a lot of them were. How scary it was to go through Macon, Georgia— with the state troopers all around the place. We were told that if we did anything wrong to really watch out because if you can't pay your fine there and then, on the spot, you'd be locked up. We heard all sorts of things like that.

the woods, or the bush, and we went swimming in the ocean—much to everyone's disgust because it was so cold. Just basically, I have been doing a lot of "New Zealand things" and getting to know what New Zealand is like, and loving every minute of it.

[Doing] New Zealand things: A lot of it has to do with the out-of-doors and involves the ocean—like eating fresh mussels [that I] actually collected, sailing on yachts, and maybe trekking through the bush. The bush is very different than our woods. The bush, with the pohutakawa trees and the large tree ferns, was very interesting for me because it is such very different vegetation. Just studying the different things is just great. And the weather is a New Zealand thing!

On Sunday, December 29, I joined 49 others on a 12-day [organized] tour. As New Zealand tends to be an "outdoors" country, most of [the activities] involve excitement outdoors. I went up in a helicopter, zoomed down rivers in a jet boat, white-water rafted, went parasailing, climbed Fox Glacier, and went trail riding. I also had the thrill of seeing four sperm whales, over 100 dolphins, and some seals in their natural environment.

New Zealand is an ever-changing landscape of plains, hills, volcanoes, rivers, oceans, forests, dairy lands, rugged sheep lands, and mountains. The North and South Islands are very different but equally as beautiful.

After the tour I spent 3 nights with a cousin of Sue's, and then went

It was quite scary when we went into the shopping center [in Macon] the day before Christmas. I've never seen so many black, black people. I'm used to seeing colored people, but these people were so black. They were quite hostile too. We felt quite threatened. They probably didn't mean it, but they were looking sideways [at us]. As soon as we opened our mouths people looked at us—it was quite a scary place to be.

We enjoyed a wonderful 2 weeks in the States but needed a holiday when we returned. We spent a week in Florida going to all the tourist attractions and traveled back through Washington, DC, where we spent 2 great days.

We have had a terrific week with friends at their cottage in Port Loring, [Ontario]. The cottage is on the edge of the Pickering River about an hour from North Bay. The sky is blue! We enjoyed doing "winter things" with them—snowmobiling, cross-country skiing, sledding, etc. We went to visit a hermit who has 100 acres on the other side of the river, accessible only by water in summer and ice in winter. He has all sorts of gadgets to improve his situation as he has no power. The wildlife is so friendly they feed from your hands. It felt really great to be part of an extended family again (all in all, there were 21 of us in three cottages). We will be going back in July to do "summer things." We are so lucky to have made such good friends.

south to Timaru. I spent 4 nights at a sheep station with another cousin of Sue's and had a wonderful time feeding the pigs, moving the cows from pasture to pasture and the sheep from hillside to hillside. Driving along makeshift roads in a four-wheel drive truck high in the hills with the drop to the valley about a meter away is something I will never forget. The view from the top will also stay in my mind long after I leave New Zealand.

[Then] I headed for Dunedin [where I] stayed with Sue's great aunt. I made my way back northward again, stopping at the sheep station for one last night. Then it was train and ferry to Wellington. I'm glad I had people to visit after the tour because, then, I had someone to talk to about my new adventures. After Wellington I took the bus to Taupo and spent 4 nights on a dairy farm near Reprora. I went to Mt. Tarawera (a volcano that last erupted about 106 years ago), climbed with others to the top and then slid deep into the crater. It was eerie but beautiful standing on the crater's floor looking skyward.

Finally, January 29, I decided I had to arrive back in Auckland. School begins February 3.

Usually we feel pleased to be coming home at the end of a holiday but this time we returned reluctantly. I guess it was great to be part of a family again. Reading this again, I now realize the things we miss the most—family times. Today is the first time I have really felt homesick.

We drove to Niagara Falls. They are magnificent! We went on The Maid of the Mist [tour boat that goes under the Falls]. We were so close to the Falls, it was unbelievable. And the noise was so loud! We also went up in the [viewing tower] and, again, the view was unbelievable!

We're getting really good at traveling on the subway [system in Toronto]. [On this trip to Toronto] we drove to [a city outside Toronto], had lunch with some other [teacher] exchangees, and then took the [commuter train] into Toronto. Then, we traveled by subway to see the Ice Capades [a professional skating troupe].

We booked our flight to Scotland today [to leave after school finishes], returning from London 2 weeks later.

Grace spent many evenings and weekends with newfound friends in the Auckland area, visiting and "doing New Zealand things." Invariably these activities involved the outdoors. The summer vacation (mid-December to the beginning of February) provided opportunities to travel further afield. That she chose an organized travel tour may indicate her value for being within a group of like explorers.

Nevertheless, it did represent an extensive and adventuresome excursion into rugged and rural New Zealand.

From the first weeks of their landing in Canada, Sue and her family frequently spent whole weekends exploring nearby and distant places. Indeed, she initially traveled so much that she suspected that "it may have prevented us from meeting people in the community." It was this early period, however, that set the initial tone of the exchange experience, and which Sue found very difficult. She was not able to establish and develop the kinds of solid friendships with Ontarians that she desired. Thus for her, attention to finding out about the greater contexts of Canada and experiencing them was a double-edged sword. Because they were "away most weekends," they were not able to quickly establish themselves as "permanent" and *bona fide* residents in the town. Becoming familiar with the more distant initially inhibited them from becoming familiar in and with the local context.

Experiencing the new settings as extensively as they did also had strong influences on Grace's and Sue's personal and professional identities. We include the following brief accounts because they highlight, once again, but on a larger scale, the role of experience in the ongoing reconstruction of meaning.

"Being Me" in New Zealand

[Being in New Zealand] has really allowed me to open up a little bit; whereas, I have not had that chance in Canada. I don't think that anyone in New Zealand would ever think that I was shy and quiet, and yet, that is probably the way most people in Canada think I am. I think because I have always lived in a small town [where] people have known me, I have always been a little more reserved than I am here. Just basic things [have happened] that have re-

Being New Zealanders in Canada

We watched the opening of the World Cup rugby on television—such patriotism! Pete sat up late watching New Zealand and England [play], [and a few nights later] we watched New Zealand walk all over the United States [team].

[The whole family] watched the opening ceremony for the Winter Olympics [and later in the week] we watched the slalom and downhill racing and the bobsled teams. The girls were very patriotic when the New

ally helped me to, maybe, broaden my own thinking about things or broaden my own needs, and [have] allowed me to be me.

Zealand girl won the women's downhill event.

We have become very patriotic since we left New Zealand. We don't make a big fuss [about patriotism] at home but, here, if we see anything about New Zealand, we really perk up.

My parents send a lot of cuttings from the newspaper and some magazines. I don't buy [Canadian] magazines although I sometimes get them from people. I never really read them; I just flick through them. When a New Zealand magazine comes here, [however,] I read it from cover to cover.

I am getting used to driving on the left side of the road. It's fun to wind up into the hills as the scenery changes before you. I really like the beaches and the chance to be by the ocean. Walking along the sandy beach while the waves crash at your feet and the wind blows through your hair gives you a real sense of freedom. I have always liked to be near water, and New Zealand has only deepened that desire. I feel far more relaxed with water around than in a city of concrete.

I seem to be a bit behind in my correspondence. We have been out more I guess. I write every week to my family but friends get rotated every couple of weeks so there is always a letter on the go. I love getting mail from New Zealand.

Discovering Personal and National Identities

More than anything, Grace's narratives give evidence of the value of living briefly in a different environment. In Canada, her physical and cultural environments were bounded. She grew up, lived, and worked in a small rural community—a relative speck on a continental land mass with large commercial and industrial cities in relatively close proximity, the Great Lakes nearby, and the Atlantic Ocean more than 1,000 miles to the east. North America dwarfs New Zealand. Climatically, she was used to being in a cool, temperate, continental zone. In contrast, Auckland, with its warm, temperate, almost subtropical, maritime climate and easy access to a variety of landscape forms, made possible a different kind of lifestyle—one that was less structured by the extremes of weather and distance. These conditions formed a context for Grace to "be me."

Aside from the professional aspects of the experience, being "on exchange" provided opportunities for Grace to extend personal and psychological boundaries. In a strange, new, and vastly different place, unshackled from familiar surroundings and expectations, she was able to explore elements of her psyche: her identity, self-concept, and interpersonal orientations. Grace's narratives in this section remind us of the experience of self-discovery on which Alice Koller (1981) embarked when she left familiar surroundings in search of "An Unknown Woman."

Sue's experience of "becoming patriotic" was not a surprise to us. Indeed, numerous recent New Zealand authors have written about the place of the OE (Overseas Experience) in the process of "becoming Pakeha." And further, for example, King (1985, 1991) argues that a sojourn in a foreign country has the place and role of establishing more firm appreciations of the peculiar New Zealand culture and lifestyle:

> The effect of my travels . . . was unexpected. I felt more, not less, a New Zealander. I became more deeply conscious of my roots in my own country because I had experienced their absence. I missed physical things, like empty land and seascapes, driftwood fires, bush, New Zealand birdsong. And I missed common perspectives with Maori and Pakeha New Zealanders. . . .
>
> With the perspective of distance, New Zealanders seem to have gone much further towards developing cultural traits than they had at home. . . . (1985, pp. 171-172)

Thus, King suggests, such distance from home as represented in foreign travels or sojourns induces thinking about the relationships of *Pakeha* to Maori and insights into one's nationality. (This is particularly relevant because it is only a few years ago that New Zealanders typically described an OE to the United Kingdom as a trip "home.") Likewise, the experiences of Ireland (1991), Laidlaw (1991), and Spoonley (1991) attest to a kind of bold patriotism that strikes when individuals (in these cases, New Zealanders) are out of their country. And, we suspect, this is similar to the experiences of those of other nationalities who find themselves great distances from their homelands.

Both of us, living away from our respective ancestral homes, are vigorously patriotic toward them, as we suspect Grace to be, and as Sue evidenced. Being patriotic is simply one way in which we can affirm our roots when in a foreign place. Also, not surprisingly, at the height of Sue's patriotism her attention was focused on the sports accomplishments of a compatriot at the Winter Olympics. As Sinclair (1986) points out, New Zealand and New Zealanders have long relied on athletic prowess to help define their identity. Nevertheless, it was Sue's sojourn into the "Northland" of Ontario with her family, visiting with Canadian friends, that provided her an opportunity for the first time to feel homesick, longing for family and friends of New Zealand.

These thoughts withstanding, "the experience of being foreign has the potential for working a significant transformation at the deepest level of an individual's sense of being" (Lewis & Jungman, 1986, p. xvi). And "no matter how strong the attachment to one's native land, one cannot live away from it very long and still resist what is seen every day." (Czeslaw Milosz, quoted in Lewis & Jungman, 1986, p. xvi).

Educational Exchange

Finally, we stand back and look at teacher exchange programs that are promoted as opportunities to

> improve one's professional ability and competence and to gain greater understanding of another country. . . . Teacher

exchange has a two-fold advantage—the benefits to the pupils and the school system brought by the fresh and different approaches of a teacher from another country, and the added stimulus injected when the teacher returns with new ideas and a revitalized outlook. (Canadian Education Association, 1991)

Grace's Teacher Exchange

When I heard of these exchanges, I thought it was the ideal time to go [to New Zealand] because I would be working in their system but I would also be able to see their country and meet the people, the sheep, and everything else. I expected a system much like ours, and very friendly people.

One of the advantages of being on an exchange is that you just kind of fit in. You don't try to change anything and you don't really notice

Sue's Teacher Exchange

I have applied for a deputy principal job [in New Zealand]. People say that you shouldn't go back permanently [to your old job] but that you should grow and regroup from that job. [By regroup I mean, for example,] when you are in school, especially in a small school, you carve out a little niche for yourself. (I did all of the physical education, and all of the outdoor education, and the art, and I used to buy all of the art equipment and I had a kiln in my classroom.) [You do those] things because you are interested [in them]. (Somebody else filled my position and took over all of the good jobs that I had) so [when] you go back to start again [it's difficult]. As someone said, "It's better to start again in another school."

[Because] I got out of the country and did something different, I probably have increased my chances of promotion. [The perception is that] I would bring back something new to the school, something good and interesting.

I have learned from [the exchange] but, really, I don't see that I have learned a lot from other people [in the school] here. I don't think

[that] things [are] so different because you feel so at ease in what you are doing. Some of the things that have stood out are working with these children—which is always a joy for me no matter where I am—getting to know them, and seeing them develop. I have especially enjoyed working with the ESL children, watching how they progress and how they really get excited when they understand something and want to go on [learning].

they have had anything to offer that we have not had in New Zealand. They are not doing things better [in Ontario], but I was told that before I came. The other exchangees find the same thing. You get so much out of this exchange, but not academically for your classroom. I think New Zealand is quite a lot further ahead than the system here.

There are courses offered [through the school board]. Every night of the week there is an opportunity for people to get further training. I am going to computer courses at night.

[On one professional development day] I went to [one of the Board's secondary schools] to visit one of the best art departments in southern Ontario. Art has been my field, so that was really interesting for me. I also spent a day with a "mentor" who is also at our school. I go in and out of her room quite a lot now. She has been teaching me [to work with] pastels, which I have never been able to use successfully myself or in the classroom.

Ardra and Gary came this afternoon. I find that after talking with them I have to question some of my own attitudes. It is good to get other perspectives as you can become very insular and see things in a one-sided manner!

[You need to think about] expectations [for the exchange]. I haven't been disappointed. Everything that we've wanted to do, we've been able to do. We've been lucky.

I think, in just working with another staff and another administrative system, getting a chance to talk to the different teachers and the headmaster here, you get a better feeling of the education system. I think growth as a teacher has [come about by] working with a different culture of children, [which has] helped me to think about things, or look at things a little bit differently, especially in relation to who these children are.

I have developed as a teacher, I think, just with the experience of a change. A chance to go to a new country and be part of that different education system has helped me to become more confident in myself. I am not an outgoing person. I would rather fit in than be the leader, and that will not change. I don't like to stick out, although I may when I get back home. Probably it helped me to meet people and talk to people. I have learned assessment methods used in New Zealand, what they call reading records and running records. I am not sure whether I totally agree with them but I have learned how to do them.

———————

Probably there are a number of things that I will take back home. I really enjoy their reading program. Ours is something like it but they do have the New Zealand *School Journal* that they work with and the stories are all catalogued by age level and reading interest level. I think those are a good thing. In fact, I will take a few back with me. Other things I like are all the senior teachers getting together every week and discussing what is going on. I like the

I don't think anybody should go on an exchange unless they have a really good relationship with their family and spouse, because it can be tough. You depend on each other all the time. [As a family] we've had to be so independent and self-sufficient. The experiences the girls have had [have been wonderful].

———————

I guess the traveling and the living side of it is what we will always remember. And the good friends—because they really are very special now. ———————

planning. That would not happen in
Canada because our curriculum for
Grade 8 is different from Grades 6
and 7, and so there is no sense in
getting together to plan it; although,
once a year our whole school gets
together. We take 2 or 3 weeks and
plan a whole unit that we all do,
from kindergarten to Grade 8. The
idea of doing fitness, having a sports
afternoon, I think that is a great idea
for the children.

Teacher Exchange Programs
and Personal-Professional Development

Both New Zealand and Canada support educational exchange programs of various kinds. Being citizens of a small isolated country, New
Zealanders have a broad appreciation for extending their experiences
beyond the country's oceanic border. Thus formal exchange programs in all kinds of professions and settings—or informal kinds of
exchanges—are viewed as offering opportunities for, as many New
Zealanders might say, an OE, an overseas experience. In reality, this
kind of sojourn is akin to a rite of passage. Many New Zealand citizens
have spent considerable periods of time out of the country.

It is commonly thought that exchanges, such as the one made by
Sue, tend to have far-reaching effects on thinking and practices within
Aotearoa, New Zealand. Indeed, outside perspectives tend to be given
more credence than they sometimes deserve.

Similarly, we sense Canadians also generally value exchanges with
those of alternative backgrounds and perspectives, and similar patterns of formal and informal exchanges are evident in Canada.

Although it was not our intention to conduct an intensive analysis
of Grace's and Sue's narrative accounts of their experiences in each
other's contexts, as we interacted with them and their text we were
struck by two things: the similarity of the topics they chose to write
about and how they responded to or made sense of their experiences
within and outside the classroom. Each teacher left home with well-

established understandings about teaching, learning, and schools, and about herself as a person and a professional, as well as some preconceived ideas about the new context she would be entering. Exposure to and participation in different experiences challenged some of their understandings and provided opportunities for them to extend their thinking and construct new meanings. Thus we see teacher exchange programs as educative opportunities, which, drawing on Dewey (1938), emphasize "connectedness in growth," and epitomize the continuous and interactive nature of learning and development.

In our efforts to better understand the educative nature of teacher exchange opportunities, we adopted a research approach that we thought would "come close" to apprehending and representing these same qualities of connectedness, continuity, and interaction. Thus we took a narrative approach to understanding and representing the time Sue and Grace spent in each other's school, home, and country. Teachers' narratives of experience are becoming increasingly prevalent in the literature on teacher development (e.g., Connelly & Clandinin, 1988; Knowles & Cole with Presswood, 1994; Miller, 1990; Newman, 1990; Schubert & Ayers, 1992; Witherell & Noddings, 1991). These books, and others like them, illustrate the power of narrative as a tool for reflection and increased personal and professional understandings. In our re-presentation of Sue's and Grace's narratives of experience we, and presumably they, have gained considerable insights into teacher exchange programs and experiences. In addition, and perhaps just as important, we have defined a role for narrative in understanding such experiences.

Notes

1. Initially the plan was for both teachers to work in each other's classroom for the year. While Sue went into Grace's classroom in Ontario, a change of other staff at the Auckland, New Zealand school forced a different placement for Grace. A new assistant principal was appointed who apparently wanted to teach older children, as in Sue's classroom, and so Grace was assigned a class of younger children.

2. The period represented the full academic year in Ontario and from the middle of one school year to the middle of the next in New Zealand.

250 THE NARRATIVE STUDY OF LIVES

3. At the same time we also knew from personal experience that the two different contexts would probably not be perceived as massively dissimilar, a fact that we thought may promote professional development. In contrast, contexts that were very dissimilar, we thought, might prove dysfunctional (see, e.g., Forman & Chapman, 1981; Leroy, 1988).

4. The conversation with Grace that took place in New Zealand did not include Ardra.

References

Canadian Education Association. (1991). *Teacher exchange* [Pamphlet available from the author, 252 Bloor St. W., 8-200, Toronto, Ontario, Canada M5S 1V5].

Cole, A. L., & Knowles, J. G. (1993). Shattered images: Understanding expectations and realities of field experiences. *Teaching and Teacher Education, 9*(5/6), 457-471.

Connelly, F. M., & Clandinin, D. J. (1988). *Teachers as curriculum planners: Narratives of experience.* New York: Teachers College Press.

Dewey, J. (1938). *Experience and education.* New York: Collier.

Forman, D. D., & Chapman, D. W. (1981). Perspectives on teaching in another culture. *Alternative Higher Education, 6*(62), 67-78.

Holly, M. L. (1989). *Writing to grow: Keeping a personal professional journal.* Portsmouth, NH: Heinemann.

Ireland, K. (1991). Echoes from a snail's shell. In M. King (Ed.), *Pakeha: The quest for identity in New Zealand* (pp. 9-22). Auckland, New Zealand: Penquin.

James, M. (1983). An English English teacher. *Journal of English, 72*(2), 56-57.

King, M. (1985). *Being Pakeha.* Auckland, New Zealand: Hodder and Stroughton.

King, M. (1991). Being Pakeha. In M. King (Ed.), *Pakeha: The quest for identity in New Zealand* (pp. 9-22). Auckland, New Zealand: Penquin.

Knowles, J. G., & Cole, A. L., with Presswood, C. S. (1994). *Through preservice teachers' eyes: Exploring field experiences through narrative and inquiry.* New York: Merrill.

Koller, A. (1981). *An unknown woman.* New York: Bantam.

Laidlaw, C. (1991). Stepping out from shadow. In M. King (Ed.), *Pakeha: The quest for identity in New Zealand* (pp. 157-170). Auckland, New Zealand: Penquin.

Leroy, C. (1988). Kisii and me. *The Alberta Teachers' Association Magazine, 68*(4), 12-14.

Lewis, T. J., & Jungman, R. E. (1986). Introduction. In T. J. Lewis & R. E. Jungman (Eds.), *On being foreign: Culture shock in short fiction* (pp. xiii-xxv). Yarmouth, ME: Intercultural Press.

Miller, J. M. (1990). *Creating spaces and finding voices.* Albany: State University of New York Press.

Nesdoly, C. (1988). Greece and the great myth. *The Alberta Teachers' Association Magazine, 68*(4), 30-33.

Newman, J. M. (Ed.). (1990). *Finding our own way: Teachers exploring their assumptions.* Portsmouth, NH: Heinemann.

Schubert, W. H., & Ayers, W. C. (Eds.). (1992). Teacher lore: *Learning from our own experience.* White Plains, NY: Longman.

Sinclair, K. (1986). *A destiny apart: New Zealand's search for national identity.* Wellington, New Zealand: Unwin Paperbacks/The Port Nicholson Press.

Spoonley, P. (1991). Being here and being Pakeha. In M. King (Ed.), *Pakeha: The quest for New Zealand* (pp. 146-156). Auckland, New Zealand: Penquin.

Teaching on exchange: A change in jobs and lifestyles. (1978). *Education Manitoba, 4*(3), 8-12.

Witherell, C., & Noddings, N. (Eds.). (1991). *Stories lives tell: Narrative and dialogue in education.* New York: Teachers College Press.

Index

About the Contributors

Adital Tirosh Ben-Ari is a faculty member of the School of Social Work at the University of Haifa, Israel, where she has introduced courses concerning narrative approaches in social work into the school curricula. She received her Ph.D. from the University of California at Berkeley in 1989, where she also did her postdoctoral training and had a teaching position.

Susan E. Chase is Associate Professor of Sociology and cofounder of the Women's Studies Program at the University of Tulsa. Her recent book, *Ambiguous Empowerment: The Work Narratives of Women School Superintendents,* explores how successful professional women narrate their contradictory experiences of achievement and discrimination.

Ardra L. Cole is Professor in the Department of Applied Psychology at The Ontario Institute for Studies in Education, Toronto, Canada. Her research, writing, and teaching are in the areas of teacher education and development, and qualitative approaches to educational research, particularly autobiographical, narrative, and life history methods. Among her recent publications is a book, coauthored with J. Gary Knowles, *Through Preservice Teachers' Eyes: Exploring Field Experi-*

ences Through Narrative and Inquiry. She is currently conducting a life history study of university teacher educators.

Jaber F. Gubrium is Professor of Sociology at the University of Florida. His research centers on the descriptive organization of social forms. Gubrium has conducted fieldwork in diverse institutional settings and has recently authored *Out of Control: Family Therapy and Domestic Disorder* and *Speaking of Life: Horizons of Meaning for Nursing Home Residents.*

James A. Holstein is Professor of Sociology at Marquette University. His recent research focuses on the social construction of social forms, particularly the family, the life course, social problems, mental illness, and the self. Recent publications include *Court-Ordered Insanity: Interpretive Practice and Involuntary Commitment; Reconsidering Social Constructionism,* with G. Miller; *What is Family?; Constructing the Life Course;* and *The Active Interview;* all are coauthored with Jaber Gubrium.

Ruthellen Josselson is Professor of Psychology at Towson State University. Recipient of the APA Henry A. Murray Award (1994) and a Fulbright Research Fellowship (1989-1990), she has also recently been Visiting Professor at the Harvard Graduate School of Education and Forchheimer Professor of Psychology at the Hebrew University of Jerusalem. She is author of *Finding Herself: Pathways to Identity Development in Women* and *The Space Between Us: Exploring the Dimensions of Human Relationships.*

J. Gary Knowles is Professor in the School of Education, University of Michigan, Ann Arbor. He teaches graduate courses in teacher education and development, and qualitative research (particularly autobiographical, narrative, and life history methods), and has written extensively in both of these areas. He also does research in the area of home education. Among his recent publications is a book on preservice teacher education coauthored with Ardra L. Cole. His current research activities include an autoethnographic study of teacher educators as well as an autobiographical exploration of the place of artistic endeavor and aesthetic influences within qualitative research enterprises.

Amia Lieblich is a member of the faculty of the Department of Psychology at the Hebrew University of Jerusalem, where she served as chairperson in 1982-1985. She is the author of several psychology books that deal in narrative form with specific issues of Israeli society, such as war, military service, and the kibbutz. Her most recent work is *Seasons of Captivity: The Inner World of POWs*.

Sarah Mkhonza is a lecturer at the University of Swaziland. She is presently a doctoral student at Michigan State University. Her area of interest is Language Planning. She has published several papers in language planning and women's issues in Swaziland. Her other publications include two novels, short stories, and poems that are in siSwati and English. She has worked as an English teacher in several schools in Swaziland. Her interest in narratives about women has come from observing women in a southern African context that is influenced by issues of race, patriarchy, and class—all of which are reflected in her writing.

Steven Weiland is Professor of Higher Education at Michigan State University, where his work focuses on adult development and aging, the history and rhetoric of the academic disciplines, and biography and life history methods. He is the author of *Intellectual Craftsman: Ways and Works in American Scholarship, 1935-1990* (1991) and essays in the humanities, the social sciences, and education.

Hadas Wiseman is Lecturer in Counseling and Psychotherapy at the School of Education at the University of Haifa, Israel, and a registered clinical psychologist in private practice. She received her Ph.D. from York University, Toronto, Canada. Current research interests are in relatedness, loneliness, and in psychotherapy research.

Ada H. Zohar is at the Department of Psychology at Hebrew University of Jerusalem and is the Coordinator of the Scheinfeld Center of Human Genetics in the Social Sciences. After obtaining her Ph.D.

from Hebrew University on Outstanding Mathematical Reasoning Ability, she was a postdoctoral fellow at the Child Study Center at Yale Medical School. Her work focuses on environmental and genetic influences on individual differences, and combines quantitative and narrative methodologies.